THE FAMILY OF
RICHARD III

T0117590

MICHAEL HICKS is Professor of History at King Alfred's College, Winchester. He has written extensively on medieval England and is regarded by many as the leading expert on the Yorkist dynasty. He is a Fellow of the Royal Historical Society. He lives in Taunton.

PRAISE FOR MICHAEL HICKS

Richard III
'A most important book… compulsive reading' DESMOND SEWARD, *BBC HISTORY MAGAZINE*

'A fascinating odyssey into English history' *HISTORY TODAY*

Anne Neville: Queen to Richard III
'A masterful and poignant story' ALISON WEIR
'Does little for Richard III's tattered reputation' *BBC HISTORY MAGAZINE*

Warwick the Kingmaker
'Immensely well-researched' *THE RICARDIAN*

Edward IV
'Michael Hicks' greatest strength is in his eye for detail and ability to discern order from the chaos of the detail' *HISTORY: JOURNAL OF THE HISTORICAL ASSOCIATION*

The Prince in the Tower
'The first time in ages that a publisher has sent me a book that I actually want to read!' DAVID STARKEY

THE FAMILY OF RICHARD III

MICHAEL HICKS

AMBERLEY

First published 2015
This edition published 2017

Amberley Publishing
The Hill, Stroud
Gloucestershire, GL5 4EP

www.amberley-books.com

Copyright © Michael Hicks, 2015, 2017

The right of Michael Hicks to be identified as
the Author of this work has been asserted in
accordance with the Copyrights, Designs and
Patents Act 1988.

ISBN 978 1 4456 6015 8 (paperback)
ISBN 978 1 4456 2134 0 (ebook)

British Library Cataloguing in Publication Data.
A catalogue record for this book is available
from the British Library.

Typesetting and Origination by Amberley
Publishing.
Printed in the UK.

CONTENTS

PREFACE

This is not the first book that I have written about Richard III or about members of his family: both brothers, his father-in-law, his nephew, and his queen. Obviously it takes account of these works, builds on them, repeats and summarises them. I have not re-examined everything I have written before. This is not the book to seek blow-by-blow discussions of Richard III in the north, the usurpation or the fate of the Princes in the Tower, which I have discussed elsewhere. This book is not based on profound new research. However, it takes a different perspective, sets Richard into different contexts, and thus has different things to say. What makes complete sense from one biographical angle is less satisfactory from another and forces a reassessment, both in detail and in interpretation. Long ago Professor Barrie Dobson dubbed me a re-revisionist. There is some new data in this book. More important, there is a lot of rethinking, even on such well-trodden topics as the fall of Clarence. I have learnt from revisiting old themes. Richard was a man of his time who needs to be viewed through the lens of contemporary expectations. In some ways he was conventional, even unthinkingly uncritical, yet in others he departed from the norm. Among other things this book charts a progression to the most casual ruthlessness to one's relatives that was a legacy of the Wars of the Roses to the Tudors.

This is a book about people: lots of people. Richard III had a great many relatives and has a huge number of connections even today. The book is full of names, titles, and dates of death. This is where I am happiest: Jack Lander called me a genealogical historian. I hope that I have provided all the necessary signposts in the text, the tables, and the index. Such data is drawn overwhelmingly from the *Complete Peerage*, the new *Oxford Dictionary of National Biography*, the biographies compiled by the History of Parliament Trust, and other standard compilations. I have tried to check all these; undoubtedly errors remain, for which I apologise. They and any other errors of fact or interpretation are my own.

This is also a book about bastardy. It was not intended to be so. Obviously bastardy and allegations were always part of the story, but recently they were plastered across the television news, the national press, and all over the ether. As it happens, bastardy is a topic I know about – the proofs of a paper on the subject reached me in the final stages of writing – and I hope therefore that I have proved equal to the challenge. Legitimacy, Christian sexual morality, and chastity were actually fifteenth-century norms and expectations. They were also an area where Richard's relatives, the scandalous House of York, appear always to have fallen short.

Understanding Richard III is a collaborative project that has involved many hands. A host of authors have contributed to *The Ricardian* over the years and there have been far more biographies, plays, and novels than I have been able to read. Almost all contain some nugget of information hitherto overlooked or some original insight. The Richard III Society has published or made possible the publication of modern editions of the principal sources. Years later it is often difficult to recall who said what and when. What this author has read thoroughly and repeatedly are the works of his academic peers – notably John Armstrong, Michael Bennett, Sean Cunningham, Barrie Dobson, Keith Dockray, Peter Hammond, Alison Hanham, Gerald Harriss, David Hipshon, Rosemary Horrox, Michael Jones, Paul Murray Kendall, Jack Lander, Alec Myers, Tony Pollard, T. B. Pugh, Colin Richmond, Charles Ross, James Ross, Anne Sutton, and Livia Visser-Fuchs

– whose labours in this particular vineyard are foundations to this book. Thank you all. A lightly referenced book undoubtedly understates my debts to you. Some of you have died: you have been often in my thoughts. It is too much to expect that you will all agree with the results, but I acknowledge your contributions gratefully. For over thirty years I learnt about Richard III and the Wars of the Roses from cumulatively hundreds of students at Winchester. Most recently I have learnt from Dr Gordon McKelvie and Mr Alexander Bronderbit. My late parents, my wife Cynthia and my children have been critical sounding boards for the ideas and arguments rehearsed here. The book has intervened in our retirement: I dedicate it to Cynthia.

Scientists have intervened in this topic and chapter 9 is devoted mainly to their work on the bones allegedly of Richard III discovered at Leicester. The present author is not a hard or STEM scientist in the modern sense – not an archaeologist, biologist, biochemist, geneticist, pathologist, statistician, or any other variety of scientific technician – and his knowledge of the relevant science rests on the extremely lucid explanations of John Ashdown-Hill, Philippa Langley, Richard Buckley and Mathew Morris, Michael Pitts, and the whole Leicester team in their copious articles, books, podcasts, television programmes, radio broadcasts and other media, for which I gratefully thank them. I enjoyed reading their books and wish them huge readerships. The general public and I are much better informed in consequence. I do not pretend to be the academic peer of the archaeologists and scientists: I am not competent to peer review or to criticise their research, which appears excellent as far as I can tell, and I do not criticise it. Professor Jon Arch, University of Buckingham, and my completed research student the former forensic chemist Dr David Cousins, have advised me fruitfully. I am, however, a critical scientific historian and have taken a critical scientific eye to their conclusions, pointing out what seems to me obvious but which somehow has been missed. Chapter 9, where this occurs, is probably the most controversial part of the book, and the least enduring. If not already outdated at publication, I hope that the necessary research is taken quickly to supersede it.

Jonathan Reeve kindly suggested that I write this book before all the fuss about the bones blew up. That has changed this book significantly: I am grateful for him to allow me to include chapter 9 on this topic, which was written, very appropriately, just as the Leicester team issued their misleading announcement that DNA had proved the bones to be Richard's. By making me an Emeritus Professor on my retirement, the University of Winchester enabled me to keep track of a fast-moving debate.

Taunton, December 2014

LIST OF PEDIGREES

LIST OF TABLES

PEDIGREES

Pedigree 1. Kings of England, 1377–1547

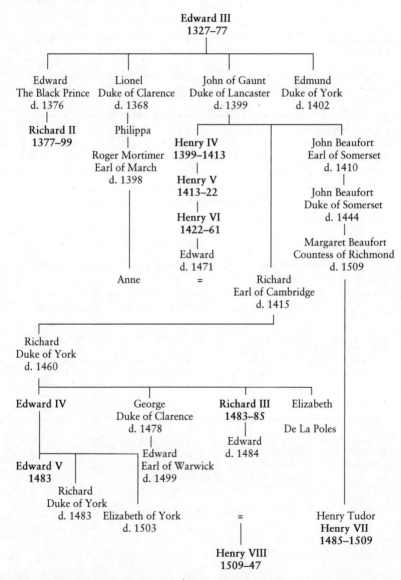

Pedigree 2. The House of York 1452–64

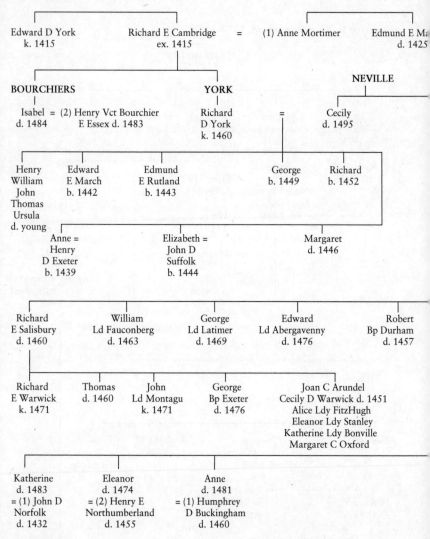

Edward D York k. 1415		Richard E Cambridge ex. 1415	=	(1) Anne Mortimer	Edmund E Ma d. 1425

BOURCHIERS

Isabel = (2) Henry Vct Bourchier
d. 1484   E Essex d. 1483

YORK

Richard
D York
k. 1460

=   Cecily
d. 1495

NEVILLE

Henry
William
John
Thomas
Ursula
d. young

Edward
E March
b. 1442

Edmund
E Rutland
b. 1443

George
b. 1449

Richard
b. 1452

Anne =
Henry
D Exeter
b. 1439

Elizabeth =
John D
Suffolk
b. 1444

Margaret
d. 1446

Richard
E Salisbury
d. 1460

William
Ld Fauconberg
d. 1463

George
Ld Latimer
d. 1469

Edward
Ld Abergavenny
d. 1476

Robert
Bp Durham
d. 1457

Richard
E Warwick
k. 1471

Thomas
d. 1460

John
Ld Montagu
k. 1471

George
Bp Exeter
d. 1476

Joan C Arundel
Cecily D Warwick d. 1451
Alice Ldy FitzHugh
Eleanor Ldy Stanley
Katherine Ldy Bonville
Margaret C Oxford

Katherine
d. 1483
= (1) John D
Norfolk
d. 1432

Eleanor
d. 1474
= (2) Henry E
Northumberland
d. 1455

Anne
d. 1481
= (1) Humphrey
D Buckingham
d. 1460

C = countess; D = duke, duchess; E = earl; Ld = lord; Ldy = lady; M = marquis.

Pedigree 3. Richard's Grey and Wydeville in-laws in the 1460s

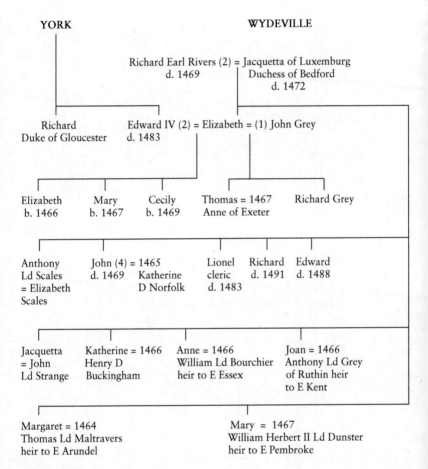

YORK   WYDEVILLE

Richard Earl Rivers (2) = Jacquetta of Luxemburg
             d. 1469   Duchess of Bedford
                                          d. 1472

Richard   Edward IV (2) = Elizabeth = (1) John Grey
Duke of Gloucester   d. 1483

Elizabeth   Mary   Cecily   Thomas = 1467   Richard Grey
b. 1466   b. 1467   b. 1469   Anne of Exeter

Anthony   John (4) = 1465   Lionel   Richard   Edward
Ld Scales   d. 1469   Katherine   cleric   d. 1491   d. 1488
= Elizabeth   D Norfolk   d. 1483
Scales

Jacquetta   Katherine = 1466   Anne = 1466   Joan = 1466
= John   Henry D   William Ld Bourchier   Anthony Ld Grey
Ld Strange   Buckingham   heir to E Essex   of Ruthin heir
                                                           to E Kent

Margaret = 1464   Mary = 1467
Thomas Ld Maltravers   William Herbert II Ld Dunster
heir to E Arundel   heir to E Pembroke

Key:
C = countess; D = duke, duchess; E = earl; Ld = lord; Ldy = lady; M = marquis.

Pedigree 4. The Neville inheritance in the 1470s

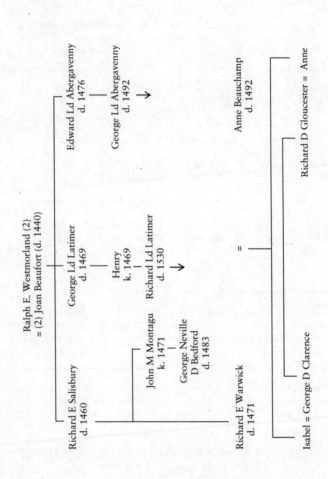

NEVILLE

Ralph E. Westmorland (2)
= (2) Joan Beaufort (d. 1440)

Richard E Salisbury
d. 1460

George Ld Latimer
d. 1469

Henry
k. 1469

Richard Ld Latimer
d. 1530

→

Edward Ld Abergavenny
d. 1476

George Ld Abergavenny
d. 1492

→

John M Montagu
k. 1471

George Neville
D Bedford
d. 1483

Richard E Warwick
d. 1471

Anne Beauchamp
d. 1492

Isabel = George D Clarence

Richard D Gloucester = Anne

=

C = countess; D = duke, duchess; E = earl; Ld = lord; Ldy = lady; M = marquis

Pedigree 5. The family of King Richard III in 1484–85

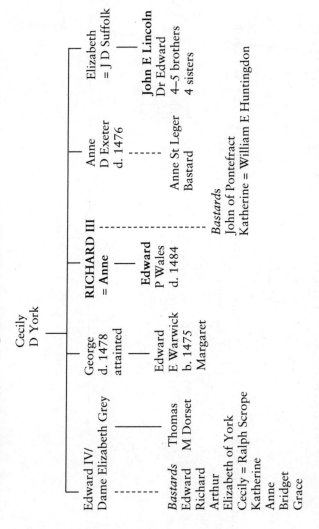

Key: dotted line signifies illegitimacy
C = countess; D = duke, duchess; E = earl; Ld = lord; Ldy = lady; M = marquis

The Family of Richard III

Pedigree 6. The family of Henry VII

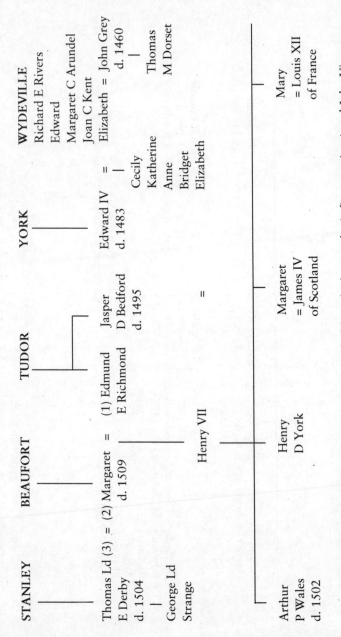

STANLEY **BEAUFORT** **TUDOR** **YORK** **WYDEVILLE**

Richard E Rivers
Edward
Margaret C Arundel
Joan C Kent

Thomas Ld (3) = (2) Margaret = (1) Edmund   Jasper   Edward IV   Elizabeth = John Grey
E Derby   d. 1509   E Richmond   D Bedford   d. 1483   d. 1460
d. 1504   d. 1495 |
| Thomas
George Ld   =   M Dorset
Strange |
                                                                                  Cecily
                    Henry VII   =   Katherine
                                                                                  Anne
                                                                                  Bridget
                                                                                  Elizabeth

Arthur   Henry   Margaret   Mary
P Wales   D York   = James IV   = Louis XII
d. 1502   of Scotland   of France

Not shown: The St Johns (Margaret Beaufort's half-siblings by her mother's first marriage) and John Viscount
Welles (Margaret Beaufort's half-siblings by her mother's third marriage)

I

RICHARD III IN CONTEXT

King Richard III (1483–85) is one figure from history that we today feel that we really know. Richard's deeds proclaim his character. It was Richard III who usurped the throne in 1483, Richard who slew his innocent nephews, who planned to discard his wife and to marry in her place his niece, and Richard who perished at the Battle of Bosworth in 1485. Many contemporaries came to know him as violent, acquisitive and self-interested, a deceiver and perjurer, a monstrous tyrant, a homicide, a regicide, perhaps a matricide. Such was the prevailing orthodoxy from Sir Thomas More and William Shakespeare to James Gairdner in 1878 and A. L. Rowse in 1966.[1] Such denunciations of course came from Richard's enemies or at least those who, knowing about his disastrous end, regarded Bosworth as indisputable evidence of God's disapproval and therefore of Richard's wickedness. Very few plaudits are recorded from Richard's own life, inevitably from his allies and employees,[2] and virtually none after his death. Nevertheless to many other people today Richard stands out as a loyal subject of his brother (Edward IV, 1461–83), as a disinterested arbiter, a straightforward soldier, who ascended the throne as his public duty, a young hero, more sinned against than sinning, and indeed as 'Good King Richard'.[3] These wildly different perceptions do convey a genuine complexity in the original character.

Of course it is seldom helpful to focus purely on Richard as an individual. He needs to be seen in context. Richard was not a twenty-first-century man transported like Dr Who to another time or like Gulliver to another country. Richard was the product of a particular time and place – fifteenth-century England – and specifically of the Wars of the Roses. Our full appreciation of him demands our understanding of the code of conduct, values and standards to which he was brought up, and against which his contemporaries appraised him. Richard was part of a political system. There were particular circumstances that do need to be taken into account, above all the distinct era called the Wars of the Roses to which he belonged and in which he played such crucial roles. As guides on how to behave in politics in such challenging times, Richard had precedents, even models, in how other magnates in similar crises had behaved, notably his father Richard Duke of York (1411–60) in 1450–61 and his father-in-law Warwick the Kingmaker (1428–71) in 1469–71. Richard had witnessed them both in operation. Richard's political stage was crowded with personalities from his own class, the aristocracy, many of whom were his relatives. Their brief lives were complicated by their inter-relationships – which among so many ties were those that mattered and which determined their actions? – and by frequent changes of name and rank as they succeeded, married, and were promoted.

Richard himself acted many parts, as a child and minor, as son, brother and uncle, husband and father and childless widower, as a subject, royal duke, commander-in-chief, and king. The eighth son and eleventh child of his parents, as insignificant and limited in prospects as the son of a duke could be, he became a prince, a royal duke, and ultimately a king. All individuals at all times are members of society, all interact with others, and it is through these relationships that historians can study them. Those interactions that can best be investigated are predominantly formal and material, and are deduced from actual events and actions. Straightforward statements of motive are rare indeed. Infusing such ties with the sentiment that gave them motion, establishing precisely which bonds determined alliances or collaboration and which left the actors unmoved, and pinpointing affection or other emotional ingredients are much more difficult and indeed can rarely be achieved. The rivalry, anger, and revenge that fatefully divided the brothers Edward IV, George Duke of Clarence (1449–78), and Gloucester (1452–85) was spawned from emotionally charged encounters in childhood when they coexisted under the same roof. Richard served the first two Yorkist kings and was also served himself, as Rosemary Horrox has documented.[4] His career is also a study of self-service. And of course Richard had his own family or families and fitted into many other people's families. It is the House of York, of which Richard was the product; his own family that he formed and planned for, the royal family that he worked with and that ultimately failed him.

Richard III had many families, as this book will show. In thirty years his family of origin was transmuted into a destination family, with identifiable stages in between. He fitted into nuclear families, multiple lineages, families of affinity and consanguinity, and is an ingredient in many thousands of families today. This book seeks to examine them all.

2

TYPES OF FAMILIES

Locating Richard

Richard III we all know about. Born at Fotheringhay in
Northamptonshire in 1452, he was the youngest son of Richard
Plantagenet, 3rd Duke of York, Earl of March and Ulster (d. 1460)
and Cecily Neville (d. 1495). On the accession of his eldest brother
Edward Earl of March as King Edward IV (1461–83), Richard
became a royal prince and Duke of Gloucester, bossed the north
of England from 1471 to 1483, deposed his nephew Edward V
(1483), and in his two final years reigned as King Richard III.
He has had 529 years of afterlife as England's most villainous
monarch. Of his own family, most readers will remember his
parents, his brothers Edward IV and George Duke of Clarence, his
consort Queen Anne, and his two innocent nephews the Princes
in the Tower. Shakespeare's *Henry VI, Part 3* brings in a third
brother, Edmund Earl of Rutland, and Richard's father-in-law,
Warwick the Kingmaker. Readers of Philippa Gregory's historical
novels, and fans of the television series *The White Queen* based
on them, will have some knowledge of his sister-in-law Queen
Elizabeth (Wydeville) and his niece Elizabeth of York, eventually
queen to Henry VII. Those better informed may recall a third
sister, Margaret Duchess of Burgundy, and Richard's own son

and heir, Edward of Middleham. Even these, however, are mere fragments of his whole family. Missing from public memory are Richard's uncles, aunts, cousins, two other sisters, nephews and nieces, many in-laws, and his own illegitimate by-blows.

Moreover the term 'family' at this date embraced one's whole household, servants in their scores, to whom the head of the household stood in the relation of a father to his children and to whom his menials owed the obedience due from children. For such a household man (and they were almost all male) to kill his master was even categorised as petty treason, which was as serious and carried the same penalties as treason proper. These domestic servants were Richard's *familiares*. Richard was to cherish the souls of those who perished at his side in the battles of 1471.[1] Some of these additions really mattered in Richard's career, others being minor royals whose names even Richard would have struggled to remember. The caste changed constantly as new members were added by birth and marriage and others died. Life expectancy in the Middle Ages was very short. The Wars of the Roses curtailed it further.

There is also of course a genetic component to the family. We are all the products of DNA passed down by our parents and mixed in an infinite variety of ways. Until now, such knowledge has been of limited value to medievalists, who know only that in appearance Richard III resembled his father Richard Duke of York, unlike his two brothers Edward IV and George Duke of Clarence, and that Elizabeth of York was alike in physique and colouring to her aunt by marriage and cousin Anne Neville.[2] Now, however, science has entered the fray, with particular reference to the bones of Richard III, and connections via the Y chromosome, mitochondrial DNA, and haplogroups can be expected to enrich discussions. Outside chapter 9, however, this book confines itself to more traditional definitions of the family and its operations.

What Is a Family?[3]

This is a deceptively easy question with an apparently simple answer. All of us (like Richard) have two parents, a father and a mother, usually bound in wedlock (the conjugal couple), and most of us also have at least a brother and/or a sister, our siblings. That is our family and one definition of Richard's family too. Each of our families is unique to us. This unit is known as the nuclear family. The nuclear family is an institution whose members reside together, eat, sleep and play together, are brought up together, and are the fundamental presumption of everyday life.

There is a sentimental component to such cohabiting units – a glue of shared experiences and heightened emotions that gives them cohesion. Close proximity over many years most likely generated strong emotional relationships in the past also, both affection and sibling rivalries. Members of the same nuclear family had common interests to defend against those outside the nuclear family, including cousins and other less closely related, common interests that they were all bound to advance. If not concerned about school catchment areas, medieval parents already schemed their best for their children. Junior members were imbued with family loyalty and were yoked into the cooperative family enterprise. The strength of such bonds diminished with time as the component members grew up and were routinely superseded as they established nuclear families of their own. Marriage, a voluntary commitment contracted by almost every medieval person, signalled a couple's movement from their two nuclear families of origin to the new one that they had founded for themselves. Nuclear families were born, waxed and waned, and died in succession to one another.

Marriage converted the family of one partner into the relatives of the other. These were affinal kindred or affines. Hence the terms father-in-law and mother-in-law, son-in-law and daughter-in-law, and brother- and sister-in-law. The offspring of one partner became kin of the other: Henry Tudor, son of Edmund Tudor and Margaret Beaufort, was the stepson of Margaret's later husbands Sir Henry Stafford and Thomas Lord Stanley. The 'in-law' is significant: Henry Stafford called his stepson his son, York called his son-in-law Exeter his son, and Henry IV called his wife's mother, Joan Countess of Hereford, 'the king's mother', and his brother-in-law Ralph Earl of Westmorland he called his brother. The Church treated affines (those in-laws related by marriage or affinity) and blood relations (by consanguinity) as equally related. Sex with affines was just as incestuous and fell within the prohibited degrees. The husbands of sisters-in-law, such as those of Queen Elizabeth Wydeville's sisters, who had no blood relationship to Richard III and would not be regarded as kin today, nevertheless were Richard's relatives too. They have been called brothers-in-law here (and, vice versa, the 'in-law' has also been used in this book for her brothers' wives). Knowing who was related in this way became evermore difficult as the generations passed, let alone knowing who was theoretically debarred by sexual intercourse without the benefit of marriage. Henry VIII married his deceased brother's wife, which was declared illegal in favour of a marriage to Anne Boleyn, who should also have been barred because he had inseminated without benefit of wedlock her sister Mary. Godparenthood – standing sponsor at the font – also created a spiritual relationship that barred future marriage which, however, scarcely features in this book.

The prohibited degrees were a rule of the Church deriving from the biblical book of Leviticus that set limits to who could marry whom. Originally this barred marriage between those related in the seventh degree, both by blood (consanguinity) and marriage (affinity), between those sharing great-great-great-great-great-great-grandparents, 128 forebears in all. Even today few people could identify 128 ancestors and in 1215 this was adjusted to a more manageable four prohibited degrees, sixteen in all. The degrees sought to prevent inbreeding, which can magnify genetic deficiencies disastrously: witness Tutankhamun, the Egyptian pharaoh born to a brother and sister, and the Spanish Hapsburg King Charles II. To marry within these degrees created an invalid marriage and was sinful: any offspring resulting were bastardised. Such matches were immoral, incestuous, and deeply shocking. Important people, such as princes and noblemen, could evade these restrictions by securing dispensations from the Pope, ideally beforehand but often enough afterwards, when unrecognised impediments were discovered and often revealed because of the conscientious qualms of the two partners. Henry VII had to secure three dispensations to plug all the gaps.[4] Applications for dispensations in the fourth and third degrees were routinely approved; in the second degree, between first cousins, sometimes; and in the first degree, only once: the marriage of Henry IV's son Thomas Duke of Clarence in 1411 to his aunt by marriage Margaret Holland.[5] Both Richard III's first marriage to Anne Neville and his proposed remarriage to Elizabeth were too close to be dispensed. He was a serial incestor.[6] A generation later, however, Joanna Queen of Naples was dispensed to marry her nephew and thereafter royalty commonly received such dispensations. The impotent and simple-minded Charles II was a dreadful consequence.

Rarely do families consist merely of conjugal units that succeed one another. This requires only children of only children to wed only children of only children, which can occasionally happen by accident rather than design. Most families are messier than this today and were much messier in the Middle Ages, when large broods and premature mortality complicated the picture. Three generations may have coexisted, albeit briefly: the vertically extended family. All Richard III's grandparents had died before he was born. Outside the nuclear family there were usually uncles and aunts, married or single, cousins, nephews and nieces, great-aunts and uncles, step-parents and step-siblings, half-brothers and half-sisters. Extension horizontally of the family tree embraced all such collateral relatives. The remarriage of the widowed and further reproduction often produced complex families, frequently co-resident domestic groups, in which the children need have no blood relationship at all. The household of Arthur Viscount Lisle in the mid-1530s consisted not only of offspring of the viscount and viscountess but of each of them by former spouses and the children of such former spouses by previous marriages.[7] Often contemporary family trees move from the direct line to record all living relatives at the time when compiled.[8]

Such collaterals, however, were secondary in importance and in their emotional attachment. The term 'boundary awareness' marks the distinction between each nuclear family and those outside it: a common outlook, common interests, unity of purpose, and even affection was concentrated or even confined within the nuclear family. As each brother and sister married and bred and each sibling's issue became a separate nuclear family, they came to matter more than collateral networks. Their resources, loyalty and love were more concentrated, and exercised on behalf of other members. Because primogeniture did concentrate resources, titles, and honour on the senior line, normally collateral relatives at least deferred to the head of the main line and hoped to share in his largesse. The shared name and self-interest reinforced this particular tie. Yet the junior house of Neville, derived from Richard Earl of Salisbury, a middle son of Ralph Earl of Westmorland (d. 1425), did not hesitate to despoil the senior Westmorland and junior Abergavenny lines of his brothers of their northern and Welsh inheritances.[9] The Courtenays of Tiverton, Powderham, and Bocannoc waged war on each other. We are all Staffords or Courtenays or Nevilles or Hickses in love and hate. To certain relatives at certain times Richard was passionately attached – to his offspring legitimate and baseborn. He subordinated himself appropriately to his elder brother Edward IV, who was the source of his wealth; but towards more distant kin (and even some close kin) he was 'muche what indifferent', as Thomas More said,[10] and even ruthless.

Family relationships and kinships can divide as well as unite. In this period conflicting rights of inheritance were powerful causes of dissension and even bloodshed, as demonstrated by the history of Richard's family and indeed Richard's own career. The Wars of the Roses were civil wars. The House of York, even by contemporary standards, was the most dysfunctional of families.

The Lineage

The nuclear family is itself a staging post on a much larger family, the lineage or clan that extends back over millennia and that will continue to unfold into the future. Actually all of us are the culmination of many separate lineages. Like all of us Richard had two parents (a couple), along with three brothers and four sisters, together a rather large nuclear family – very large by modern standards. Each nuclear family is part of a much larger family – an extended family – that encompasses not just past ancestors and future descendants that feature in genealogical pedigrees but also collateral connections – uncles, aunts, nieces, nephews and cousins – parcelled around a whole series of conjugal couples in different nuclear families. We all have two parents, four grandparents, eight great-grandparents, sixteen great-great-grandparents, thirty-two great-great-great-grandparents and so on. Anybody tracing their ancestry is forced to prioritise which line to pursue even if, improbably, they eventually sought out them all. The television series *Who Do You Think You Are?* selects from diverse possibilities the line of most interest, the line that makes the best television. After seventeen generations, perhaps the five hundred years back to 1485, each of us have 131,072 direct ancestors. It is hardly surprising that the present author, neither royal nor noble, is descended through three lines from Edward III. There comes a point where such collateral relationships – first, second, third and further cousins, especially cousins by marriage (affinity) rather than blood (consanguinity) – fade into obscurity and cease to be recognised as relationships. How many of us today can name all our eight great-grandparents or keep track of all their descendants? It required a considerable effort of genealogy in 2014 to identify all the posthumous thirty-two grand-, great-grand, and great-great-grandchildren of the Somerset private William John Newman, who perished in the early days of the First World War.[11] Very few of us retain memories beyond our grandparents or can enumerate all our second cousins. Rigorous research among current undergraduates reduces this score close to zero. Few family historians even today look beyond the family trees of their parents, their paternal and maternal lines, let alone the sixteen or 131,072 relatives outlined above.

The Church had denounced as prohibited and incestuous any marriages and sexual relations between those related within the seventh degree – all those descended from 128 blood ancestors or 128 kin by marriage across two centuries. Even in the Middle Ages nobody could keep track of them, so in 1215 the Church reduced the test to the fourth degree – descendants of sixteen blood ancestors and sixteen in-laws – but even then it was too easy to offend by accident and to require a retrospect dispensation. Lionel Duke of Clarence, through whom the Yorkists claimed their throne, was one of their thirty-two. In the Middle Ages the Church banned marriage with all such remote kin who fell under its laws of incest. Medieval royals and nobles nevertheless tended to intermarry and therefore needed papal dispensations to legitimise their unions and their children: for example, Richard's parents were distant cousins. Edward III and Queen Philippa crop up three times on Richard's family tree. Such papal dispensations usually recognised more than one different relationship created by common descent and the intermarriage of cousins. It was not uncommon to later discover yet more relationships that needed dispensing – Henry VII had to return three times to the Pope to legalise his marriage to Elizabeth of York. No family tree ever devised can depict satisfactorily everyone and express the full complexity of these connections. The Marquis of Ruvigny, who tracked the blood royal of England from Edward III to the early twentieth century, divided his endeavours into volumes – the Isabel Plantagenet, Clarence, and Anne of Exeter volumes – and within them into dozens of (sub)tables. Many individuals featured in several tables, one of them fifteen times.[12]

Remember that everyone in the Middle Ages claimed descent from Adam: humankind was a vast, interconnected family, royal dynasties being the senior lines or trunks. Royal lines of descent are the trunk roads in this endless network of connections. The motor was inheritance: family names, status, renown, land, chattels and heirlooms were inherited. Inheritance was sacred. It is to track the descent of the family, its titles, estates, and often its name, that the pedigree or family tree was developed. It was a key accompaniment to deeds of title and demonstrated the accumulated battle honours, etc., of the aristocratic house. Many such pedigrees survive from medieval England, sometimes as original illuminated rolls, more often as copies within chronicles or the collections of early modern heralds. The evolution of the family is traced from earlier times at the top to the present day at the foot, linked by vertical lines signifying successive generations and horizontal lines collaterals, those identified being encircled in roundels and the union of houses through marriage clearly apparent. Running over many generations, they can be membranes of parchment long, but they are commonly rolled up. Genealogists in all eras focus on those lineages that appear significant, usually because they transmit titles of honour, surnames, rank and landed property. They are also the easiest to research. Most easy to trace is the direct line of descent of those with the same surname. In actual fact, however, the nuclear family is and was the staging post in many lineages. Highly decorative national genealogies were mass produced professionally around St Paul's Cathedral in London, skilfully updated and adapted to the needs of particular families.[13]

All those in such pedigrees since King Henry II (1154–89) were

Plantagenets, members of a royal house with no name. They were either members of the senior trunk or the principal branches, twigs or twiglets distanced further in every generation from the crown.

Starting off with a simple emblem such as a white lion or a sleeve, coats of arms were greatly elaborated during the fourteenth and fifteenth centuries by quartering the arms of families with which intermarriage had taken place, with marks of cadency for junior lines, and other differentiation for illegitimacy. The most elaborate of the coats of arms of the House of York contain sixteen quarterings that lay claim to the armorial bearings of those ancestral dynasties considered significant in enhancing the titles, possessions, and honour of the family.

Coats of arms were one mechanism to mark the territory of the nobility and to perpetuate their memory. Noblemen plastered their coats of arms and crests on their newly built houses, castles and churches, their tombs, their tapestries, windows and bed hangings, their table services and any vestments, communion or christening plate they gave away, often beside or in addition to earlier arms of their ancestors. Noble boys like Richard III were taught to recognise such emblems, many of which of course relate to defunct names and titles otherwise too easily forgotten. Monasteries recorded the genealogies of their founders, located their often unmarked tombs, and publicised them through chronicles and pedigrees that were the principal source of information not just for those monks who were bound to pray for them, pilgrims and casual visitors, but also the aristocratic heirs who often enough were hereditary patrons of the monastic house. Relevant to Richard's lineages are the abbeys of St Augustine at Bristol, Alnwick (Northum.), Bisham (Bucks.), Coverham, Whitby and St Mary York (Yorks.), Tewkesbury (Gloucs.), Wigmore (Salop.), and Clare friary in Suffolk. From the later Middle Ages there survive genealogies of the Plantagenets, the House of York, the Mortimers (Wigmore) and the de Clares (the *Clare Roll*), the Beauchamps (the *Rows Roll*), the Montagus (the *Salisbury Roll*), the Nevilles and the Percys – all progenitors of Richard III and Queen Anne. Others record other lines of descent. Richard was descended many times over from the well-documented kingdoms of France and Spain. The propagandist *Brief Treatise* of Edward IV stressed his descent from the royal houses of England, France and Castile.[14] Duke Charles the Bold of Burgundy cherished rights to the crowns of England and Portugal. Such claims were latent: the opportunities never arose to impose or even assert them against those who actually ruled these realms.

There could have been no Richard III without all these ancestors, but only a few contributed to the titles, estates, renown, and coats of arms of the House of York of which Richard of Fotheringhay was almost the last and most insignificant member. The eighth son of Richard Duke of York, he was the fourth to achieve maturity and never higher than third in line to the family's inheritances until he acceded in 1483. Fortunately there were always rules that determined priority among these hosts of relatives – four rules in particular: primogeniture, the direct male line, the royal line of succession, and the mitochondrial DNA of the direct female (maternal) line. Each is now discussed in turn.

The Principal Branches

Nobody in the Middle Ages was aware of DNA, let alone mitochondrial DNA. Everybody inherits genetically from all our ancestors. Mitochondrial DNA, so modern scientists assert, is transmitted only through females and never changes through the generations. Richard III's mitochondrial DNA was therefore inherited from his mother Cecily Neville, Duchess of York, his grandmother Joan Beaufort, Countess of Westmorland, his great-grandmother Katherine Swinford, Duchess of Lancaster (d. 1403), his great-great-grandmother the wife of the herald Payn Roet of Hainault in modern Belgium, and backwards though unidentified females who were probably Belgian.[15] Investigation of the female lines leads quickly into uncharted territories, into foreign origins and social obscurity; much more difficult to trace than the lines of descent in contemporary pedigrees, in the *Complete Peerage*, or the *History of Parliament*. A lady would share her husband's obsession with the future of his lineage, the lineage to which they had added a generation, but less interest was shown in its past. Often they recalled their mothers and grandmothers, invoking prayers for their souls, but no further back. The direct female line was of almost no interest in late medieval England and therefore generally went unrecorded. Looking forward, the family's genealogists recorded primarily the line of inheritance – rarely female, especially after the adoption of the male entail – and the genealogists of their husbands' families recorded only the irruption into the line of another wife. Past genealogies are little help in tracing mitochondrial DNA. All descendants of these ladies through the female line up to the present day should share the same mitochondrial DNA. Looking forwards again, all the descendants in the unbroken female line from Richard's sisters should share it too – a crucial forensic argument in the identification of the bones under the Leicester car park discussed in chapter 9. It is ironic that this obscure and neglected phenomenon should have become so important today and moreover that it apparently determined key aspects of our ancestors' physical make-up.

Royalty and noblemen in late medieval England inherited their rank, wealth, and right to rule. There were strict rules that determined the order of inheritance. Land was inherited in late medieval England according to strict rules. There were inheritance customs that allowed all children or all males to inherit equally, for chattels (moveable goods) and in Kent for land (gavelkind), but these never applied to large estates. The rules that applied to lands held by knight service, which meant almost every sizeable property, was primogeniture, which was so normal that it was often termed the law of England. Primogeniture was the default position that was assumed unless there were good reasons not to apply it, for example an entail. Asked who was heir to a deceased tenant-in-chief, inquisition juries automatically identified the heir by primogeniture. Primogeniture produced single rather than multiple heirs. Priority was given to the direct line of descent, to males in each generation in order of birth before females, and permitted inheritance by females or through the female line; for example, the daughter of an eldest son took precedence over younger sons, and sisters inherited equally as coheiresses. Most issue were younger sons and daughters who, their fathers hoped, would not inherit. Life expectancy being short, mortality ever present, and fertility erratic, often enough younger sons or daughters defied such intentions and predictions and did inherit nevertheless. Noblemen died often enough without issue, but rarely without male heirs – collaterals could succeed when the direct line was exhausted – or without heirs at all since relatives through female lines could succeed. 'Landowners,' declared K. B. McFarlane, 'rarely if ever died without heirs. Without issue, yes, often enough; but without any blood relations, virtually never. And the longer the Conqueror's followers were established in England, the wider the network of their blood-ties spread. An escheat, that is to say, could not happen naturally; it had to be engineered.'[16]

Ancient dynasties like the Beauchamps, Mortimers or Nevilles gradually accrued through the female line the estates of other families that failed in the direct male line. The monster estates of Richard Duke of York and Warwick the Kingmaker were agglomerations of multiple inheritances that had been accumulated in this way. Duke Richard inherited much more from his mother Anne Mortimer than from his uncle Edward Duke of York. It was by primogeniture that he was Earl of Ulster in Ireland, Earl of March in Wales, and lord of the honour of Clare in England.

Sexual equality is our modern expectation and in 2013 the law of succession was amended to give to princesses the same rights as princes to reign. In late medieval England, in contrast, that women could inherit was perceived as a weakness of primogeniture. There were three problems with it. Firstly, a woman carried her inheritance to her husband, who was likely to exercise it without regard for junior or collateral members of her birth family, such as uncles or younger sons. Secondly, coheiresses broke up the estate into equal shares. Thirdly, female succession interrupted the family name. All three phenomena can be illustrated by the Beauchamp earls of Warwick, who strove on several occasions to maintain a line of succession dating from 1268 that demographic accidents threatened to terminate. They entailed their estates on the male line and provided generously for their disinherited daughters in other ways. From the late thirteenth century, however, many landholders entailed their lands. They limited the succession to their descendants, male or female, and increasingly in tail male – to their direct male line of sons, grandsons, etc. Entails were practised by men and women. They were frequently used by second wives to divert inheritances to the offspring of second marriages.[17] Elizabeth Lady Ferrers of Groby famously preferred her second husband and her younger sons to the offspring of her eldest son John, whose potentially destitute widow Elizabeth Wydeville was driven into the arms of Edward IV.[18]

Edward III was enthusiastic about male entails. In 1337 he restricted five new earldoms to the male lines of the new earls. Similarly, the dukedoms of Clarence and York that he bestowed on his junior sons Lionel and Edmund and the estates and annuities that were settled on Edmund Duke of York were all in tail male. Lionel had a daughter, Philippa, but being only twenty he was expected to father sons. Edward's entail meant, firstly, that the duchy of Clarence died with Duke Lionel in 1368; it did not pass to his daughter Philippa, to her heirs by primogeniture the Mortimers, or hence to their heir Richard Duke of York. Duke Richard inherited nothing from Lionel and Philippa. He was therefore not entitled to the coat of arms of Clarence and had never used them, as the lords in Parliament pointed out. There is a parallel in the royal permission required for Henry Duke of Buckingham to adopt, with a difference, the royal arms of his great-great-grandfather Thomas of Woodstock, Duke of Gloucester (d. 1397), youngest son of Edward III.[19] Secondly, the entail meant that only the descendants of the third son, John of Gaunt, and the fourth, Edmund of Langley, retained their duchies into the fifteenth century. With the passage of the generations, these lines grew apart. Richard Duke of York, second cousin twice removed of King Henry VI, became a rather distant collateral relative of the Crown, still an inheritor of royal blood but no longer categorised as a member of the inner royal family. Duke Richard, as a duke, was a high and mighty prince, but his youngest son Richard of Fotheringhay was not a prince at all. Demographic accident, in particular the childless deaths of the three brothers of King Henry V, made Richard Duke of York the senior surviving duke, the premier duke with precedence over all the other dukes that Henry VI was to create. Indeed King Henry recognised that York was special and allowed to his elder sons Edward and Edmund the courtesy titles of earl, respectively of March and Rutland.

The English Royal Family

Medieval Europe was almost the same as Christendom. All medieval Europeans, like Richard III, were Christians and believed the stories in the Bible from Genesis on to be literally true. They tagged their own genealogies on to national histories that continued down to themselves. Humankind was a vast, interconnected family. All lines of descent started, so medieval people believed, in the Garden of Eden with Adam (the first father) and Eve (the first mother), with Noah and his three sons, and the myriad generations that lay between. Supposedly monarchs reigned by conquest (possession) and election or acclamation, not just by inheritance alone, but actually inheritance was the key. The *King*

Lear situation, where a kingdom was divided between daughters just like any other piece of property, was never acceptable. For the royal house were constructed the grandest genealogies of all, mass-produced by professional scriveners and illuminators. All such rolls traced the succession of kings of England, their queens, and their offspring. Some such rolls were customised for particular purchasers, tracing their lines beyond the birth of their princely ancestors and itemising their own growing broods with sufficient accuracy to enable us to date approximately the composition of particular rolls. For kings and those who were royal, this line of succession and the principal princely houses stood out from the mass of noble, genteel, and plebeian pedigrees. These were the trunks, the main roads to which lesser families tried to attach themselves and thus share their royal blood, albeit diffused and diluted.

The English royal family (the Plantagenets) was itself a considerable network of approximately 200 individuals all claiming to be royal. These 200 were descended from previous English kings both in 1300 and in 1500. That the number did not increase significantly was because such aristocrats tended to intermarry. All were cousins: more than seven generations comprehended those descended from 256 great-great-great-great-great-grandparents. Table 1 illustrates this: bar two generations of Roets and Padillas, all the sixty-four great-great-great-great-grandparents of Richard III were born to parents who were monarchs or members of the English House of Lords.

The Wars of the Roses were wars among cousins, all descendants of Henry II (the first Plantagenet) and all those who really mattered from Edward III (1327–77). Edward III was the patriarch of the nobility of fifteenth-century England (see Pedigree 1). Nobody in fifteenth-century England disputed the kingship of any ruler before him: only with his tyrannical grandson Richard II (1377–99) did the succession become a political issue. All royal, none used the name Plantagenet, dividing instead into separate branches of the

Table 1. Lineages culminating in Richard III.

No.	Parents 2	Grandparents 4	Gt-Grandparents 8	Gt-Grandparents 16	Gt-Grandparents 32	Gt-Grandparents 64
1						Edward I 1272–1307
2					Edward II 1307–27	Eleanor of Castile d. 1290
3				Edward III 1327–77		Philip IV d. 1314
4			Edmund D. York d. 1402		Isabella of France d. 1358	Joan of Navarre d. 1305
5						John II Ct Hainault d. 1324
6					William III Ct. Hainault d. 1337	Philippa of Luxemberg d. 1311
7		Richard E. Cambridge d. 1415		Philippa of Hainault d. 1369		Charles Ct of Valois d. 1325
8					Jeanne of Valois d. 1352	Margaret of Anjou d. 1299
9						Ferdinand IV of Castile d. 1312
10					Alfonso XI of Castille d. 1350	Constance of Portugal d. 1313
11				Pedro I of Castille d. 1369		Alfonso IV of Portugal d. 1357
12					Maria of Portugal d. 1357	Beatrice of Castile d. 1359
13			Isabel of Castile d. 1392			Unknown
14					Juan Garcia de Padilla	Unknown
15				Maria de Padilla d.1361		Unknown
16	Richard D. York				Maria Garcia de Henestoza	Unknown
17						Roger E. March d. 1330
18		Anne Mortimer d. 1411		Edmund E. March d. 1381	Roger E. Match d. 1360	Joan de Geneville d. 1356
19						William E. Salisbury d. 1344
20			Roger E. March d. 1398		Philippa Montagu d.1382	Katherine Grandisson d. 1349
21				Philippa d. 1381		Edward III 1327–77
22					Lionel D. Clarence d. 1368	Philippa of Hainault d. 1369
23					William E. Ulster d. 1333	
24					Elizabeth de Burgh d. 1363	Maud Chaworth d. 1377
25						Robert Ld Holland d. 1328
26					Thomas Holland E. Kent d. 1360	Maud Zouche d. 1349
27				Thomas E. Kent d. 1397		Edmund E. Kent d. 1330
28					Joan of Kent d. 1385	Margaret Wake d. 1349
29						Edmund E. Arundel d. 1326
30			Eleanor Holland d. 1405	Alice Arundel d. 1416	Richard E. Arundel d. 1376	Alice Warenne
31					Eleanor of Lancaster	Henry E. Lancaster d. 1345
32						Maud Chaworth

No.	Parents	Grandparents	Gt-Grandparents	Gt-Grandparents	Gt-Grandparents	Gt-Grandparents
	2	4	8	16	32	64
33						Robert Neville d. 1271
34					Randal Ld Neville d. 1331	Mary Fitz Randolf d. 1320
35						Robert FitzRoger d. 1310
36				Ralph Ld. Neville d. 1367	Euphemia Clavering	Margery Zouche
37						James Audley
38					Hugh Ld Audley d. 1326	Ela Longespée
39			John Ld Neville d. 1388	Alice Audley d. 1374		Edmund Mortimer d. 1304
40					Isolt Mortimer fl.1336	Margaret Fiennes d.1334
41						Henry Percy d. 1272
42				Henry Ld Percy d. 1352	Henry Ld Percy d.1314	Eleanor Warenne
43			Maud Percy d. 1379			Richard E. Arundel d. 1302
44					Eleanor Arundel d. 1328	Alasia of Saluzzo d. 1292
45						Robert Ld Clifford d. 1314
46					Robert Ld Clifford d. 1344	Maud de Clare d. 1327
47				Idonia Clifford d. 1365		Maurice Ld Berkeley d. 1326
48		Ralph E. Westmorland d. 1425			Isabel Berkeley d. 1362	Eva Zouche d. 1314
49	Cecily Neville					Edward I 1272–1307
50					Edward II 1327–77	Eleanor of Castille d. 1290
51						Philip IV d. 1314
52				Edward III 1327–77	Isabella of France d. 1358	Joan of Navarre d. 1305
53						John II Ct Hainault d. 1324
54			John D. Lancaster d. 1399		William III Ct Hainault d. 1337	Philippa of Luxemberg d. 1311
55				Philippa of Hainault d. 1369		Charles Ct Valois d. 1325
56					Jeanne Valois d. 1352	Margaret of Anjou d. 1299
57		Joan Beaufort d. 1440				Unknown
58					Payne Roet I	Unknown
59						Unknown
60			Katherine Swinford d. 1403	Payne Roet II	Unknown	Unknown
61						Unknown
62					Unknown	Unknown
63				Unknown		Unknown
64					Unknown	Unknown

Key: D = duke; M = marquis; E = earl; Ld = lord; Ct = count

royal family tree comprising the Lancastrian kings, Mortimers, Beauforts, Hollands, and Staffords. All were descended from Edward III – each with its own interests and priorities, each striving to become the royal line itself. They all cherished memories of their royal descent and royal blood. The Mowbray dukes of Norfolk made much of the arms of England (the three leopards) with a label of cadency that they inherited from Edward I's second surviving son, Thomas of Brotherton, and that marked them out as royal even though the Lancastrian kings who bore updated arms of England and France quarterly regarded them merely as distant cousins and not royal at all.[20]

Kings nevertheless remembered more distant ties than ordinary people, titling as cousins or *consanguinei* those whose kinship was somewhat distant. This was how they addressed the Mowbray dukes – most probably when implementing petitions in which the dukes named themselves in these terms. Richard III's father Richard Duke of York was merely a cousin of Henry VI. During the Wars of the Roses, cousins did kill cousins, brother-in-laws killed brothers-in-law, and ultimately brother slew brother. Shared family trees did unify their outlooks and aspirations. Such pedigrees did demonstrate the relationship of each nobleman to successive rightful kings to whom each owed obedience and fidelity. The family tree was thus the framework within which political action took place and helps explain much of that action.

It was also a cause of dissension and the wars – because Henry VI was the first of several kings whose right to rule was not universally acknowledged and because the question of who should rule instead gave rise to answers that varied according to the inheritance system that was applied. Although the Wars of the Roses began about good governance, it degenerated into a dynastic struggle. The claim of Richard Duke of York to succeed Henry VI differed from his claim to supplant him as Lord Protector: Edward of Lancaster, Henry Holland, and Margaret Beaufort did not agree. Different, contrasting and rival rules were invoked to justify the reigns of

Edward IV, Henry VI (again), Richard III and Henry VII. Richard III was first the beneficiary of this family rivalry and then its victim. Henry Tudor, who had been sheltered abroad, was left the last man standing and wed the senior surviving Yorkist, Edward IV's daughter Elizabeth. Their son Henry VIII was acknowledged as heir of both the warring houses, but the Yorkist pretenders of Henry VII's reign and the volumes of pedigrees of Edward III's descendants published around 1900 by the Marquis of Ruvigny and Raineval remind us how widely royal blood had been diffused.

Yet York was probably the male heir of Henry VI in 1447 and hence of Edward III. In England there was no Salic law like that invented in fourteenth-century France, which confined the succession to the direct male line, but Edward III, although claiming the French crown through his mother, desired to exclude women and claimants via women from his English throne. In 1376 King Edward appears to have entailed the crown in tail male on the male heirs of each of his sons.[21]The Black Prince and Duke Lionel were already dead. King Edward feared that a woman might inherit, specifically Philippa of Clarence. The ancient precedent of the Empress Matilda showed that women could not rule. Should the boy Richard II die childless, then Edward III decreed that the succession should pass over Philippa of Clarence first to the line of his third son John of Gaunt, then to that of his fourth son Edmund of Langley, and then to his fifth son. This entail was fulfilled in 1399 by the accession of Gaunt's son as King Henry IV and justified the rule of the three Lancastrian kings. The Lancastrians, however, failed to reproduce. Their blood ran very thin. From 1453 it was represented only by King Henry VI himself and his infant son Edward of Lancaster. What would happen if the Lancastrians expired? One option was that the crown would pass to Edmund Beaufort, Duke of Somerset, the grandson of John of Gaunt by his third marriage. But Gaunt's Beaufort children had been born before their parents married and bastards were unable to inherit in medieval England. They had been legitimated – the only bastards in medieval England to be legitimated both by the Church and Parliament[22] – but Henry IV had tried to exclude them from the throne, with doubtful legality but probably in accordance with public opinion. If they were discounted, then Richard Duke of York was next male heir to the crown under the 1376 entail. It was probably for this reason that York's retainer Thomas Young MP demanded that the duke be recognised as heir apparent.[23] It was probably the prime factor also in York's selection as Lord Protector in 1454. This 'high and mighty prince' certainly felt he could govern better than the inadequate man who was his sole and unquestionable superior. Each of his coups was preceded by public declarations of his loyalty, submissiveness and obedience to Henry VI. That high and mighty princess Duchess Cecily similarly presented herself as 'your lowly obedient servant and bedewoman' to Queen Margaret of Anjou.[24]

But was the 1376 entail valid? Indeed, were the acts of Parliament by which the succession was vested in Henry IV's male heirs? Actually it is doubtful whether kings could settle the crown or anything else beyond their own lifetime. Neither Henry V, Edward IV, nor Henry VIII, each of whom left underage heirs, were able to shape the management of the minorities or even the fulfilment of the pious intentions of their last wills. In 1460 York asserted that primogeniture, the law of England, was in accordance with the laws of God and nature, which took precedence over any such human arrangements. It was at this point that York laid claim to the crown by primogeniture as the great-grandson, through Philippa, of Lionel Duke of Clarence, second son to Edward III and elder brother of John of Gaunt.[25] Philippa's seniority was known – her priority over the Lancastrians features in the Mortimer chronicle of Wigmore Abbey[26] – but York had never before dared assert what amounted to an act of treason. In 1460, in the absence of the Lancastrian lords, those present in Parliament (most of whom held their lands by primogeniture) agreed. York's title could not be defeated and would take effect only after Henry VI's death. York's four sons, Richard of Fotheringhay included, became princes of the blood royal. Primogeniture prevailed.

The Yorkists won the Wars of the Roses and the winners wrote the history. Historians have therefore accepted this argument, but it came to prevail only over time. The Lancastrians rejected it, both in 1460 and until their extermination in 1471, and Chief Justice Fortescue wrote a whole series of treatises that rejected the Philippa claim. Much of its relevance moreover disappeared in 1471, when the deaths of Henry VI, his son, and the last Beauforts left Edward IV as heir both by primogeniture and in tail male. Even so, women could still not reign. Wherever Henry VII derived his title, from his mother Margaret Beaufort or his consort Elizabeth of York, they did not reign or even attempt to reign but transmitted their title to him. Henry VIII's desperation for a male heir is well known. Queens regnant came to England (as everywhere) only when there were no male alternatives.

The Creation of the Plantagenets

Until 1460 the royal family had no surname, known simply by their Christian name and place of birth: Lionel of Antwerp, John of Gaunt (Ghent) and Edmund of Langley for instance. It was Duke Richard who, in 1460, invented the surname of Plantagenet for the royal house. It is a surname that does not occur earlier. It harked back to the *planta genista*, or yellow broom, that Geoffrey Count of Anjou sported as his badge. Count Geoffrey was the father of King Henry II (1154–89), the ancestor of every later English king. What Duke Richard wished to convey was that he was the rightful heir through Philippa of Henry II. He also donned the livery colours of Lionel Duke of Clarence. Strictly speaking only the male line were entitled to the surname. Plantagenet became the name of a dynasty that included both the houses of Lancaster and York. Richard's offspring then became Plantagenets: Richard of Fotheringhay, the subject of this book, became Richard Plantagenet. Even the Beauforts and their descendants the illegitimate Somersets are regarded today as genetic Plantagenets in the Y-chromosome tests on the bones allegedly of Richard III.[27]

Richard III was the last Plantagenet king. The Plantagenet line is usually held to have ended with his death at the Battle of Bosworth in 1485; he was very largely responsible for the extinction of the Plantagenets. Not quite entirely, however, for his brother Clarence's son Edward Plantagenet, Earl of Warwick, survived until 1499 and every subsequent monarch of every dynasty traces its descent from Henry II and his father Count Geoffrey. The royal line of Plantagenet was the trunk of which the House of York was a branch that became, thanks to the pollarding of the Wars of the Roses, first the principal and then the only branch.

Bastards

Bastards are children born to parents who are not married. They were quite a prominent feature of fifteenth-century England. Princes and noblemen, including Henry V's three brothers, soldiers in the French wars and Lancastrian exiles, admitted to fathering quite a few, mainly boys. Distanced from wives, unmarried, or ineligible for their natural equals, they sated their sexual urges with those they need not marry. Such aristocrats benefited from a double standard that condoned the sexual peccadilloes of men while forbidding it for ladies. Edward IV, his boon companions the Wydeville men, Warwick the Kingmaker and Richard Duke of Gloucester, all fathered bastards. Yet chastity was *de rigueur* for aristocratic girls, who were devalued on the marriage market if deflowered and carefully chaperoned, and within marriage also, since the succession to family property and titles was at risk. Mistakes did happen – witness the shotgun wedding in a pre-shotgun era of Elizabeth of Lancaster, sister of Henry IV, to her lover John Holland, and the cases of Constance Despenser (*née* of York) and Anne Duchess of Exeter (again *née* of York) – but rarely. It was presumably sexual desire that prompted financially independent young dowagers to become the *femmes couvertes* of attractive young men of lower rank, especially successful jousters, as Elizabeth of Lancaster (twice), Queen Katherine of France, Jacquetta of Luxemberg, Elizabeth Wydeville, and Cecily of York all did. The moral code of the Church was strict. Sexual intercourse outside marriage (fornication), within marriage (adultery), homosexuality, bestiality, and much else was forbidden and the rules were enforced with the aid of a public that found such conduct genuinely shocking and shopped the offenders. Lust was the one deadly sin that obsessed the Church authorities. Babies were such conspicuous evidence of sin. Early modern statistics derived from parish registers indicate astonishingly low illegitimacy rates of 1 per cent, although these are inflated four-fold for babies conceived outside wedlock but born within it. Such prenuptial pregnancies, Peter Laslett argued, were undertaken with marriage in view and were thus almost respectable. Sex with married women, of course, was always much more difficult to prove: the baby was generally attributed to the husband.

Illegitimacy was a terrible slur. The Church itself was quite tolerant to bastard begetters who subsequently married, legitimising their children, but the English refused to comply. They denied that bastards could ever be legitimated; the only exceptions, the Beauforts, needed a special act of parliament to legitimise them at the common law, yet public opinion seems never to have accepted them. Bastards could not inherit. They had no heirs able automatically to inherit from them. They had no landed inheritances, therefore no manorial descents by which they can be tracked. The inseminator had no obligation to pay maintenance or otherwise support them. Bastards did not count as family and indeed had no family. The fathers of bastards, it appears, seldom acknowledged their bastards, especially when female. Bastard sons are better recorded than bastard daughters, probably because they were more often acknowledged and eased into military careers. Bastard daughters, if recognised, had to be expensively married off: Humphrey Duke of Gloucester's daughter Antigone and Warwick the Kingmaker's daughter Margaret are examples. Single mothers were left holding their baby, husbands the babies (presumably unsuspected) of their wives that had been fathered by other men. Some of the inseminators cherished their by-blows and tried to provide for them, with difficulty. Richard III falls into this category. Once king, he divulged his bastards, treated them as family, made a good marriage for his daughter and offered advancement to his son. He was as harsh to the bastards of others as anyone else, however. Richard's summary execution of his illegitimate cousin Thomas Neville, Bastard of Fauconberg, is reminiscent of the contempt and unkindness shown to the by-blows of Edward III, John Duke of Bedford, or Humphrey Duke of Gloucester. Richard moreover reduced his brother Edward's offspring to bastards, thus destroying their social status, inheritances, and marriageability. This was extremely cruel treatment to his blameless nephews and nieces. Unsubstantiated slurs of bastardy, almost a political commonplace, were ruinous to the victims. There was normally no room for bastards within nuclear or conjugal families, collateral families, or lineages.

3

CADET OF THE HOUSE OF YORK

The Demography of Richard III

Richard of Fotheringhay, the focus of this book, figured in many families of different types that succeeded one another and overlapped with each other. He was born the eighth son and eleventh child of Richard and Cecily. He was almost the last and most insignificant addition to their brood:[1] a cadet of the House of York. His thirty-two years of life, which seem so short to us, exceeded the life expectancy of the population as a whole. We cannot tell how many of his eleven siblings still existed during his own lifetime or were known to him – unusually, it is their births that are recorded, not their deaths – but we know five that left home and married before him. His father, three of his brothers, and two of his four sisters predeceased him. So did all of his aunts and uncles. Nephews, nieces, and cousins too numerous to easily categorise were born, some of whom also died in infancy. Richard's brothers and sisters, their spouses and in-laws, and their progeny became Richard's extended family. His own nuclear family was truncated. He was not young to marry at about twenty, to have fathered a legitimate child at twenty-five, to be widowed at thirty-two, nor was he unique to be planning a second family at his death. Richard was never a grandfather, nor apparently even a great-uncle if Mary of Burgundy, stepdaughter of his sister, is disallowed.

Richard III's parents, Richard Duke of York and Cecily Neville, were probably married in 1429 when Cecily was fourteen and Richard was eighteen,[2] but babies took their time to appear. Pseudo-Worcester writes of years of barrenness, no pregnancies or at least no live births, but between 1439 and 1455 Richard and Cecily had twelve children who lived long enough to be baptised. Additionally there were three gaps long enough to fit in miscarriages or stillbirths. The chronology of Cecily's pregnancies and the order of her live births are set out below (Table 2). The dates and locations of birth are recorded. The date of conception is calculated on a gestation period of thirty-eight weeks: babies, however, are notoriously unreliable in timing their first appearance, so variations of a few weeks could have occurred. John Rows stated much later that Richard was two years in the womb,[3] which is not possible biologically nor (as Table 2 shows) mathematically, but there was ample time for a longer-than-normal gestation. Churching, the purification of the mother, is calculated at forty days after the birth, a period for which marital intercourse should have been suspended.

Cecily was pregnant for 122 months during these years, 66 per cent of the entire period; perhaps another fifteen months of recuperation should be allowed for her twelve purifications (churchings). It was a relentless schedule that may not have left her much time for other thoughts, activities, or political engagement. We cannot know how incapacitated Cecily was in the early stages of pregnancy. Only in the last phase of pregnancy were medieval ladies actually confined, but without the benefit of antenatal classes or vigorous post-natal exercise perhaps they (and particularly Cecily) were not in best physical condition. A letter of encouragement from Cecily to the pregnant Queen Margaret draws on her own experience.[4] Although the letter is undated, it could be Richard's carriage that was so wearisome to her. Of course Cecily did not

Table 2: The Children of Cecily Duchess of York (and Richard Duke of York)

Name	Date of conception (calculated)	Place of birth	Date of birth	Date of churching (calculated)
Anne	10 Dec 1438	Fotheringhay	10 Aug 1439	29 Sept 1438
Henry	10 May 1440	Hatfield	10 Feb 1441	22 Mar 1441
Edward	28 Jul 1441	Rouen	28 Apr 1442	7 May 1442
Edmund	17 Aug 1442	Rouen	17 May 1443	11 Jun 1443
Elizabeth	22 Jul 1443	Rouen	22 Apr 1444	1 Jun 1444
Margaret	3 Aug 1445	Fotheringhay	3 May 1446	12 Jun 1446
William	7 Oct 1446	Fotheringhay	7 Jul 1447	16 Aug 1447
John	7 Feb 1448	Neyte	7 Nov 1448	17 Dec 1448
George	21 Jan 1449	Dublin	21 Oct 1449	21 Jan 1449
Thomas	Feb 1450 or later		Jan 1451 or later	
Richard	2 Jan 1452	Fotheringhay	2 Oct 1452	2 Jan 1453
Ursula	20 Nov 1454		20 Jul 1455	29 Aug 1455

Sources: Osbert Bokenham, 'The Clare Roll', in W. Dugdale, *Monasticon Anglicanum*, ed. W. Thomas (1830), vii.1600–02; *Annales*, ii (2).762–65, 767.

suckle her own offspring – the aristocracy routinely delegated that task to wet nurses – and so there was no amenorrhoea to reduce her fertility or to impede the conveyor belt of reproduction. Slight evidence indicates that her children nevertheless resided with her. Cecily had a separate household and a separate itinerary from her husband. The frequency of conceptions shows the duke was often around. Richard's birthplace at Fotheringhay seems a more probable base than Sandal in Yorkshire or Ludlow in Wales,[5] where several of his documents are dated.

Richard of Fotheringhay's hectic passage through all the ages of man illustrates how life was concentrated, even transistorised, in late medieval England. Living was always risky and unpredictable. Sudden death loomed at any time. The most commonplace injuries or maladies were killers then. Everyone was vulnerable to disease and accidents at all ages, often succumbing to infections or injuries that pose no risk today. Sudden and speedy deaths were common.

The most hazardous experience of everyday life was its beginning. Perhaps as many pregnancies ended prematurely in miscarriages and abortively in stillborn infants as resulted in live births. Such misfortunes may fill the gaps in the fertile cycle of Richard's mother Cecily. Miscarriages and stillbirths generally went unrecorded. Parish registers had not yet been invented and the parish and private service books in which baptisms were irregularly recorded have seldom survived the centuries. However, chronicles and pedigrees derived from them sometimes do. As king, Richard III entered his date of birth (2 October 1452) in the calendar of his book of hours.[6] To be remembered babies had to be born alive, baptised, and named. Christenings were held as soon as babies were born, often on the actual day of their birth, a process that made them Christian and eligible for salvation. There are two records of the births of twelve children of the House of York in Osbert Bokenham's *Clare Roll* or pseudo-Worcester's *Annales*. Edward, Edmund and Elizabeth were born at Rouen in Normandy during Duke Richard's lieutenancy of France; George was born at Dublin during the duke's lieutenancy of Ireland; one other was born at Westminster and the other four at Fotheringhay. Five of Richard's siblings died in infancy or early childhood: Henry (born 1441), William (1447), John (1448), Thomas (1451?), and Ursula (1455). Thomas did not live long enough to be noticed in Worcester's list but Ursula was still living in the *Clare Roll*, presumably dying a toddler. Of those to survive only Edmund, slain at the Battle of Wakefield in 1460, failed to achieve maturity, but half of the York offspring had died by their mid-twenties, the life expectancy being low. Three died violently, and only Elizabeth (1444–1503) and Margaret (1446–1503) reached their fifties – a marker of old age.

Probably only six of these ten older brothers and sisters were still living when Richard was born: Anne (already married), Edward,

Edmund, Elizabeth, Margaret, and George. An undated letter from the duchess to the queen, dated to 1453 on the basis that Margaret's sole live birth was also her only pregnancy, refers to 'th'encomeous labour' that had prevented Cecily attending the queen. The language is obscure. Perhaps it referred to sickness when bearing Richard, the difficulty being that that birth happened several months before the queen's only recorded pregnancy began.[7] It is possible, of course, that either the queen or the duchess or both had other abortive pregnancies that are unrecorded. Long afterwards John Rows and Thomas More reported that Richard gave Cecily a difficult pregnancy and difficult childbirth, as the baby was overdue (and therefore perhaps large), positioned feet-first (the breach position), 'could not be delivered uncut' (probably an episiotomy rather than a Caesarean), and with teeth and hair (which were immaterial in birth). These observations, some current in 1486 and the others afterwards,[8] are usually regarded as later elaborations to supply the unnatural beginning felt necessary for someone so evil. They were reported by men who were not eyewitnesses and knew little of the topic, since men were excluded from birthing chambers and Rows anyway was a celibate priest. Yet there may have been a grain of truth to the story. Richard was to acquire only one further sibling, the short-lived Ursula, born after a three-year interval in 1455, when Cecily was forty. Only two of Cecily's last five babies survived infancy, and only Richard out of the last three. Perhaps Cecily was in poor shape for these final pregnancies: medieval ladies may well have become progressively less fit for labour rather than benefiting from past experiences. It may well have been a surprise therefore that 'Richard liveth yet', as Bokenham wrote, a much quoted comment perhaps indicating his continued frailty, but which may merely have been written because the comment needed to fit the verse. If the bones are indeed his, Richard was undersized, slender and delicate.

Richard, his brothers Edward and George, and his sisters Anne, Elizabeth and Margaret all departed their family of birth to become conjugal partners of new nuclear families. All except

Richard and Margaret bore children who married and formed their own nuclear families.

So great was infant, childhood, and adolescent mortality that historians once opined that parents could not afford to invest love in their offspring. Against that needs to be set evidence from the proofs of age that the christenings even of younger children were occasions for joy, celebration, and lavish expenditure. Churches were decked out with expensive hangings and messengers hastily assembled guests who were regaled with exotic sweet wines. The mothers were virtually never present – they were exhausted and not infrequently died. It was customary for gifts of wine and poultry to augment their diet. Towards the birth pregnant mothers were confined and often therefore geographically distant from their husbands. Husbands were anyway redundant at the birth; excluded from the labour room and unwilling to await the convenience of the baby, they were often absent, hunting or engaged in business at quarter sessions or Parliament, and had to be notified and/or fetched by messengers who were often lavishly rewarded. The proofs indicate just as much fuss over younger children as the firstborn. Richard Duke of York had a separate household, separate residences and a separate itinerary. Although apparently nearby at the births of Edmund and George, he was surely absent from that of Ursula and probably those of several others. Quite likely he did attend Richard's christening on 2 October 1452 at Fotheringhay since he issued documents there on 11 August and 18 December.[9] It would be nice to presume that the duke selected Richard's name, to commemorate his own name or that of his father, but most of his offspring seem to have had not family names but those of their godparents or names selected by their godparents.[10] The birth of a fourth son was not an important event, if indeed Richard of Fotheringhay ranked as high as fourth at birth – we do not know when his elder brothers William and John (or indeed Henry and Thomas) died. The years before Duke Richard's death and his earliest memories were marked by a dozen christenings and churchings of his mother, occasions for family celebration in which, of course, he had not shared.

The nobility were expected to provide for all their children as was appropriate to their rank. This was expensive, yet not to do so was to father's and family's 'disworship'. It could detract from their standing and reputation. York had no need to make special provisions for his eldest son Edward, who was destined to inherit everything, but the younger sons were a problem. A conquered lordship in Normandy was earmarked at first for Edmund,[11] but this was lost inevitably in the reconquest. Perhaps the elevation of Edmund to the earldom of Rutland implied an obligation for Henry VI to endow him, but nothing had been done for George and Richard by 1460, when Duke Richard died. He did marry his two eldest daughters, Anne and Elizabeth, to the dukes of Exeter and Suffolk, the noblest husbands around, contracting to pay the highest known marriage portion, of £4,333 13s 4d, to Exeter.[12] All dowries were payable in instalments – hence a continuing burden on the family estate – and neither was fully paid when York died still heavily in debt. Such matches were prestigious political alliances, but they were also massive investments in York's daughters' futures and illustrate how the sole inheritor was harnessing all his resources to the benefit of his whole family.

Richard himself was to marry, acquiring a wife, in-laws and a son, and formed his own nuclear family early in the 1470s. An important component was conjugal intercourse between Richard and his consort Anne Neville, which continued almost as long as Richard's marriage, but sex alone with his mistress(es) was possible without the ideological and material commitment that was involved in marriage. Richard and Anne cherished their only son Edward, invested in him hopes for his and the family's future, and were distraught when he died.[13] It was in 1484–85 that both Richard's wife and son died, leaving him alone. Evidently Richard intended to marry again and thus to create further children: a new nuclear family. Nuclear families constantly expired as new ones grew out of them, grandchildren in due course becoming grandparents. Even when a lonely widower, therefore, Richard still had a family and was a component in many other families as Uncle Richard and Cousin Richard. He still possessed two sisters, numerous nieces and nephews, brothers- and sisters-in-law. There were also his own bastards. However, mistresses and by-blows did not count as family: in law a bastard had no parents and no heirs. Richard III had not one family but many families. Richard had scores if not hundreds of kin. The remainder of this chapter itemises the families with which he started.

The House of York

Richard of Fotheringhay features almost last among the children of Duke Richard and Duchess Cecily on the royal pedigree rolls. The youngest son was the most insignificant and had the most uncertain future. His childhood was nevertheless privileged, since he basked in the exalted rank, lavish lifestyle, noble connections and hereditary renown of his paternal line.

The House of York originated in Edmund of Langley (d. 1402), the fourth son of Edward III. Duke Edmund was meagrely endowed, most of his income coming in annuities that were irregularly paid by the exchequer, and had relatively few estates. Attempts were made to find him a foreign principality by marrying him to Margaret of Flanders, England's natural ally, but she fell instead to the Valois prince Philip of Burgundy: a case in which an Avignon pope, Urban V, showed himself to be decidedly Francophile.[14] Edmund did marry Isabella de Padilla, the younger illegitimate daughter to King Pedro the Cruel of Castile, and never renounced his title as his brother John of Gaunt did on behalf of Isabella's sister Constance of Castile. This distant and unrealistic claim was fostered by both Duke Richard and Edward IV.[15] Duke Edmund did remarry to an heiress Joan Holland, the match being childless. Within England, Fotheringhay in Northamptonshire, where our Richard was born, was a principal seat. The family stayed quite frequently at Fotheringhay Castle, which has completely disappeared, and raised the parish church into the collegiate church that was fashionable around 1400. Fotheringhay College was their mausoleum. Unfortunately the east end and their original tombs were destroyed in the Reformation, the bones removed to the nave, but the splendid Perpendicular western limb and central tower remain. It was surely here that Richard was baptised and certainly here that he was principal mourner at the reinterment of his father and elder brother Edmund in 1476.

Generation by generation the Yorks should have removed far beyond the inner royal family. The failure of the main Lancastrian line to reproduce, however – all three Lancastrian royal dukes died without legitimate heirs – raised Duke Richard instead to the status of premier duke, the first subject of Henry VI and the senior legitimate male line after the king's own. Henry VI had treated York as special. Such distinction made York's rebellion in 1459 all the more ungrateful and heinous.

Although royal and ducal, the Yorks were not particularly distinguished. Duke Edmund had fought in France and Spain and Duke Edward perished a war hero at Agincourt, albeit in a humiliating fashion. Unhorsed, the fat duke was suffocated in his armour. All three children of Duke Edmund – Duke Edward, Richard of Conisborough (Yorks.), and Constance Despenser – were fickle politically and of doubtful loyalty. Duke Edward, the favourite of Richard II, was lucky to escape his master's fate and appears also to have dabbled in treason under Henry IV. Duke Edmund surely made some provision for his second son Richard, but it cannot have been much. His mother Isabella, illegitimate daughter of King Pedro the Cruel of Castile and his mistress Maud de Padilla, had so poor a moral reputation at the time that 'the possibility that her ruffianly lover' John Holland 'was the father of the duchess's younger (and favourite son) [Richard of Conisborough] cannot

be ignored'. Infidelity was suspected by the chronicler Thomas
Walsingham and the poet Geoffrey Chaucer among contemporaries
(and among modern historians by T. B. Pugh and Professor Mark
Ormrod too).[16] Henry V cannot have credited the story, since he
raised Richard to the earldom of Cambridge in 1414: this lesser
family title anticipated the succession of the earl and his young
son (the future Richard Duke of York) as heir apparent to the
duchy on Duke Edward's death. Henry V did not endow him.
Cambridge plotted against Henry V – the Southampton Plot of
1415 – and was executed for treason. Their sister Constance Lady
Despenser committed treason too against Henry IV. She also bore
an illegitimate child by Edmund Earl of Kent – she seems to have
thought they were contracted – but he chose to marry elsewhere. The
dubious liaisons of Richard's sister Anne await proper examination.

Of these three children of Duke Edmund, it was this second son
and traitor Cambridge who was the father of Richard Duke of York
and grandfather of Richard III. York had always to live with his
father's treason. He was brought up by Ralph Earl of Westmorland
and Joan Beaufort, Henry V's uncle and aunt, loyal stalwarts to
whom the Lancastrian kings confided the upbringing of other sons
of traitors. The Westmorlands married him safely to their youngest
daughter Cecily. Contracting him to Cecily, also of the royal blood
of Lancaster, was a mechanism to integrate Duke Richard into the
loyal royal family. Only in 1461 did Edward IV have Cambridge's
sentence revoked: the justification then, in a rewriting of history,
being that Cambridge died backing the rightful Mortimer cause
against the wrongful Lancastrian usurpers. King Edward provided
for masses for his grandfather's soul at Southampton, Westminster,
and elsewhere.[17] Duke Edward had perished shortly after his
brother. Cambridge's four-year-old son Richard did inherit the
duchy of York, its modest endowment, and dubious reputation,
but it was the inheritance of his mother Anne Mortimer (d. 1411)
that enabled him to live up to his rank and made him the greatest
nobleman of his day. She was the sister and eventual sole heiress

of Edmund Mortimer, earl of March and Ulster (d. 1425), the greatest landholder in both Wales and Ireland and with substantial estates at Clare (Suff.) and elsewhere in England, all of which accrued to Duke Richard on his majority. Ludlow (Salop.) was the capital of York's great Welsh estates from which he launched his *coups d'état* in 1452, 1455 and 1459. The York title and Mortimer estates underpinned Richard's appointments twice as lieutenant of France and as lieutenant of Ireland.

The Mortimer inheritance itself was composite. The Welsh marcher lordships were indeed Mortimer possessions, but the earldom of Ulster and the honour of Clare had been the inheritance of Elizabeth de Burgh, Duchess of Clarence, whose daughter Philippa had married an earlier Earl Edmund (d. 1381). Philippa's father Lionel Duke of Clarence was the second son of Edward III, but she had inherited neither his own title nor his own lands since these had been entailed in the male line. Neither she nor her descendants were entitled to the arms of Clarence, which Richard Duke of York appropriated only in 1460. It was through Philippa and Anne Mortimer – two female descents – that Duke Richard laid claim to the crown by primogeniture in 1460 even though Edward III, Henry IV and the parliament of 1406 had firmly ruled them out in favour of the Lancastrian male line. These ramifications of Richard's ancestry were well known within the family and the religious houses that cultivated its memory. The *Clare Roll* of their friary at Clare in Suffolk traced the descent of Clare from Edward I's daughter Joan of Acre through Elizabeth de Burgh, Philippa, and Anne Mortimer to Richard Duke of York and his children. The Mortimer chronicle compiled at Wigmore Abbey proclaimed the validity of Duke Richard's claim to the throne,[18] albeit to a very small readership. When Duke Richard asserted his claim in 1460, as 'verray heir', there were many who resisted. Within two months he was defeated at Wakefield and executed. Duke Richard's eldest son Edward did make himself king in 1461, but he was opposed by the Lancastrians for another decade.

York's great inheritance was not merely the accident of heredity, but had been planned. Kings and nobles were the product of selective breeding. There were scarcely any love matches in late medieval England. Any that happened were condemned for being based on mere partiality rather than the rule of reason. Royal and aristocratic marriages were *arranged*, on the basis of lineage and connections, rank and title, inheritance, dowry, and political usefulness. They were contracted with others within the same circle, among equals, designed to ensure the support of both parties and any resulting offspring, to mutual advantage. The House of York was the culmination of many generations of selective breeding designed to foster important connections rather than the perfect human being. Richard Duke of York and his youngest son Richard III were apparently small, dark, slight and not at all handsome. Human pedigrees, not unlike Cruft's, need not select the finest physiques, the most handsome or beautiful, the strongest and most militarily adept, the cleverest, the most religious or most artistic, the most trustworthy, or the most sexually potent and faithful to take the accolades and rule. Individual kings of the Wars of the Roses met some of these criteria. None met them all.

Richard of Fotheringhay imbibed all this family lore at an early age. Important though they were, all his grandparents were already dead: Anne Mortimer in 1411, her husband Richard Earl of Cambridge in 1415, Ralph Earl of Westmorland in 1425, and his second countess Joan Beaufort in 1440. He would have learnt about them – indeed unquestionably did know about them – because he was taught about them. He was reminded of more distant ancestors in the direct line by manuscript pedigrees – the royal pedigrees mentioned above, the *Clare Roll*, the *Wigmore Chronicle*, the Neville pedigree, and royal rolls. Noble children were taught heraldry so that they could read effortlessly the family names, lineages, and connections recorded in the quarterings of the coats of arms and the badges that adorned the shields, the caparisons of horses, banners, communion and table plate, vestments, castles and churches that surrounded them on every side. Monuments in their churches commemorated ancestors for whom they were constantly enjoined to pray. Whenever Richard visited Fotheringhay he was reminded of his York forebears, at Ludlow of the Mortimers. At Durham there was a Neville chapel, at York St William's College, at Lincoln Joan Beaufort's tomb, at Westminster those of his kingly ancestors. Monastic and family chroniclers strove to ensure that the memory of these predecessors stayed alive. Continuations of these pedigrees added in the marriages and youngest generations of his lineage. Richard did his bit. *The Rows Roll* and the pedigree in the *Beauchamp Pageant* record Richard's marriage. Both culminate with his son Prince Edward of Middleham. Noble youths needed to know all their connections, their names and titles, and their coats of arms: to them these were visual aids by which pedigrees could be read and relationships identified. Even if he did not know every connection in person, Richard surely knew where they fitted. In the 1470s Richard applied such knowledge to ensure that rights and inheritances devolved properly on him.

Collateral Relatives

There were not many members of the House of York outside Richard's nuclear family. Great-aunt Constance Lady Despenser's bastard daughter Eleanor was married to James Tuchet Lord Audley, who was killed by the Yorkists at the Battle of Blore Heath in 1459. Perhaps this distant connection explains why John Lord Audley was close to Edward IV – close enough to be threatened with death alongside Edward's other favourites in 1469 – but there is no concrete evidence of this and no obvious benefit for Audley. Eleanor apparently predeceased her husband.

In the next generation Duke Richard of York had one sister, Isabel, who married Henry Bourchier, in due course viscount,

Count of Eu, and Earl of Essex. Their marriage lasted from 1426 to 1483 – a remarkably long time in the fifteenth century. Bourchier was already Isabel's second cousin, since his mother, Anne Stafford, was daughter of Thomas of Woodstock, fifth son of Edward III. They had three brothers, Duke Richard's brothers-in-law/second cousins, in Thomas Archbishop of Canterbury (d. 1486), William Lord FitzWarren (d. 1469), and John Lord Berners (d. 1474), and a half-brother in Humphrey Stafford, Duke of Buckingham (d. 1460). All had royal blood. Essex, FitzWarren, Berners, and Buckingham all had issue, Duke Richard's nephews and also his cousins. There are too many of them to display in pedigree 2. The Bourchiers and the Staffords remained on amicable terms for the rest of the century. Earl Henry and his brother Archbishop Thomas were trusted by Henry VI in the 1450s and were advanced by Edward IV. Henry's son Humphrey Lord Cromwell, and Berners' son, another Humphrey Bourchier, both perished on the Yorkist side at the Battle of Barnet in 1471. The two key figures, Earl Henry and Countess Isabel, died at great age in 1483–84. Essex's demise five days before Edward IV's own removed a potential stabilising influence in the crises that followed.

The Bourchier–Stafford connection compensated somewhat for any lack of blood relatives, but they were dwarfed by the family of the Duchess Cecily. Her father Ralph Earl of Westmorland (d. 1425) had fathered some twenty-five children. Several died young. The principal progeny of his first wife, the line that inherited the earldom, were in dispute with offspring of his second wife, the Countess Joan Beaufort. Ralph and Joan's children married remarkably well. In right of their wives, Richard (d. 1460), William (d. 1463), George (d. 1469) and Edward (d. 1476) were respectively Earl of Salisbury, Lord Fauconberg, Lord Latimer, and Lord Bergavenny, while Robert was Bishop of Durham (d. 1457). Cecily's whole sisters Katherine, Eleanor, and Anne married respectively John Earl Marshal (later Duke of Norfolk, d. 1432), Henry Percy, Earl of Northumberland (d. 1455), and Humphrey

Duke of Buckingham, mentioned above, in his own right second cousin to Duke Richard. Cecily of course had married Richard Duke of York.[19] Cecily's siblings, brothers and sisters-in-law constituted eight uncles and seven aunts. All these marriages were fruitful, some very fertile indeed: Salisbury, for instance, had four sons and six daughters who also married well and started producing second cousins once removed for Richard of Fotheringhay during the 1450s.

The key to this splendid network was Joan Beaufort (d. 1440), who was not only exceptionally fecund but was also royal and a source of royal favour to her family. It had been conspicuous royal favour that secured recognition for Richard Neville himself as Earl of Salisbury in 1428/43 and acknowledgement of his son Richard Neville (the Kingmaker) as Earl of Warwick in 1449–51. A key moment occurred in 1452, when King Henry VI acknowledged his Tudor half-brothers and made earls of the two eldest. Owen had become a monk. Henry also gave Edmund and Jasper Tudor precedence over the premier earl (Warwick the Kingmaker). This action suggested that the Nevilles, accustomed to inclusion among Henry's near kin, had been relegated to the ranks of minor royals. It was a fateful error that may have given York the support that he needed. It was also a painful realisation for the Nevilles,[20] surely replicated many times over as new princes supplanted old.

Through the Bourchiers and the Nevilles, Richard of Fotheringhay was related to almost everyone who was anyone, often several times over. His two sisters, Anne in 1445 and Elizabeth in about 1458, were married to their distant cousins Henry Duke of Exeter (d. 1475) and John Duke of Suffolk (d. 1491–92). How well Richard knew them – or whether they knew him or were aware of him – is difficult to assess. Richard lived with his mother, Duchess Cecily, whose itinerary is unknown. She is more likely to have resided in the provinces than the capital, where all the peerage came. Presumably there was a grand (but undocumented) wedding for her daughter Elizabeth that Richard and his principal relatives had to attend.

Richard had scores of first cousins and a host of second, third and fourth cousins who partook of his royal blood but counted for hardly anything in dynastic, political, or family terms and whom he may scarcely have known. Almost anybody who counted was a relative within the criteria of the prohibited degrees.

Kinship: Cement or Solvent?

This is an era when disputes between landholders are much better documented than amicable coexistence. The records of the central courts – all about conflict – are vast and there were a couple of dozen large-scale disputes that got wholly out of hand. Every landholder possessed a portfolio of rights that overlapped and could conflict with others, such as boundaries, watercourses, common pastures, rights of way, hunting, etc., and most engaged from time to time in lawsuits with their neighbours, which did not necessarily interfere with cordial relations at a personal level. Most estates descended automatically, without question, from heir to heir. The great aristocratic feuds were exceptional, but they generated far more records, more comment and more noise than the orderly passage of the generations. All properties descended within families by inheritance. At key junctures, however, there were multiple heirs, who usually shared the inheritance out without acrimony, but sometimes they became rivals who fought to the death. What was at risk with the land was the income, wealth, rank, and status that derived from it. Disputes were exacerbated by what was perceived as unfairness: when elder sons lost out to a younger stepbrother of a later marriage (the Neville–Neville dispute), when elder daughters were supplanted by a younger sister through the preference of the whole blood over stepsiblings (the Beauchamp Inheritance), or a daughter by a male cousin (male entail). Disputed inheritances could not only divide the closest of relatives – siblings and cousins – but could make them into mortal enemies.

Kinship can therefore unite or divide, be a cement or a solvent.[21] The family unity and the shared interests that children were born into became strained when each established their own families with their own interests that perhaps conflicted. The Bourchier brothers do seem normally to have worked together. The three elder Neville brothers Salisbury, Fauconberg, and Latimer consistently collaborated. From 1452 if not earlier Salisbury, his son Warwick, and York cooperated in national politics. York seems to have supported the two Neville earls in their feuds with the Percys in Northumberland and with the Duke of Somerset in Glamorgan, so the Nevilles backed York in his feud with Somerset and in his national political ambitions. Faced with disaster in 1459, York refused terms that excluded Salisbury. Yet young Richard's uncles – the eight brothers and brothers-in-law who sat in the Lords in the 1450s – did not operate as a bloc.[22] There was moreover a rift in the Neville family, the Neville–Neville feud, between the senior Westmorland branch and the junior Salisbury branch, since the latter through the medium of Joan Beaufort had secured the transfer to themselves of some of the family inheritance. Warwick likewise managed to defraud his cousin George Neville of Abergavenny of his inheritance even though their fathers were brothers.[23]

Such tensions emerge particularly clearly in a letter that York wrote on 8 May 1454. In his capacity as Lord Protector of England Duke Richard was confronted by the 'violent reule and mysgovernaunce' of his 'cousin and sone', so inappropriate in a high and mighty prince. The recipient of York's letter was not his twelve-year-old son Edward Earl of March, the future Edward IV, but his son-in-law Henry Duke of Exeter, to whom he wrote with 'faderly and cosynly affection' trusting 'that your cosynly favour and affection is such towardes me as God knoweth myn is towards you'. Exeter did not feel the same way and persisted in his misconduct, so York took action against the rebels and imprisoned him. The letter does reveal the sentimental ties within the relationship,

York's willingness to favour his daughter's husband and, in what was an open letter, to publicise both his effort to restore peace and the fact that his punitive measures were inescapable.[24] In this case, at least, York seems to have been in the right.

These divisions were taken very seriously and pursued with few holds barred. Actual violence, however, was targeted, with minimal bloodshed and that confined to the principals, such as Sir Robert Harcourt in 1469 and Thomas Viscount Lisle in 1470. Although notorious, the Courtenay–Bonville feud in the West Country, which included a private battle just outside Exeter and the siege of Caister Castle in 1469, featured virtually no mortality. So too the Battle of Heworth outside York in 1453 that was the peak of the Percy–Neville feud. The principal contenders there were Salisbury's sons Thomas and John and the Percy sons of Salisbury's sister Eleanor. This division escalated in 1455 into the First Battle of St Albans, an altogether more serious affair. Duke Richard and the two Neville earls attacked the court. The objective was to eliminate Edmund Duke of Somerset, who was indeed slain. He was a Beaufort second cousin of both York and Salisbury: he was also brother-in-law to Warwick, their wives being sisters and rivals to the Beauchamp inheritance. The death in the same battle of Henry Percy, Earl of Northumberland and brother-in-law to Salisbury, later claimed to be unintentional, was probably deliberate. What followed had some of the character of a family feud, as the widowed Duchess of Somerset, her son the new duke, and the new Earl of Northumberland sought vengeance on the brother-in-law, uncles, and cousin responsible for their deaths. This was supposedly patched up at the Loveday of St Pauls in 1458. The next Neville uprising divided the nobility between the minority rebels and a majority who supported the king, many of whom seem to have tempered the severity of the measures taken against their kin. The Battle of Northampton in 1460 repeated some of the features of the First Battle of St Albans. Three of the four peers who were cut down were close relatives of the Yorkists:

Humphrey Duke of Buckingham, cousin and brother-in-law of York and Salisbury, John Viscount Beaumont (another brother-in-law), and Thomas Lord Egremont, nephew of both.

It was the Yorkists who first resorted to such violence and slew quite close kindred in pursuit of their goals. They sought to eliminate a succession of Henry VI's so-called evil councillors, including quite close kin – assassination was the surest means to remove them from power – and did indeed kill them. The heirs of the victims bayed for justice and revenge, but Henry VI was much more merciful. He imprisoned a whole string of disorderly noblemen during the 1450s and forgave York several times over, thus allowing the duke to rebel again and again. Henry was not prepared to rule out reconciliation even after the senior Yorkists had been condemned at the Parliament of Devils. York's claim for the crown in 1460 exposed his deeper motives beyond question. Revenge for Northampton came at the Battle of Wakefield on 30 December 1460, after which York was executed and Salisbury murdered by a Lancastrian army led by their nephew Northumberland and cousin Somerset. It was at this battle that Richard III's elder brother Edmund Earl of Rutland and cousin Sir Thomas Neville were slain. Edmund, aged seventeen and a participant in the conflicts of 1459–60, was not the innocent child slaughtered in Shakespeare's play *Henry VI, Part 3*. At last Yorkists too suffered the political deaths they had inflicted on others. Some Lancastrian victims were indeed guiltless. The Yorkist victory at Towton and the mopping-up operations that followed resulted in more deaths among the nobility, some inevitably distant relatives of Richard.

Clearly there were limits to this bloodletting. There were still taboos. Salisbury's sons worked together against Northumberland's sons. Brothers did not kill brothers nor fathers their own sons, even when serious disputes (e.g. about inheritance) arose. Evidently the marriage tie, which originally allied families to mutual advantage, slackened with time. Mere cousinage arising from a distant ancestor was not a bond that determined family policy and political commitment beyond the first generation. All the rivals for the many disputed inheritances shared common ancestors. They competed rather than cooperated or compromised about this key to their wealth, rank, status and title. Warwick the Kingmaker excluded his Neville cousins and Beauchamp in-laws from their family inheritances. Perhaps brothers-in-law and nephews were not targeted in these conflicts – though some evidence suggests that they were – but the risk of collateral damage was accepted. The family trees that connected Richard to his relatives explains many of the conflicts that arose. Kinship can explain some of the alliances of the Wars of the Roses, but it also explains why some brothers-in-law and cousins ended up on different sides. Cousins did kill cousins and brothers-in-law killed brothers-in-law. The royal family tree was not just the framework within which the political action took place: it was the reason why the actions occurred and gave them meaning that even today we can understand.

Conclusion

In today's parlance, Richard of Fotheringhay was a very minor royal. He descended through three different lines from King Edward III (1327–77) and hence from Henry II, William the Conqueror, Alfred the Great and other English monarchs. He was of the blood royal of England and also, so the Yorks claimed, of France and Castile. Yet he was also a younger son at a time when the only career opportunities were through military service, through marriage, or through the Church. We cannot know which Duke Richard had in mind – if he had any in mind in 1459, when the boy was still only seven. When the duke made himself heir in 1460 and when Edward acceded in 1461, everything changed for Richard of Fotheringhay. He was still not his father's heir, nor indeed later to be heir to the crown. Even after the Lancastrians slew his second brother, Edmund Earl of Rutland, in 1460, and after his eldest brother, Edward IV, executed their third brother, George Duke of Clarence, in 1478 and disinherited Clarence's children, Richard was still only tenth in line for the throne. The throne was attained only by discounting more senior heirs, some eliminated by force, on the model of the Ealing comedy *Kind Hearts and Coronets* and the film *The Ruling Class*. But Richard himself most probably eliminated his nephews Edward V and Richard Duke of York and disqualified all Edward's daughters, and thus, so Richard argued, the family inheritance – the crown of England – devolved on him. That Richard had a career worthy of separate notice owes everything to his place in his family pedigree.

4

EDWARD IV'S NEW FAMILY IN THE
1460s

The Evolution of the Yorkist Dynasty

The Yorkist regime of the 1460s was founded on the Old
Yorkists, the family and retainers of Duke Richard and Duchess
Cecily. These Old Yorkists suffered serious casualties during the
First War of 1459–61. The future Richard III's family shrank
significantly. His father, Duke Richard, and elder brother Edmund
Earl of Rutland were both killed. On his maternal side, his uncle
Richard Earl of Salisbury and his uncles-in-law Humphrey Duke
of Buckingham, John Viscount Beaumont, and Henry 2nd Earl of
Northumberland died, together with his cousins John Lord Neville
(senior branch), Sir Thomas Neville (junior branch), John Duke
of Norfolk (naturally), Henry 3rd Earl of Northumberland, and
Thomas Lord Egremont, along with others more remotely related.
Brother Edward became king and established a new royal family
from his new in-laws and his own offspring. It is this burgeoning
royal family of the 1460s that is the focus of this chapter. Besides
the new king, young but mature, there were his two brothers
George and Richard – two royal princes and royal dukes – who
were declared of age at sixteen respectively in 1466 and 1468.[1]
Neither fathered legitimate children until the 1470s. George and

Margaret, Richard's youngest sister, married. Five months before his accession Edward is reported to have visited George and Richard, his third and fourth brothers, every day.[2] Once king Edward kept his eye also on those wider kin that were potentially useful to him: his eldest nephew John, created Earl of Lincoln in 1467;[3] his big sister Anne; his senior niece Anne Holland, who was to marry his own stepson Thomas Grey; and on those cousins that were matched to his in-laws. He attended especially his queen, her sons, and her siblings, whom he undertook to provide for (although, in the event, he could not find uses for them all). The 1460s also witnessed the beginnings of Edward's own children – Elizabeth, Mary and Cecily. Probably he also fathered bastards by several mistresses, but there is little evidence of this.

The rout at Ludford in 1459 had not been the Yorkists' finest hour. Their claim to be loyal subjects to the Lancastrian monarchy was hardly tenable when they drew up in battle formation facing the army of the king with his banner displayed. They were faced with two apparent choices, both unappetising: to fight – unquestionably an act of treason that their supporters had not signed up for – or to submit and trust in the mercy of Henry VI. The latter option was certainly the safer. Amazingly they selected a third option, the most cowardly route, and fled during the night. York and his second son Edmund fled to Ireland, his first son Edward Earl of March and Warwick choosing Calais. The Yorkist leaders deserted their army and left their followers and indeed York's town of Ludlow defenceless. Leaderless, next day the Yorkist army capitulated. Nobody was executed, but those of rank were captured and, to the number of twenty-one, were attainted by the Parliament of Devils at Coventry, suffering forfeiture of their lands. Scanty evidence indicates that some Yorkists were ransomed and that Ludlow was looted. These were not all whom York abandoned. Among those apprehended at Ludlow were his duchess Cecily, her youngest sons George and Richard, and probably Margaret of York also. This was the first appearance in the sources of these children outside the genealogies and the commencement of their political careers. Margaret was aged thirteen, George was ten, and Richard was seven. Edward, their eldest brother, was only seventeen. The lives of these young captives were spared, of course, but they were placed with their mother in the protective custody of her elder sister Anne Duchess of Buckingham, a measure designed to ensure that Cecily could advance no monetary or other help to her erring husband.

Of course, the Wars of the Roses were civil wars. If Richard's father, eldest brothers, uncles Salisbury and Fauconberg, and cousin Warwick went into exile, within England there remained plenty of loyal relatives – the Bourchiers, the Nevilles, Duchess Cecily's sisters, and young Richard's brothers-in-law Exeter and Suffolk. Probably it was some of these and/or the bishops who argued so forcefully for mercy towards the Yorkists in Parliament. Two parchment contributions to the debate survive. Such discussions can be detected in the reduction in number of those to be condemned and in the changes of view apparent from the records of Parliament itself. The Yorkist sympathisers lost the argument – their cumulative rebellions had passed the point of acceptability – but the king himself evidently thought attainder too severe a penalty and was prepared to show mercy wherever he could to whoever would submit. But the Yorkists refused the terms on offer. The Yorkist earls invaded England in June 1460 and overthrew the government. In October 1460 York agreed with Henry VI in the *Accord* that the House of York rather than Henry VI's son Edward of Lancaster was to succeed on Henry's death. In the meantime York was to rule and was to receive all the revenues hitherto earmarked for the Prince of Wales. While York himself was unlikely ever to reign – he was ten years older than King Henry and the *Accord* explicitly safeguarded Henry against enforced abdication – York's eldest son Edward Earl of March was bound in due course to become king. Although unmentioned in the *Accord*, York's youngest sons George and Richard were destined to become royal princes.

York, of course, miscalculated. The *Accord* was an agreement approved by York's supporters, not by the Lancastrians. No provision had been made for Queen Margaret, Prince Edward, nor the Beaufort and Holland royal dukes that cherished ambitions to the crown. The queen and her son had to resist. When they did resist, Richard went northwards to police them. The opposition was expected to quail. Instead of submitting, as in 1454 and 1455, the insurgents attacked – and the duke, his second son Edmund, and Richard Earl of Salisbury were killed. What next? Nobody knew for sure. But if the Yorkists were to persist in their claim to the throne, York's younger sons George and Richard had suddenly acquired a real political importance. Both were despatched hastily to the Low Countries, where they could operate as figureheads for their dynasty and cause if necessity required. Once their brother Edward had made himself king, their Burgundian hosts treated the two boys with great honour and ceremony as the representatives of what had become a ruling house.[4]

The change in status of Richard's family transformed his rank and prospects. There was all the difference in the world between the fourth son of a royal duke, however wealthy and well born, and the younger brother of a reigning king. It was Edward now who was in control: it was he who made decisions on Richard's upbringing, he who assessed his political value, he who shaped Richard's career. Fatherless, Richard was not motherless, but his mother Cecily, now elevated to the mother of the king, was no longer responsible for his upbringing. George, Richard, and Margaret were royal princes and princesses and were treated as such. They were brought up like royal wards in an offshoot of the royal household. They were housed in luxury in the tower of the brand-new Greenwich Palace, where they were brought up in company with four henxmen – wards and aristocrats of their own age. They emerged for major court ceremonies such as Christmas and the New Year and for the great council at Leicester in 1463 and were therefore visible to those who mattered politically. If the bones discovered at Leicester are Richard's, it was probably his puberty in these years that was accompanied by the onset of the scoliosis (otherwise unrecorded) that was to distort his body forever.

Second in age but first in status of these three children was George, who had a special significance: first in line for the throne and heir apparent, he was created a duke with the highly symbolic title of Clarence – a reminder of the Yorkist claim from Lionel Duke of Clarence – and was knighted, made knight of the Garter, and appointed steward of England. Richard, second in line of succession and now aged nine, was scarcely less important. He was knighted and created duke after a few months' delay. Was Edward uncertain whether Richard was to be a lay magnate or alternatively a great churchman? Regardless, Edward quickly made up his mind. Richard, like George, was to be a royal duke and a great nobleman. The king reserved lands and offices for them and declared both of them of age when sixteen, George in 1466 and Richard in 1468. They were to be territorial magnates. They and their descendants, new dynasties of the blood royal, were destined to be buttresses to his throne.

Edward IV had a strategy for his brothers. Probably he did not realise it or had not codified so clearly the prejudices and principles that determined his intentions for them. His usurping dynasty needed heirs and a line of succession that extended beyond himself personally, in the form of heirs of his own body and/or his brothers, and of adult princes who could support and deputise for him. Edward himself had been brought up as a nobleman rather than a prospective king. He shared the outlook of the nobility, mixed easily with other noblemen, and esteemed noble life and culture. He expected the House of York to be reinforced by his brothers as his greatest subjects. Clarence and Gloucester in that order were given precedence at court, in Parliament, and in great public ceremonies over all other dukes – over Buckingham and Norfolk, both of royal descent, and even over his sister's brother Suffolk – and also over Warwick, the premier earl. They could fill such great offices and commands as steward of England and lieutenant of

Ireland (Clarence) and admiral of England (Gloucester): deputies initially took on the work. Edward showered both at once with estates all over the country, most of them forfeited by his Lancastrian enemies, as he sought to make them, firstly, into great territorial magnates with the resources for a role that demanded the most conspicuous consumption and display, and, secondly, into rulers of particular regions: the king's representative and medium of royal authority in each. In the short run, his brothers were too young to officiate themselves, but Edward consistently worked towards this objective. Edward's plans were not developed all at once – he revised what he had given each brother on several occasions – so that Clarence, for instance, may originally have been destined to be warden of the East March in place of the Percys and then in 1464 to rule the palatinate of Chester. At their majorities, Clarence's regional hegemony was focused on Staffordshire and Derbyshire (the honours of Tutbury and Duffield) and Gloucester's on north-west England, the honours of Halton and Clitheroe in Cheshire and Lancashire. Edward wanted his brothers to breed and to establish their own families and dynasties in the belief that these would strengthen the royal house. He wanted to set at a distance those existing magnates whose hereditary power, wealth, and influence owed nothing to his patronage. Moreover Edward wanted the support of his brothers as soon as possible, which was why he knighted them and created them dukes forthwith, endowed them quickly, and declared them of age at sixteen rather than the usual twenty-one. Edward's strategy resembled that of Edward III. It contrasts sharply with the strategy of Henry IV and Henry V, who did value their junior princes but as individuals rather than as founders of cadet dynasties or local potentates.[5] No doubt both dukes appreciated such trust and promotion, Clarence rushing at once to Tutbury after rendering homage and Gloucester probably proceeding apace to the north-west.

Edward may have miscalculated somewhat, as both immature magnates embroiled themselves at once in local factional fighting to disruptive effect.[6] They had not yet learned to exercise their power with discretion. Richard's first surviving letter, a trivial entreaty for a loan, captures the urgency and passion of the king's much later postscript about Buckingham's rebellion to his chancellor.[7] Moreover Edward clearly expected his brothers to accept his authority, to follow his lead, to comply with any reconfigurations of their estates, and to remain available for any diplomatic marriages in the interests of the royal house that might not necessarily fit their own evaluation of their interests. Both dukes, in time, married as they chose, not as the king determined. The development of their own dynasties, which Edward so desired, inevitably brought some differentiation between their own interests and strategies and those of the king. What to do with one's heirs and one's spares remains a quandary for hereditary monarchs even unto the present day.

Richard's Adolescence

Edward IV himself was only nineteen years old at his accession and relied heavily in his early years on older kinsmen with more experience. The best-known were his Neville first cousins Richard Earl of Warwick (Warwick the Kingmaker), who directed the destruction of remaining Lancastrians in the north and was the new regime's principal diplomat; George, his chancellor, who presided over the central government machine; and John Lord Montagu, who was his field commander. All were in their thirties, older than the York boys but not so much older, and still in their prime of life. William Earl of Kent (formerly Lord Fauconberg), Richard's middle-aged uncle and the last of the previous generation, died in 1463. This era has been called the rule of the Nevilles, although their control was less complete than was supposed by some external observers. Less visible but important nevertheless were the king's uncle by marriage Henry Bourchier, Earl of Essex, treasurer of England 1461–62, and his brother

Thomas, Archbishop of Canterbury. William Lord Hastings, the king's chamberlain, was both an Old Yorkist and now a cousin by marriage, the second husband of Warwick's sister Katherine Lady Harrington. All these kindred of Edward IV were related in the same degree to Richard of Fotheringhay. Whether or not they knew or were even conscious of Richard in the 1450s, they certainly knew him now. He was a royal prince scheduled for a brilliant future. Other prominent figures in the new regime were the Old Yorkists William Lord Herbert and Humphrey Lord Stafford of Southwick and the complete outsider John Tiptoft, Earl of Worcester. They all matured during the 1460s. For excellent service, John Neville was created Earl of Northumberland in 1464, George Neville promoted to Archbishop of York in 1464, Herbert to Earl of Pembroke (1468) and Stafford to Earl of Devon (1469). It was in 1464 that Edward married against everyone's advice and in 1467 that he shook off the tutelage of his Neville cousins. The faction that had made him king was divided.

Richard, however, remained close to the Nevilles because the later stage of his upbringing had been consigned to Warwick himself. It was customary for young aristocrats to spend a few years in honourable service in another household, where they could hone the courtesy, courtliness and athletic pursuits expected of their station under critical rather than overindulgent parental eyes. It was certainly unusual for a royal prince to be treated in this way, perhaps even unprecedented. Richard had entered Warwick's custody by 1465, maybe as early as 1463.[8] Warwick, of course, was the best of examples for a young prince to emulate. He was the right-hand man of the new regime. He was a soldier, diplomat and statesman who set an example of unremitting attention to duty. He also lived in a more sumptuous style, more princely, than any other contemporary. He was a model that Richard was later to replicate when he too was warden and lieutenant of the northern marches towards Scotland and lord of the north and when Warwick's castles of Barnard (Durh.), Penrith (Cumb.), Middleham, and

Sheriff Hutton (York.) had become his own. Almost nothing is known of this period in Richard's life other than his appearance with the earl and countess and their two daughters Isabel and Anne at the resplendent enthronement at Cawood Palace (Yorks.) of Warwick's brother George Neville as archbishop, at York and at Warwick.⁹ That was when the earl and countess – and therefore their households – were combined, which may have been unusual. The relationship of a noble attendant to the heads of a household was intimate: it was comparable to that of a son to a father and mother. Isabel and Anne Neville may have been akin to sisters to Richard. How well acquainted they became and whether there was more to their relationships cannot be known.

King Edward intended this sojourn with Warwick merely to be a finishing school for Richard, not for him to find a bride in Warwick's daughter, but Warwick may have supposed otherwise. Edward had plans for his siblings, both Clarence and Margaret being destined for diplomatic marriages: Margaret did indeed marry Charles the Bold, Duke of Burgundy, in 1468. Clarence was not prepared to wait for such a match, which anyway would suit Edward more than him. By 1467 Clarence certainly proposed to wed Isabel Neville, Warwick's elder daughter, and did indeed marry her despite Edward's disapproval in 1469. One source, the Burgundian chronicler Jehan de Waurin, says that Warwick also wanted Richard for Anne Neville. Waurin certainly sets any such plan too early, in 1464,¹⁰ and it is perhaps implausible: only born in 1456, four years after Richard, Anne Neville was not yet a teenager when Richard left the earl's household. That they knew one another was to be important in the next decade. Of course Richard also knew Anne Countess of Warwick well, but his maltreatment of her from 1473 seems untinged by any sentiment developed in his adolescence.

Apart from Duchess Cecily and collaterals, the House of York itself consisted in 1461 only of the six siblings, three of them female, five of them unmarried, and three of them underage, but it expanded during the 1460s and even more in the 1470s. Richard's elder sisters the duchesses Anne and Elizabeth were already married before Edward's accession and in 1468 the youngest sister Margaret wed Duke Charles and left the English scene forever to reside abroad. It was a splendid match that cemented the alliance of Burgundy with England against France. It was this sort of diplomatic marriage designed to secure the recognition abroad of the usurping Yorkist regime that was thought appropriate for the king and that was vigorously pursued by Warwick and his other ambassadors. Negotiations had proceeded far enough by September 1464 for Edward to be asked to commit himself to one of these ladies. Presumably Edward had originally intended this kind of match both for himself and his two brothers, who potentially were useful diplomatic pawns.

The husband of his eldest sister Anne was Henry Holland, Duke of Exeter, a Lancastrian royal duke who had chosen to support his Lancastrian cousins rather than his father-in-law York. Exeter shared the Lancastrian defeat at Towton and fought on afterwards. When he was attainted and escaped abroad, his duchess remained in England. Their relationship had been poor – there was no risk that she would send him money or otherwise help him – and she soon replaced him sexually with the courtier Thomas St Leger. Anne exercised the influence of an elder sister over her brother the king. She secured the lion's share of the Holland inheritance and had the custody of her daughter and heiress, Anne Holland, Richard's niece. Young Anne Holland was an extremely attractive catch on the marriage market: first she was betrothed to the much younger George Neville, born only in 1465, the sole son of John Neville and heir to much of Warwick's inheritance, but this match was gazumped in 1466 by the queen for her son Thomas Grey. Such a connection was very attractive to the duchess too: she was paid 4,000 marks (£2,666 13s 4d) by the new queen for it,[11] most probably in instalments.

The next sister, Elizabeth Duchess of Suffolk, embarked on a clutch of nieces and nephews for Edward IV and Richard: there were to be six (possibly seven) sons and four daughters who reached maturity. Her first son – and the first nephew of the king and Richard – was John de la Pole, who was created Earl of Lincoln in 1467: an earnest of favour to the Suffolks that never added up to much.

King Edward himself was already a womaniser. He seems to have fathered at least one child early in the 1460s,[12] but bastards were not recognised as full members of the royal house.

Lancastrian resistance persisted throughout the 1460s, most of the leaders being related in some degree to Richard Duke of Gloucester and the House of York. Obviously this was true of the inner royal family of Henry VI, his queen Margaret of Anjou, his son Edward of Lancaster, and his brother Jasper Tudor, Earl of Pembroke, all of whom survived the decade, along with Henry Duke of Somerset (ex. 1464) and his brothers, and Richard's brother-in-law Henry Duke of Exeter. Sir Ralph Percy, first cousin, and Thomas Lord Roos, the countess' nephew, were beheaded in 1464. All the Lancastrian royalty except Henry (after 1465) ended up in exile. They knew well that their blood ties to the Yorkists were no impediment to their execution, although Somerset found that reconciliation and forgiveness was not impossible. The Wars of the Roses were not waged on women, who retained their inheritances and estates: the two Northumberland dowager countesses, the elder being Duchess Cecily's sister, and her two other sisters Katherine Duchess of Norfolk (also widow of Viscount Beaumont) and Anne Duchess of Buckingham illustrate this point. Some such ladies were consigned to custodians. Moreover, such blameless children as Henry Tudor and Henry Percy, 4th Earl of Northumberland, Richard's cousin, were looked after as though still heirs and acculturated to the new regime in the same manner that the Westmorland had raised such sons of traitors to the Lancastrian kings as Richard's own father Richard Duke of York. Certainly Tudor's guardian William Herbert gambled on their restoration and planned to marry both Tudor and Percy to his own daughters.

The Explosion of the Yorkist Royal Family

What revolutionised the inner royal family was the king's own marriage in 1464 to the young widow Elizabeth Grey (*née* Wydeville). This was not planned and was not the sort of marriage that kings were supposed to contract. Edward IV was the first king to marry within his realm since King John (although the Black Prince, had he lived another year, would have been a second). The Italian Dominic Mancini rightly reported that English kings generally married foreign princesses who were virgins and whose virtue was above reproach. Elizabeth was not royal. She was not even noble. Her father, Richard Lord Rivers, was a marginal first-generation peer who owed his promotion in part to his marriage to her mother Jacquetta and who was financially almost wholly dependent on Jacquetta's dower. Jacquetta of Luxemberg was the sister of the Count of St Pol, a continental nobleman of the second rank (but of impeccable lineage traceable back to Charlemagne). Jacquetta had been very briefly married to the Lancastrian royal duke John Duke of Bedford (the Regent Bedford, d. 1435) before wedding his official Richard Wydeville to the outrage of even Henry VI. The proper level of the Wydevilles was the lowest baronage or the upper gentry, not the crown. Their lineage displays little of the blue and royal blood that almost monopolises tables 1 and 4, the lineages of Richard III and Anne Neville. Moreover, Elizabeth was no virgin. She had married first Sir John Grey, heir to the Ferrers of Groby barony, a good match for a Wydeville, and had borne him two young sons. Sir John Grey had died before inheriting. She did not have possession of even her own modest jointure. She was no fit consort for a king. The match was highly imprudent, motivated principally by love or lust and 'not by rule of reason' – the unquestioned standard of the arranged marriage that was a king's public duty to observe. There was not much to distinguish Elizabeth from other noble ladies bedded by the king in the early years of his reign. It was also a clandestine marriage that Edward had concealed for as long as possible from his councillors and lords, whom he expected to disapprove. They did indeed, and apparently tried to annul it.[13] However, the marriage was valid and legally watertight and therefore had to be accepted. Elizabeth was undoubtedly queen.

Lust has its points. Queens were expected to secure the succession by providing heirs and to do that they needed to have frequent sexual intercourse with the king, which Elizabeth evidently did. Elizabeth proved to be exceptionally fertile. She duly delivered the king both an heir and a spare, in total ten children in addition to her existing two sons. There was a brief delay until the birth of their eldest daughter, Elizabeth of York, in 1466 and thereafter almost annual births until 1480, when Queen Elizabeth must have been in her early forties. Most of these children – and indeed the first three – were daughters, the future Edward V arriving only in 1470. These offspring pushed Clarence and Gloucester well down the order of succession. They are tabulated in tables 3, 6.

Far more noticeable in the short run was the integration of Elizabeth's luxuriant family into the royal house. Both her parents were still living: Richard Lord Rivers, the king's father(-in-law) and Jacquetta, the king's mother(-in-law). Elizabeth had two sons, now the king's stepsons, Thomas and Richard Grey. She had five brothers, now the king's – and Richard's – brothers(-in-law): Anthony Lord Scales (already married), John, Richard, Lionel (b. c. 1450) and Edward, probably in that order. She had six sisters, now the king's – and Richard's – sisters(-in-law): Jacquetta, already Lady Strange of Knockin, Margaret, Katherine, Anne, Joan, and Mary.[14] The new queen also had plenty of cousins, notably the Kentish family of Haute, products of the union of Earl Rivers' sister Jane and Sir William Haute of Bishopsbourne (Kent),[15] now connections of the king and duke. Lord and Lady Rivers brought twelve children to maturity. We know of no stillbirths, miscarriages or deaths in childhood (although there were surely some), nor the date of the last live birth. And as they married, a host of their new relatives became affinal kinsfolk of the king and Richard too. The royal family was enormously increased.

Elizabeth's son Thomas Grey, after all heir to a barony, was married almost at once to Anne Holland, daughter of the king's sister Anne and the heiress of the dukedom of Exeter. She was unlikely ever to be supplanted by a brother, so Thomas was destined to be Duke of Exeter and was indeed advanced to the Holland earldom of Huntingdon in 1471. No provision at this stage was made for Elizabeth's younger son Richard, who was still unmarried at his death in 1483 but for whom some property had been earmarked.[16] Elizabeth's father was created Earl Rivers and appointed Lord Treasurer and constable of England. Of the new queen's siblings, her eldest brother Anthony Lord Scales and Jacquetta Lady Strange of Knockin were already married and endowed. The next brothers were probably Sir John Wydeville, who married the thrice-widowed elderly dowager (and Richard's aunt) Katherine Duchess of Norfolk; Richard who sought to appropriate the priorate of the crusading order of St John; and Lionel, who had entered the church, accumulated benefices, and in 1481 became Bishop of Salisbury. The youngest brother was Sir Edward Wydeville, who received nothing much from the king. There were five sisters besides Queen Elizabeth and Lady Strange who were now married to the heirs of the Earl of Arundel, Kent (formerly Grey of Ruthin), Essex, and Pembroke (formerly Herbert), and to Henry Duke of Buckingham.[17] Assuming normal gestation at thirty-eight weeks, and forty days' abstinence before purification of the mother (churching), it took Jacquetta at least ten years (524 weeks) flat out to produce her brood: indeed we know it took her longer than that. Any stillbirths or miscarriages, as usual, went unrecorded. The dates of birth are not recorded. The elder daughters were fourteen years old (the age of the majority) in the mid-1460s, but the youngest were probably not. Of their spouses, only William Bourchier seems likely to have been of age at marriage. All but Buckingham were in the custody of their fathers, each of whom chose to contract a Wydeville marriage and perhaps picked over the litter before selecting their daughters-in-law. Buckingham, the greatest of royal wards, had no such option and was made to marry whom Edward chose.[18] It seems likely therefore that Margaret, who married in September 1464, was the oldest, that the three who married in February 1466 were in age order Katherine (who bagged a duke), Joan, and Anne, and that Mary, married September 1466, was the youngest.[19]

Perhaps, as contemporaries complained, some of these were elevated above their station. What mattered was that Edward recognised them as kindred and accepted the obligation to provide for them as royal. It was surely their royal connections and their anticipated royal influence that prompted the earls of Arundel and Essex at least to contract their heirs to ladies of modest antecedents who were not heiresses. Edward sweetened the Arundel, Essex, Kent and Pembroke deals by settling royal lands jointly on the young couples and their issue.[20] Such financial gains apart, it does not appear that any of these fathers-in-law gained much political influence in the short term that they did not already possess. Thomas Arundel, Lord Maltravers, appears prominently in court ceremony in the next decade. In the 1470s, when these Wydevilles had grown up and started begetting their own offspring, they should have dominated the Yorkist court. Actually they suffered a disappointment. None of the five Wydeville boys fathered legitimate offspring. Joan and Mary brought no children to their husbands. Chapter 6 moreover reveals how the queen's siblings, collateral relatives of Edward and Richard, were increasingly sidelined by the offspring born to the king and queen.

Edward had an exceptionally high estimation on what it was to be royal. Much later, in 1483, a sumptuary law distinguished between royal dukes, who could wear purple, and common or garden dukes, who could not. King Edward III had made his sons into earls and had endowed them as such (1,000 marks or £666 13s 4d a year). All five in due course became dukes, four financed by the marriage to heiresses, York at the minimum level for a duke (2,000 marks or £1,333 6s 8d a year). It was fifteen years after the revolution of 1399 that King Henry V elevated his youngest two brothers to dukedoms. King Henry VI had been able only to make his stepbrothers earls at the minimum 1,000 marks level. Edward IV, as we have seen, made both his brothers dukes, and he endowed them at the level of super-dukes: in 1467 Clarence was guaranteed £3,700 a year and later both he and Gloucester secured much more than this. Edward's plans for his new Wydeville and Grey in-laws were particularly lavish. We have seen how Elizabeth's father, brothers John and Lionel, and her sisters were provided for. Edward seems to have felt that an earldom was the minimum level for his sisters-in-law, promoting the fathers-in-law Edmund Grey and William Herbert to new earldoms of Kent and Pembroke, and endowing four of the new husbands with forfeited estates. From the angle of the Wydevilles, these were highly respectable marriages to well-established noble families that integrated the Wydevilles into the high nobility and refuted snobbish criticisms of them as unworthy parvenus. The queen's household was stacked with Hautes and other connections. Not only were the Wydevilles promoted, but they were highly visible at court. They were expert jousters. In 1467, the tournament at Smithfield of Anthony Wydeville, the queen's eldest brother, and Anthony Grand Bastard of Burgundy was a European event.

The greatest of the new magnates of the 1460s was William Herbert of Raglan. Originally a native Welsh retainer of Richard Duke of York – his father was William ap Thomas – this old Yorkist was Edward IV's chosen ruler first of south Wales and then the whole of Wales. It was he who defeated the Welsh Lancastrians in 1461–62 and it was he finally who took Harlech Castle in 1468 after several others had failed. His conspicuous service was rewarded with offices, with the elevation of Raglan to a new marcher lordship, with promotion to a barony and then in 1468 to the earldom of Pembroke. He built up his estates and wealth to an impressive £2,400 a year. He arranged a string of advantageous marriages for his children.[21] The matching of his son and heir, another William Herbert, to Mary Wydeville made him kinsman to the queen, to the king and to his royal brothers, and tied him into the court. His rapid advancement and his own ambitions for the future brought him into conflict with Warwick the Kingmaker in 1469 and cost him his life.

Richard's Bastards

This chapter has been itemising those born legitimate and especially those that married, but beyond this core there were other offspring who lacked the security of wedlock. Richard had at least two bastards of his own. Sex and marriage were not the same and were not interdependent. There were plenty of opportunities in fifteenth-century England for sex without committing oneself to marriage, especially for the rich and powerful. Edward IV was a notorious fornicator before his marriage and a notorious adulterer thereafter. Queen Elizabeth's ten babies are proof of frequent sexual intercourse with the king, but she was frequently (normally?) with child and hors de combat.

Between the conception of her daughter Elizabeth in 1466 and the churching for Bridget in 1480 she was with child for 103 months, being purified for another thirteen months, total 116 months out of 159, almost two-thirds of the time. Her itinerary around her own residences may not often have coincided with the king's. Her services were insufficient to assuage his lust. Thomas More identified three particular mistresses, identifiable as most probably Margaret Lucy, Eleanor Butler, and Elizabeth Shore, the first two being well-born ladies at court, but there were probably others. In

Table 3: Edward IV's Legitimate Children in his First Reign, 1461–70

Name	Conception	Birthdate	Months until next birth	Birthplace	Date of death
Elizabeth	May 1465	(11) February 1466 (expected 19 January)	10	Westminster	
Mary	December 1466	(12) August 1467	10	Windsor	1482
Cecily	(20) June 1468	(20) March 1469	10	Westminster	

an era before effective contraception, Edward should have fathered numerous bastards, but only three can safely be identified.[22] Any offspring begotten with married women were attributed to the husband of the mistress and are thus unidentifiable.

It may be that Richard started his own family in Edward's *First Reign*: a family in our modern parlance, not by fifteenth-century standards, since any such children were bastards. The first records of Richard's bastards come after his accession. John of Pontefract was made titular captain of Calais and Katherine was married as second wife to William Herbert, Earl of Huntingdon (formerly Pembroke). That Richard acknowledged them then – and recognised his obligation to provide for them – suggests that he had recognised them earlier, that he had provided them with the upbringing that fitted John to act the gentleman and Katherine to make a good marriage, and hence that they were conceived by a reputable lady and that she was still around to press her children's case. All this is speculation, of course. However, there appears in receipt of an annuity from Middleham in 1473–74 a Lady Isabel Burgh, who receives further rewards after Richard's accession. She was apparently related to the wet nurse of Richard's legitimate son. Was she the mysterious mistress? The lordships of Middleham and Pontefract point to procreation up to 1468 – when Richard was only sixteen years old and rather precocious – or from 1471, which would make Katherine below the age of majority when she wed the rather more mature earl.[23] If Isabel Burgh is the right lady, Richard apparently had a continuous relationship throughout his marriage. It is difficult to say whether Richard started his family in the 1460s, but if he did, he voluntarily accepted his responsibilities.

Richard's family – the Yorkist royal family – grew enormously in the 1460s, probably beyond the point where Richard or indeed anyone else could keep track of it all. The Wydeville and Clarence matches brought him eleven brothers-in-law, ten sisters-in-law, two nephews, and a host of cousins to add to the burgeoning brood of his sister Elizabeth. Not much emotional attachment seems to have been generated by him or indeed by his brother Clarence, who strove to destroy many of these new kinsfolk in the *Second War* of 1469–71. Richard was to cut off others in the *Third War* of 1483–85.

5

BROTHERS AT ODDS: GLOUCESTER, CLARENCE AND EDWARD IV 1469–1478

Richard's wider family of the 1460s was the framework for several distinct storylines in the 1470s and 1480s. This chapter focuses on the brothers' wars – the notorious contests between the three York brothers Edward IV, George Duke of Clarence, and Richard Duke of Gloucester – that contributed to the political upheavals and disturbed the peace for almost a decade.

The Second War of the Roses, 1469–71

The *Second War* did continue the conflict of York *versus* Lancaster with which the *First War* (1459–61) had ended, but it featured much more prominently the splitting and infighting of the victorious Yorkists. Furthermore, this was not confined to particular magnates – Warwick and Herbert, for instance – but started at the very summit of political society, among the inner royal family itself. In time it was inevitable that Edward IV and his two brothers would grow apart and develop their own families and distinct interests, as the three siblings headed collateral branches of their own, but in this instance this trifurcation happened exceptionally early, even precipitately, almost without an intervening period of cooperation and collaborative pursuit of common interests. Moreover the common interests of the three brothers in the English crown and in the Warwick inheritance became sources of rivalry and of mutual destruction.

King Edward had expected to harness the energies and resources of his two brothers in the Yorkist cause as defined by himself and under his leadership. He looked for fraternal support at court, in Parliament and council, in the great offices they held, in the regions they ruled, and as bridegrooms to the foreign princesses he would select as their brides. He wanted their support as soon as possible and declared both dukes of age at sixteen in the late 1460s. Their majorities signalled their arrival on the political stage and the commencement of careers of conspicuous support and service for himself and his dynasty.

Kinship, however, divides as well as unites.

In 1459 it had been Edward IV himself, then Earl of March, who had berated Rivers and Scales as parvenus whose criticism of the House of York was far above their station.[1] Edward IV's own marriage excited much criticism – not just the queen but her entire family were considered unworthy of royal or perhaps even noble status, and were apparently unpopular in some quarters. Many of the Lords were opposed, but had to accept the *fait accompli*, just as Warwick the Kingmaker did. He escorted the new queen into her first public presentation at Reading Abbey in 1464 and presided over her first churching in 1466. Warwick personally had private reasons to dislike several of the Wydeville marriages.[2] Twenty years later, in 1483, it was rumoured that both Edward's mother Duchess Cecily and Clarence, by then deceased, were such critics.[3] At that point Richard certainly was:[4] in 1464 he had been in Warwick's guardianship, an environment hostile to the king's choice.

Edward's marriage created a new royal conjugal couple and quickly spawned a new nuclear royal family separate from and senior to his own brothers. Thus Clarence was supplanted as heir apparent by Edward's daughter Elizabeth of York (and two sisters), which we know he resented. Richard moreover had receded by 1469 from second in line to the throne to fifth. New connections converted existing cousins such as Henry Duke of Buckingham, William Bourchier (son of the earl of Essex), and Thomas Lord Maltravers (son of Arundel) into brothers-in-law, their Wydeville wives into sisters-in-law, and the Wydeville brothers and cousins like the Hautes, mere Kentish gentry, into affines of the royal dukes, who had to treat them as such. Moreover, the lavish endowment of the two royal dukes which had been one of Edward's priorities up to his marriage now was balanced against the more urgent need to patronise his new family. Generous though the £3,700 guaranteed for Clarence was, it was also a ceiling to his expectations that was considerably below what he had sought and thought himself worth. By implication Gloucester could not expect any more.

George Duke of Clarence rapidly developed priorities and interests different from those of the king. When in 1468 feuding revived in the north Midlands among such local aristocrats as the Blounts, Cokaynes, Lord Grey of Codnor, the Langfords and Vernons, he seems not to have stood above the fray, but to have taken sides – and not the side Edward preferred.[5] He wanted as quickly as possible to fulfil Edward IV's intention to establish his own dynasty by marrying and begetting an heir and to make up for the limit set to his endowment by marrying the best heiress available. Hence he cold-shouldered the king's diplomatic proposals, which fulfilled Edward's interests rather than his own, and determined to marry Warwick's eldest daughter and heiress, Isabel Neville. Edward forbade the match. Since George and Isabel were first cousins, related in the second degree of consanguinity and several times in lesser degrees, it was possible for Edward initially to prevent the papacy granting the dispensation necessary for the match to be valid. Should Clarence put family first, marrying at his brother's direction for the benefit of the royal family (and nation), or should he put his *own* family first – marrying for the benefit of himself and his intended dynasty? Edward personally set this order of priorities. His rationale remains unclear. His decision appears spiteful rather than objective and not obviously beneficial to the Yorkist regime. It is at this moment that the interests of one member of the House of York departed from the vision of its head. George refused to be deterred, secured the dispensation surreptitiously, and married Isabel anyway. Once dispensed, the union could not be stopped. It was perhaps sensible for Edward to absent himself at the shrine of Walsingham in Norfolk – unless he alone was ignorant of the wedding. The ceremony was performed at Calais by Warwick's Archbishop Neville. The five knights of the Garter present clearly approved the match. So perhaps did Cardinal Bourchier, uncle to Edward, George and Richard, who licensed the ceremony. We cannot tell whether Duchess Cecily met Clarence at Sandwich to wish him well or to warn him not to proceed.[6]

In his defiance of the king, Clarence also aligned himself politically with Warwick, who was at odds with the king's new Wydeville and Herbert favourites, and offered Warwick a royal figurehead for his *coups d'état*. Clarence was still heir male after Edward himself to the House of York. Edward had conferred rank, status, office and precedence on his brothers to be exercised at his direction. He had not intended an independent voice for these teenagers: George, at least, considered that he lacked the political influence that he had expected. Three years younger and of age only late in 1468, Richard had not developed so far and was easily directed, although he too embroiled himself in the Harrington inheritance dispute.[7] It was after the *Second War* that he embarked on his own dynastic trajectory.

Could the *Second War of the Roses* have occurred without this family dimension? It did not start as dynastic struggle. Warwick consistently argued that he stood for reform in the footsteps of Richard Duke of York against Edward IV, who had conspicuously failed to bring good governance. He was widely believed. The first phase in 1469 did not seek to depose Edward but to sideline him. Supporters of Warwick and Clarence defeated the king's new royal family at the Battle of Edgecote. Richard's new kinsmen Earl Rivers and his son Sir John Wydeville, Pembroke and his brother Richard, together with Humphrey Earl of Devon, were defeated and ruthlessly executed. Beheading permanently excluded the king's new evil councillors from politics just as the Yorkists in 1455–60 had found killing Henry VI's advisers advantageous and decisive. Warwick and his brother Archbishop Neville imprisoned the king and ruled in his name. They seem to have hoped to make this arrangement legal and permanent in a parliament that was summoned but never met. A sorcery trial against the queen's mother Duchess Jacquetta, now widowed Countess Rivers, most probably sought to discredit Edward's marriage and to bastardise his children and thus elevate Clarence once more to heir apparent.[8] Clarence was out to remove from consideration some of his nearest and dearest: his eldest brother, his sister-in-law, and his three little nieces, together with other more distant connections. Richard seems to have played no part in these political events: probably he was in the north-west. He certainly learnt about what had happened and was to deploy some of this knowledge and some of the lessons in his own advancement to the throne in 1483.

Warwick's interim government collapsed after a couple of months and Edward reconstituted his regime, acquitted Duchess Jacquetta of sorcery, promoted new earls to replace those lost, and yielded not at all to the demands of Warwick and Clarence. Gloucester filled the vacuum in Wales left by the Herberts under the guidance of Pembroke's brother-in-law Walter Lord Ferrers of Chartley. A crucial strategy was to divide the Nevilles. Warwick's trusted brother John was elevated to Marquis Montagu, his son George Neville was created Duke of Bedford, and Bedford was betrothed to the king's eldest daughter Elizabeth of York. Warwick and Clarence were downgraded, Warwick as premier earl below his brother the new marquis, Clarence as premier duke below Bedford. Edward's stratagem offered an alternative route to the crown for the Nevilles. Simultaneously he asserted the superiority of Elizabeth's title to the crown by primogeniture over the heir male. Actually, it was playacting. John Neville was offended rather than gratified by the incidental loss of his stately earldom for inadequate compensation ('a magpie's nest') and remained attached to his brother Warwick. If the Bedford marriage was ever completed, for two four-year-olds could not give their consent, it was unlikely to make monarchs of them. King Edward and Queen Elizabeth had every intention of bearing sons. Edward's strategy rejigged the family of his brother Richard, potentially adding new relationships to his Neville cousins, confirming the priority of his nieces over Richard too, and inserting George Neville ahead of him in the order of precedence.[9]

Although backing the king, Richard was nevertheless a powerless loser.

If Edward's manoeuvring was intended to bring peace, it failed. Warwick and Clarence rebelled again next spring (the Lincolnshire Rebellion, March 1470), this time definitely to remove Edward from his throne and to substitute Clarence as king. If the Edgecote campaign of 1469 could just about be presented as an armed remonstrance in the public interest, this uprising crossed the line of acceptable conduct and amounted to treason. The younger brother sought to destroy the older, his nieces, and his in-laws. This was not how families were meant to operate. The third brother, Richard, stuck with his king, with Brother Edward rather than Brother George. When the Lincolnshire rebels were defeated, Edward offered justice and equity tempered with recognition of their close kinship, but not the compromise essential to bring Warwick and Clarence to submission. Warwick and Clarence fought on, raised the stakes, and fled into exile rather than submit to Edward's justice. Desperate, they allied themselves instead to Queen Margaret of Anjou in the Lancastrian cause, married

Warwick's other daughter Anne Neville to the Lancastrian heir Prince Edward, and successfully restored Henry VI as king in lieu of Edward IV (October 1470). Apparently Clarence secured his father's duchy of York, to which he was next heir, and the second place in the line of succession, but he proved ready to overthrow the whole House of York in pursuit of a mixture of his own interests, his obligations to Warwick as his father-in-law, and the promises he had made to King Louis XI of France and Queen Margaret. His new Lancastrian allies (also distant cousins) resented him and that his father-in-law Warwick was ready to concede to them some of his own entitlements to maintain peace. Such differences contributed to Clarence's decision to turn his coat again, rejoin his brother Edward, and to destroy his Neville and Lancastrian allies. We should not doubt the anguish it caused him: he interceded with Edward for his father-in-law Warwick, securing him Edward's 'grace, with divers good conditions and profitable for the earl if he would have accepted them'. Warwick did not,[10] and died in consequence.

Actually this was a moment of crisis for the whole House of York. Edward IV escaped into exile in Burgundy in the autumn of 1470 and sought the support of his brother-in-law Charles the Bold, Duke of Burgundy, who was very disinclined to help. Most probably Charles was pressurised by his duchess, Margaret of York, who was committed to Edward's restoration, but it was actually Warwick's attack on his own Burgundian territories, prompted by Louis XI, that drove Charles to resource Edward's return to England. No more than John Neville (as described above) were other members of the House of York persuaded to back Clarence rather than Edward. Gloucester had been left in England, but joined Edward later, whether of choice or necessity we cannot tell. At this juncture he was loyal to Edward, accompanied his invasion, fought in the battles of Barnet and Tewkesbury, and presided over the judicial despatch of the Lancastrian leadership. Warwick, Montagu, and other cousins were among those killed.

If self-interest played a big part in Clarence's defection, so too did the arguments and blandishments both to Clarence to defect and to Edward to take him back 'by right covert ways and means ... by mediations of certain priests and other well-disposed persons' of Bishop Stillington and of his closest relatives: 'the high and mighty princess my lady their mother [Duchess Cecily]'; 'my lady of Exeter [and] my lady of Suffolk, his sisters [Anne and Elizabeth]'; '[his uncles] my lord of Canterbury [Cardinal Bourchier] [and] my lord of Essex [Henry Earl of Essex]'; 'my lady of Burgundy especially [his sister Margaret]'.

Duchess Margaret indeed sent a stream of messengers from the Low Countries to both Edward and Clarence.[11] So speaks Nicholas Harpsfield, Edward IV's signet clerk in his official history *The Arrival*.[12] Crowland stresses the mediation of Clarence's elder sisters, Anne Duchess of Exeter as well as Duchess Margaret.[13] Nothing is recorded of the views of Isabel Neville, Clarence's duchess and Warwick's elder daughter. Perhaps she was not consulted about Clarence's re-defection.

The constable of England was a great honorary office that carried with it titular military leadership and the administration of the law of arms, principally through the court of chivalry. The expertise of the Wydevilles in jousting made Richard Earl Rivers a highly suitable choice of constable; so too was his son Anthony, to whom Edward granted the reversion for life. However good as jousters, both proved useless in the 1469 campaign. Edward disregarded the reversion, appointing his brother Gloucester as successor. It was therefore as constable that Gloucester fought the 1471 campaign. To him fell the oversight of the military court that summarily tried captured leaders: after the Battle of Tewkesbury Gloucester condemned and had executed the last two Beauforts Edmund Duke of Somerset and John Marquis of Dorset, John Courtenay, Earl of Devon, John Lord Wenlock, John Langstrother, prior of St John and Henry VI's treasurer, and others. This merciless bloodletting was obviously on instructions of the king, who could have extended to them the prerogative of mercy that was applied to Sir John Fortescue, Dr John Morton, and possibly the king's (and Richard's) badly wounded brother-in-law Henry Duke of Exeter. It was, however, shocking, since the Lancastrian leadership had emerged from sanctuary at Tewkesbury Abbey on royal safe-conducts that had not been honoured. Gloucester also joined in the pacification of Kent, most of the rebels being punished by the purse but some by the neck. Thomas Neville, the Bastard of Fauconberg, Warwick's naval commander and the cousin of both Warwick and Gloucester, was received into the king's grace and despatched to serve on the Scottish border under Gloucester's command. What exactly followed is not recorded – whether any further treason was committed, which seems highly unlikely, Gloucester in his capacity as constable had him executed. If Gloucester had any role in the deaths of Prince Edward of Lancaster or King Henry VI, as later alleged, it was at the command of his brother the king and at his responsibility. Like his predecessor as constable, the Earl of Worcester, the epithet 'the butcher' was applied to him.[14]

The Warwick Inheritance Dispute

The intercession of the York ladies worked. The past was forgiven. The three brothers hazarded their lives together on the field of battle and, against the odds, the reunited House of York prevailed. The *Second War* was ended and indeed the Wars of the Roses as a whole seemed over. Again. Now was the time for the two royal dukes to underpin the parent dynasty as Edward had originally planned. 'These three brothers moreover, the king and his brothers, possessed such outstanding talent that triple cord could have been broken only with the utmost difficulty of they had been able to avoid dissension.'[15] But they could not. The House of York was riven by a violent quarrel conducted in public view and indeed threatened the escalation of a private war which, as the Crowland Continuator euphemistically states, 'proved difficult to settle'.[16] This was not about who should rule. In his *Second Reign* (1471–83) Edward IV was more secure than ever before. Not only had he finished off the Lancastrians and shrugged off Warwick's tutelage, but he had assured the succession. His son Edward Prince of Wales was unquestionably heir apparent whatever hereditary system was applied, be it primogeniture or the male entail. Obviously very young, Prince Edward was joined in 1473 by a second son, Richard of Shrewsbury, and briefly in 1477 by George, another Duke of Bedford. The arrival of yet more daughters relegated Clarence to seventh in line by his death and Richard Duke of Gloucester to tenth by 1483. Gloucester duly swore allegiance to Prince Edward in 1471, 1472, 1477 and to Edward V at least three times in 1483. This second rift was an inheritance dispute: it was caused by Gloucester's pursuit of the inheritance of his intended wife Anne Neville, the younger daughter of Warwick the Kingmaker.

The year 1471 represented a fresh start for Richard Duke of Gloucester. No longer was he required as the king's man in Wales or the north-west and he was deprived of the honours of Halton and Clitheroe. This terminated his involvement in the Stanley–Harrington dispute. As compensation, he received the lands forfeited by the defeated traitors, which did not actually amount to very much partly because the Lancastrians had suffered forfeiture already and partly because some obvious culprits (such as Warwick and Montagu) were exempted. These confiscations lay mostly in eastern England, notably the de Vere earldom of Oxford and the lands of the de Vere retainers. Gloucester had no intention of residing in East Anglia. He valued such acquisitions principally for income and compounded with some of the erstwhile traitors or their heirs. He was also granted Warwick's Neville lands in tail male in the north – the lordships of Middleham and Sheriff Hutton, both in Yorkshire, and Penrith in Cumberland, worth

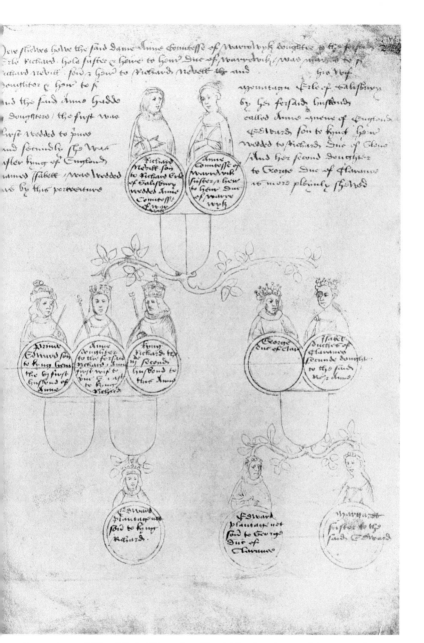

1. Descendants of Warwick the Kingmaker. King Richard III features left as second spouse of Anne Neville, their son Edward of Middleham below. To the right are Anne's elder sister Isabel Neville, her husband (and Richard's brother) Clarence and their children Edward Earl of Warwick and Margaret, later Countess of Salisbury.

2. The Lancastrian King Henry VI depicted as a saint on the rood screen of Ludham church, Norfolk (*c.* 1500).

3. King Richard III. Note the dark hair and eyes and drawn features.

4a. Fotheringhay Castle. All that remains of Richard's birthplace.

4b. Richard Duke of York's badge of the falcon and fetterlock on the choir stalls of the parish church at his town of Ludlow.

5. Richard's sister Margaret of York, Duchess of Burgundy, as a young wife.

6. Richard's brother George Duke of Clarence as Earl of Warwick.

Left: 7a. Edward IV's mistress Margaret Lucy, from her brass at Ingrave church, Essex.

Below left and right: 7b & 7c. Two shields demonstrating Margaret Lucy's noble ancestry.

8. Queen Elizabeth Wydeville and Yorkist roses from the Skinners Company fraternity register (*c.* 1472).

Right: 9a. Effigy of Joan Beaufort, Countess of Westmorland (d. 1440), grandmother of Richard III and great-grandmother of Anne Neville, at Staindrop College, Durham.

Below: 9b. Tomb of Anne Neville's maternal grandfather Richard Beauchamp, Earl of Warwick (d. 1439), in his Beauchamp Chapel, Warwick. The weepers are his offspring and in-laws.

10a. The choir of Tewkesbury Abbey and the tombs of Anne Neville's maternal grandmother Isabel Despenser and her ancestors. Anne's sister Isabel and Clarence were interred behind the high altar.

10b. Bisham Priory, burial place of Warwick the Kingmaker and Anne's maternal ancestors, from the *Salisbury Roll* (c. 1483).

11. Warwick the Kingmaker as weeper of Earl Richard Beauchamp's chapel, Warwick, *c.* 1480.

12a. Middleham Castle. The top storey of the central tower, now largely lost, was the grandest reception room of the Kingmaker and Richard Duke of Gloucester.

12b. York Minster from the north-west.

13. The Wydeville connection at court. Anthony Earl Rivers presents his translation of the *Dictes and Sayings of Philosophers* to Edward IV, Queen Elizabeth Wydeville and Prince Edward in attendance.

14. Stained-glass depiction of King Edward V at Coldridge church, Devon.

CHRISTCHURCH . MISERERIE SEAT . KING RICHARD III.

15a. King Richard III from a misericord at St George's Chapel, Windsor.

15b. Richard III's angry threat of vengeance on his brother-in-law Henry Duke of Buckingham.

Right: 16. Richard III's son Edward of Middleham, Earl of Salisbury and Prince of Wales, 1483, from the *Rows Roll*.

Below right: 17a. The skeleton alleged to be Richard III from the Leicester car park. Note the sharp curvature of the spine (scoliosis).

Below left: 17b. The supposed skull of Richard III, showing injuries incurred in life.

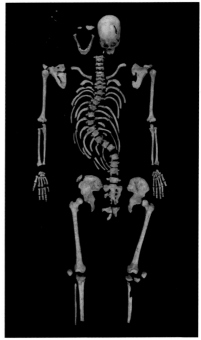

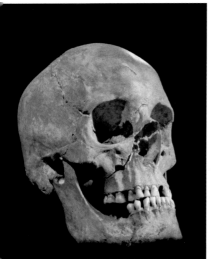

18a. Holbein's preliminary drawing of Richard III's cousin Henry VII and nephew Henry VIII for a lost mural at Whitehall.

18b. Perkin Warbeck from the *Recueil d'Arras*.

perhaps £2,000 a year – which underpinned the wardenship of the West March that Warwick had also exercised. Henceforth this was the northern powerhouse where he and King Edward chose that he should reside.[17] The heir to these should have been Warwick's brother John, also a traitor, and his son George, still Duke of Bedford but no longer destined for Elizabeth of York. Gloucester had been granted that part of Warwick's great inheritance to which Warwick's own daughters never had any claim.

The rest of the Warwick inheritance consisted of the Montagu earldom of Salisbury inherited from Warwick's mother Alice Montagu (d. 1463) in the south and Midlands and the Beauchamp and Despenser lands and earldom of Warwick concentrated in the west Midlands and Wales that belonged to Warwick's countess Anne Beauchamp.[18] At law not much was available to Warwick's daughters after excluding Countess Anne's inheritance, jointure, and dower. Alternatively since Warwick and his heir had died traitors, everything he (but not she) possessed could have been confiscated. But the law was not permitted to operate. When Clarence was forgiven and restored, still more once he had helped Edward to win, he could not be deprived of the rightful inheritance of his wife Isabel. Initially he scooped the pool: everything except the Neville lordships. Therefore Warwick and his heir Montagu were not attainted and their lands were not confiscated, with the full approval of his heirs. Clarence was also granted the custody of the other daughter, Anne Neville, Edward of Lancaster's widow, whom he intended should not succeed. There were precedents for sidelining such heiresses and precedents also for powerful suitors 'rescuing' them from their plight. Anne, however, preferred the latter option. Realising that only the greatest of husbands could force Clarence to disgorge, she committed herself to his brother Gloucester. The dowager-countess also asserted her claims, which, if admitted, would have left virtually nothing for either duke until 1492, when both dukes and both daughters were dead.

Gloucester took in Anne Neville, proposed to marry her, and laid claim to half the estates, apparently in addition to the Neville lands he already held. Clarence refused. Gloucester, he said, 'may well have my lady his sister-in-law, but they shall part no livelihood' – divide no inheritance.[19] That was not acceptable to Gloucester. The matter went in March 1472 before the royal council at Sheen, where, Crowland reports,

> So much disputation arose between the brothers and so many keen arguments were put forward on either side with the greatest acuteness in the presence of the king, sitting in judgement in the council chamber, that all who stood about, even those learned in the law, marvelled at the profusion of the arguments which the princes produced for their own cases.

It was a 'hopeless business' of 'wilful men' exercising their will.[20]

The complexity becomes understandable when it is appreciated that, in the names of their wives, the dukes were contending for what actually belonged to the Countess of Warwick and the Duke of Bedford, who must on no account have their deserts. Clarence wanted to keep all he held while Gloucester wanted to keep the Neville lands out of any partition, and Gloucester moreover was asserting the rights of Anne, whom he had not yet married and might not be allowed to marry in future. The king imposed a 50:50 partition, which satisfied neither duke, but the detailed division was not decided until 20 July 1473 and the legal technicalities until two special acts of parliament in 1474–75. The Countess of Warwick lost everything 'as though she was naturally dead': in the protection of Gloucester, it is perhaps true that he locked away his mother-in-law for the rest of his life.[21] The two dukes secured the Neville lands, Gloucester getting all but two Essex properties, for as long as the marquis Montagu had male heirs living. This excluded George Neville, but protected the rights of other Neville lines. It may have been Cardinal Bourchier, guardian of the next heir Richard Lord Latimer, who insisted on this clause. Another provision, which Clarence may have inserted, allowed for the divorce of Gloucester and Anne. Although they had married by this time, the impediments to their union had not been sufficiently dispensed to validate their union. This may be why Clarence resisted in 1473 the partition agreed in 1472. If Gloucester did not contract a valid marriage, why should Clarence give up anything at all? By then Clarence had a daughter and heiress, Margaret, so he was entitled by the law of England to all his duchess's estates should he die. Gloucester secured the same rights in the event of both Anne's death and divorce (nullity).

Gloucester's intervention secured him half the Warwick inheritance, much more than he previously had. Anne Neville was protected and assured both the status and wealth that Warwick had sought for her, including ultimately the crown, although a question mark hung over it. Clarence and Isabel lost nearly half of what they had possessed – and considerably more, when account is taken of the honours of Tutbury and Duffield that the king took back. The whole arrangement was paid for by the Countess of Warwick and George Neville, both of whom lost all their rights. So did rivals to the Beauchamp, Despenser, and Neville inheritances. The quarrel was suspended rather than permanently concluded.

In every sense, this was a family quarrel. One brother, the king, arbitrated between the other two and their duchesses, who were sisters and first cousins, to the loss of the ladies' mother – cousin to all three royal brothers – and George Neville, the first cousin once removed of the three royal brothers, the cousin of the two duchesses, and the king's putative son-in-law. There were other prohibited relationships besides this. The closest ties of consanguinity and affinity and personal acquaintance inflamed the dispute. In addition to impediments in the third and fourth degree, which were easily dispensed, both dukes were related to the Neville girls in the second degree as first cousins. Clarence, as we have seen, had difficulty in securing a dispensation to marry Isabel, his first cousin. Following Clarence's marriage to Isabel, Gloucester and Anne were additionally brother- and sister-in-law twice over – already brother and sister in contemporary parlance and by affinity – and probably beyond a valid dispensation. Gloucester appears not to have sought an extension of his dispensation, which might well have been refused and thus result in the annulment of his marriage. Clarence realised this and objected. One wonders if Anne realised. But Gloucester and Anne lived together as man and wife and duly begat Edward of Middleham, the son and heir that was the future of their dynasty, most probably in 1477. Almost certainly Edward IV was godfather.

Table 1 in chapter 2 itemised four generations of the ancestry of Richard Duke of Gloucester. Table 4 itemises the ancestors of Anne Neville. Her lineage, predominantly English, was no less noble than Richard's. One whole quarter of her lineage, which traces the Nevilles back from her father Warwick the Kingmaker, is identical to a quarter of Richard's, since his mother Cecily was sister to Warwick's father. Again Edward III occurs twice, along with Pedro the Cruel of Castile and the de Roets from Hainault, but the principal lines through which her inheritance derived – the Beauchamps, the Despensers, the Hollands, and the Montagus – are much more prominent. It was through these connections that Anne brought titles, estates, patronage of religious houses, traditions, renown, badges and coats of arms. Table 5 illustrates one such aspect: Anne's coat of arms, each quartering signalling another intermarriage.

There were three sequels to this dispute. One, the destruction of Clarence, is discussed below. The second, the confinement of the Countess of Warwick at Middleham, has been mentioned. The third relates to George Neville, Duke of Bedford. How to ensure the continuance of male heirs of the marquis Montagu and yet prevent them securing their entitlements was quite a quandary for Gloucester. George Neville was not without friends or means – he was heir to his mother, for instance, and potentially of the Earl of Worcester – and he could not renounce any rights until he came of age. There was a risk that another guardian might marry him to his daughter and would in due course seek his restoration. Richard did secure the boy's custody – a clear breach of the convention (to avoid a conflict of interest) that no guardian should have an interest in the heir's person or possessions. Richard did secure George's demotion from his dukedom and the peerage, to exclude him from a voice in Parliament. Gloucester did not interpret guardianship as placing his ward's interests first. He did not marry George off, allowing the boy to procreate his own heir, because that was potentially too dangerous. Gloucester did try to secure custody of the next heir too, Richard Lord Latimer, but he was stymied by the boy's guardian, his own uncle Cardinal Bourchier, who did have Latimer's best interests at heart. The three rivals – Gloucester, George Neville, and Latimer – were cousins several times over. Uncertain what next to do, Richard delayed: George Neville was still single when he died in 1483, aged eighteen, and Gloucester's title was reduced to a life estate.[22]

The Destruction of Clarence

The third rift in the House of York involved the destruction by Edward IV of their brother George Duke of Clarence. This act of fratricide was also the most shocking division in the House of York. 'The mind recoils from describing what followed in the next parliament,' wrote Crowland, 'so sad between two brothers of such noble character.'[23] Clarence was accused of treason, tried and executed. The charge of treason is not credible. The various individual offences, if true, do not amount to treason and there is no independent evidence of conspiracy or any other conspirators. None of the principal narrators were convinced of his guilt. All looked for explanations beyond the indictment, the most popular being that he was destroyed by his enemies – in particular Queen Elizabeth and her family, because he was perceived as an obstacle

Table 4: The Lineage of Anne Neville, Duchess of Gloucester & Queen of England

	Parents	Grandparents	Gt-Grandparents	Gt-Grandparents	Gt-Grandparents	Gt-Grandparents
No.	2	4	8	16	32	64
1						Randal Ld Neville d. 1331
2					Ralph Ld Neville d. 1367	
3						Euphemia Clavering
						Hugh Ld. Audley d. 1326
4				John Ld Neville d. 1388	Alice Audley d. 1374	
5						Isolt Mortimer fl. 1336
						S. Henry Percy d.1272
6			Ralph E. Westmorland d. 1425		Henry Ld Percy d.1314	
7				Maud Percy d. 1379		Eleanor Warenne fl. 1282
						Richard E. Arundel d.1302
8		Richard E. Salisbury d. 1460			Eleanor Arundel d. 1328	
9						Alasia of Saluzzo d. 1292
						Edward II 1307–22
10					Edward III 1327–77	
11				John D. Lancaster d. 1399		Isabella of France d. 1358
						William III Ct. Hainault d.1337
12			Joan Beaufort d. 1440		Philippa of Hainault d. 1369	
13						Jeanne Valois d. 1352
						Payne Roet I
14					Payne II *alias* Gilles Roet	Not known
15				Katherine Swinford (Roet) d. 1403	Not known	Not known
16	Richard Neville E. Warwick					Not known
17				?		William E. Salisbury d.1344
18					John Ld. Montagu d. 1390	Katherine Grandisson d. 1349
19				John E of Salisbury d. 1400		Thomas Ld Monthermer d. 1340
20			Thomas E. Salisbury d. 1428		Margaret Monthermer d. 1395	
21		Alice Montagu d. 1463				Margaret Tyas d. 1349
22					Adam Francis	Adam Francis
						Constance
23				Maud Francis d. 1424		Not known
24					Agnes	Not known
25						Robert Ld. Holland d. 1328
26					Thomas E Kent d. 1360	Maud Zouche d. 1349
27				Thomas Holland E Kent d. 1397		Edmund E Kent d. 1330
28			Eleanor Holland		Joan of Kent d. 1385	Margaret Wake d. 1349
29						Edmund E Arundel d. 1326
30					Richard E.Arundel d. 1376	Alice Warenne
31				Alice Arundel d. 1416		Henry E. Lancaster d. 1345
32					Eleanor of Lancaster d. 1372	Maud Chaworth

No.	Parents	Grandparents	Gt-Grandparents	Gt-Grandparents	Gt-Grandparents	Gt-Grandparents
	2	4	8	16	32	64
33		Richard E. Warwick				William Beauchamp E. Warwick d. 1298
34					Guy E. Warwick d. 1315	Maud Furnival d. 1302
35				Thomas I d. 1369 Beauchamp I E. Warwick		Mary d. 1283
36			Thomas II E. Warwick d. 1401		Alice Tony d. 1325	Ralph Tony d. 1295
37						Edmund Mortimer d. 1304
38					Roger E March d. 1330	Margaret de Fiennes d. 1334
39				Catherine Mortimer d. 1369		Piers Genevile d. 1292
40					Joan Geneville d. 1356	Joan of La Marche
41						William Ld. Ferrers d. 1325
42					Henry Ld. Ferrers d. 1343	Ellen Seagrave
43			Margaret Ferrers d. 1407			Theobald Verdon d. 1316
44				William Ld.Ferrers d. 1374	Isabel Verdon d. 1349	Elizabeth de Clare d. 1360
45						Robert Ld Ufford d. 1316
46					Robert E of Suffolk d. 1369	Cecily Valoignes d. 1325
47				Margaret Ufford		Walter de Norwich d. 1329
48	Anne Beauchamp				Margaret Norwich d. 1368	Catherine Hederset
49						Hugh Despenser yr d. 1326
50					Edward Despenser d. 1342	Eleanor de Clare d. 1337
51				Edward Ld Despenser d. 1375		William Ld Ferrers d. 1374
52					Anne Ferrers d. 1367	Margaret Ufford
53						Robert Ld Burghersh d. 1306
54					Bartholomew Burghersh d. 1355	Maud Badlesmere
55			Thomas Ld Despenser d. 1400	Elizabeth Burghersh d. 1409		Theobald Ld Verdon d. 1316
56		Isabel Despenser d. 1439			Elizabeth Verdon d. 1360	Maud Mortimer d. 1312
57						Edward II 1307–27
58					Edward III 1327–77	Isabella of France d. 1358
59				Edmund D. York d. 1402		William Ct Hainault d. 1337
60			Constance of York d. 1416		Philippa of Hainault d. 1369	Jeanne Valois d.1352
61						Alfonso XI of Castille d. 1350
62				Isabella de Padilla d. 1392	Pedro I (of Castile) d. 1369	Maria of Portugal d. 1357
63						Juan Garcia de Padilla
64					Maria de Padilla d. 1361	Maria Garcia de Henestoza

Key: D = duke; M = marquis; E = earl; Ld = lord; Ct = count

Table 5: The Coat of Arms of Anne Neville

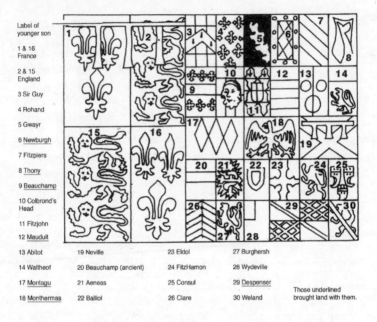

Label of younger son			
1 & 16 France			
2 & 15 England			
3 Sir Guy			
4 Rohand			
5 Gwayr			
6 Newburgh			
7 Fitzpiers			
8 Thony			
9 Beauchamp			
10 Colbrond's Head			
11 Fitzjohn			
12 Mauduit			
13 Abitot	19 Neville	23 Eldol	27 Burghersh
14 Waltheof	20 Beauchamp (ancient)	24 FitzHamon	28 Wydeville
17 Montagu	21 Aeneas	25 Consul	29 Despenser
18 Monthermas	22 Balliol	26 Clare	30 Weland

Those underlined brought land with them.

to the orderly succession of Prince Edward. The trial was fixed: in the king's high court of Parliament the word of the king could not be gainsaid. Clarence had undoubtedly been a nuisance, guilty of one of the most appalling abuses of power of the whole period in the judicial murder of Ankarette Twynho, unwise at the very least to associate himself with retainers executed for sorcery, and a bad example of dissension in the highest echelons, but these faults did not justify so extreme a penalty. Moreover, he was provoked by Edward's unreasonable conduct towards him. Of course all subjects had to bow to the king's authority, however unreasonably exercised, but Clarence was no normal subject, rather the greatest of subjects. A brother was bound to answer back.

Supposedly the reconciliation of the king and duke in 1471 had been complete. Bygones were to be bygones, the past forgotten and forgiven. Clarence recovered most of his possessions, interceded successfully for the defaulting cities of Bristol and Coventry, and was allowed his duchess' inheritance. The second quarrel over the Warwick inheritance was not resolved so cleanly. His wounds still festered. The partition that Edward imposed was equal and equitable, although Clarence lost most and substantial issues remained, but Clarence additionally lost his prime estates in Staffordshire and Derbyshire. Presumably Edward thought this an appropriate penalty for disobedience, an opportunity to reunite his duchy of Lancaster, and wished also to restrict Clarence's wealth and power, yet it was also a malign action that uniquely singled the duke out for harsher treatment. It was because of this, reported Crowland, that there were so 'many who believed that the duke's heart had turned against their former friendship'. Clarence grumbled and absented himself from the royal council, perhaps for several years.[24] However, that was all. No crisis threatened. He served on Edward's expeditionary force to France, indeed was one of Edward's choices to arbitrate on the rival claims to the French throne, and featured prominently in the 'wondrous' display of family pride and unity that intervened between the second and third rift. Detailed heraldic accounts were widely circulated.

This celebration was the reinterment in 1476 at Fotheringhay College of the patriarch of the House of York, Duke Richard, and his son Edmund Earl of Rutland, both killed at the Battle of Wakefield (1460) and humbly interred at Pontefract Priory.[25] Whereas the Nevilles had orchestrated a splendid reburial for Richard Earl of Salisbury and Sir Thomas Neville at Bisham Priory in 1463, King Edward could not afford – or had not got round to – a grand reinterment in the family mausoleum for his father and next brother. The ceremonies in July 1476 lasted ten days. At the start of the Yorkshire cortège it was Gloucester as chief mourner who headed an escort of the northern nobility. They dropped off on the way south to Northamptonshire, where it was the king and the court that took over. All three of York's sons were there

– Edward IV, Clarence, and Gloucester. John de la Pole, Duke of Suffolk, husband to Elizabeth of York, was there with his eldest son (Gloucester's senior nephew) John Earl of Lincoln – nephew to the three royal brothers – and their uncle Henry Bourchier, Earl of Essex. From the Wydeville side (Gloucester's in-laws), there was Queen Elizabeth with two daughters, her brother Anthony Earl Rivers, her eldest son Thomas Marquis of Dorset, and Anthony Grey of Ruthin, husband of the queen's sister Joan.[26] The heralds may simply have ignored the ladies. That Fotheringhay was not convenient for all and the ceremonies were protracted may explain the omission of the king's two sons, Lord Richard Grey, the queen's younger brothers, and several of her sisters' husbands. The absence of any of Duchess Cecily's Neville relatives may indicate that after the *Second War* they ceased to be accounted as royal kin.

A similar celebration of family unity accompanied the wedding early in 1478 of the king's second son, Richard Duke of York and Norfolk, and Anne Mowbray, heiress to the dukes of York.[27]

Clarence involved himself in the reinterment but was inescapably absent from the wedding and its planning, since he was a prisoner in the Tower and appeared – and was intended to appear – the one exception to the harmony and unity of the royal family. It was effective propaganda.

The rift between duke and king seems to have deepened sharply after the death (probably from the aftereffects of childbirth) of Clarence's duchess Isabel Neville, still aged only twenty-five. This was late in 1476. Clarence was genuinely distressed and gave her a splendid send-off, but, as normal in this era, he needed another wife. He was one of the most eligible unmarried men in Europe. The most magnificent opportunity arose almost at once, with the death of Charles the Bold, Duke of Burgundy, leaving as sole heiress an unmarried daughter, Mary of Burgundy. She had a war with France on her hands and needed a husband, financial and military resources, and an heir at once. Margaret of York, now dowager Duchess of Burgundy, 'who was more fond of her brother

Clarence than of any of her family, devoted all her effort and all her attention to uniting [him] in marriage [to] Mary'.[28] Viewed dispassionately, it was in England's prime interest to keep the Low Countries out of the hands of England's most powerful and most malicious neighbour, Louis XI of France. Arguments against, such as the loss of Edward IV's modest French pension and the need to subsidise Mary's defence, were surely secondary to this enormous gain. Such arguments, it seems, were never rehearsed as Edward immediately – precipitately – prohibited the match – so quickly that it features in none of the diplomatic records, nor apparently at the emergency great council convened in January 1477. Edward's motive was highly personal, so Crowland states: 'such an exalted destiny for an ungrateful brother was not to the liking of the king'.[29] A wonderful opportunity was spurned. At this point, remember, Clarence had committed no recorded crime or offence: the animosity was on the king's side. Next Clarence was offered the hand of the landless Princess Margaret of Scotland, sister of England's ally James III, but that too was forbidden by the king. In both cases Earl Rivers, belittled by Commines as 'a mere earl' and not viewed internationally as royal, was proposed in his place and summarily rejected. Surely Clarence was reminded of the king's equally unreasonable objections to his first marriage. Edward, it appeared, would bar any second marriage if he could. If Clarence felt the king was out to destroy him slowly 'like a candle consumes in burning', this overreaction was not without justification.

Clarence was arrested by the king for his abuse of power in May 1477. This did not constitute treason, but an indication that he was to be attainted was the styling on 1 July 1477 of Gloucester's son Edward of Middleham as Earl of Salisbury, one of Clarence's titles.[30] Concocting the charges took some time. A great council at Westminster in the autumn prepared for both wedding and trial to achieve the united front that ensured nobody spoke up for Clarence in the ensuing trial. The king's second son, Richard Duke of York, was additionally created Duke of Norfolk and very conveniently a third son, George, was born at Windsor. All the Lords renewed their oaths of allegiance to the king and prince. The queen's sons and brothers dominated the jousting that celebrated the wedding. A big effort was made by royal and Wydeville servants to secure seats in Parliament to secure a compliant assembly. The speaker was Sir William Allington, a chancellor of both the king's sons and a Wydeville client. Now the husbands of the queen's sisters had grown up, the Wydeville connection worked together as an extension of the king's family. Some fruits of Clarence's forfeiture were allocated in advance, certainly before his death, to his brother-in-law/cousin Henry Duke of Buckingham (steward of England this time), his brother-in-law John Duke of Suffolk (lieutenant of Ireland), and his brother Gloucester (great chamberlain of England).[31] Gloucester indeed had a whole shopping list of requests that the king conceded. All of them went along with the king's plan. Had their compliance not been assured, perhaps the trial would not have taken place.

The decision to attaint Clarence penalised his offspring as well. The duke's title was forfeited, so his three-year-old son Edward (nephew to Edward IV and Richard III) was deprived of his right to the dukedom of Clarence, and the Lancastrian forfeitures Clarence held of royal grant, worth perhaps £2,000 a year, which became the core of the crown estate that Edward now started to build up. The king could not deprive Clarence's son of his mother's half-share of the Warwick inheritance, but, as we have seen, he allowed it to be diminished in half a dozen different ways. Young Warwick was a royal ward – the greatest of royal wards – so the king had the use and income of his lands for another eighteen years and also his marriage, which he granted in 1481 to his stepson (the queen's son) Thomas Marquis of Dorset, whose infant daughter Warwick was destined to marry.[32]

Unfortunately Anne Duchess of Exeter, so important as mediator in 1471 – she was the elder sister not only of Clarence but of the king – had died in 1476 and Duchess Margaret of course was far away in Burgundy. It was down to Suffolk to speak for Elizabeth. Clarence's remaining brothers acted together. Clarence, it is said, fought back, knowing that he could not win. After sentence of death was passed against him, there was a delay. Did Edward IV have second thoughts? He is reported afterwards to have regretted Clarence's death, railing that nobody pleaded for his life. The historian Polydore Vergil interpreted this as evidence that he had been manipulated by those about him. The necessary pressure to implement the execution was applied by the speaker of the Commons – the Wydeville speaker. Duchess Cecily's intervention served only to spare Clarence the ritual dismemberment normal for traitors. That Edward experienced further qualms is suggested by compensation paid to those allegedly harmed by Clarence and payments for the completion of his tomb at Tewkesbury Abbey (Gloucs.), both for the benefit of his soul.[33]

Gloucester also professed strong regret, but this was later, in 1483, when he had good reason to dissociate himself from Clarence's death and to add it to the charges against the Wydevilles. In 1477–78 he concurred with the rest. Perhaps he felt he had no choice. He concealed his real feelings, whatever they were. The most striking evidence of his attitude at the time is the benefits that he secured – and secured, moreover, before Clarence's destruction was completed or even commenced. Several measures adjusted the partition of the Warwick inheritance in his (or rather his wife's) favour. His son was formally created Earl of Salisbury. He exchanged the marcher lordship of Elfael for that of the duchy of Lancaster and lordship of Ogmore, a convenient enclave in his great lordship of Glamorgan, and Bushey and Ware in Hertfordshire for property in Yorkshire. He secured the demotion of George Neville, not just from the dukedom of Bedford but any peerage, thus placing him more firmly in his power. Such benefits, it has been argued, do not indicate complicity in Clarence's fall, but the fact that most date from before the duke's execution and some from before his trial does, if obedience to the king's command constitutes complicity at all. Outside Parliament, Richard grabbed properties at Essendon and Shillingthorpe (Lincs.), trivial enough but evidently resenting their allocation to Clarence. Moreover, he joined with the rival claimants to the Beauchamp estates in chancery lawsuits to wrest from the trustees manors that Clarence had effectively enjoyed. All he could hope for was an eighth: his nephew twice over, Clarence's underage son Edward Earl of Warwick stood to lose seven-eighths.[34] Whatever may have been Gloucester's attitude to fellow members of the House of York, he certainly fostered the notion that he was the Warwick heir through his duchess, the source of not only his lands, but his retainers and much of his renown.

Conclusion

For nine years from 1469 to 1478 English political life was presented with scandalous divisions within the ruling house. A self-indulgent king had laid himself open to reforming replacement. Brother had contended with brother – mother and sister attempting to keep or restore the peace – and attempts had been made to dethrone the principal heir, to divorce him and to bastardise his children. The most scurrilous stories of illegitimacy, invalid marriages and living in sin, of sorcery, abuse of power and treason had been publicised or at least had been bandied about. Finally the whole house had joined together to destroy a single defaulting member in an act of fratricide that offended all contemporary standards. Could the House of York become more dysfunctional and self-destructive? Surely not. With the single dissenting voice excised, the wars concluded, and the succession secured, Edward IV himself now 'exercised his office so haughtily thereafter that he seemed to be feared by all his subjects while he himself feared no man'. The authority of crown had been asserted over even the greatest subjects, now much less formidable.[35] A brighter, more peaceful future was assured.

6

BROTHERS IN LAW: THE EVOLUTION OF THE ROYAL FAMILY DURING EDWARD IV'S SECOND REIGN

What befell Clarence in 1478 was the exception to the luxuriant expansion of the Yorkist royal family. During the 1460s Edward IV's brothers were minors and so too were several of the queen's brothers and sisters and their spouses: all, in fifteenth-century terms, Richard's kin. Over the next decade they grew up. It was at this point that the king's two brothers, his sisters Anne and Elizabeth, the queen's eldest son, sisters and younger brothers matured, reached childbearing age, and in most cases produced children. The Yorkist family was burgeoning. It follows that Richard was acquiring more relatives. This much-enlarged royal family was particularly evident at court, at the reburial of Duke Richard and at the wedding of Edward's younger son. They constituted a formidable common front for the destruction of Clarence. They should have constituted a formidable common front in support of Edward's heir, the next king Edward V, but it did not work out like that, as this book will show, for reasons outlined earlier and explored later in this chapter. This chapter looks first at the king's own nuclear family, then at those of his siblings – especially Richard Duke of Gloucester – and at the developing Wydeville connection.

King Edward's Family

On 2 October 1470 Edward IV was in exile during the *Second War* and Queen Elizabeth was in sanctuary at Westminster Abbey when the long-awaited son and heir, Prince Edward, was born. Publicly acclaimed as heir apparent on the king's return in 1471, he was created Prince of Wales, Duke of Cornwall, and Earl of Chester, and in due course in 1483 he succeeded automatically as King Edward V. The Yorkist royal house grew. King and queen performed their duty: Queen Elizabeth pumped out a baby almost every year until Princess Bridget in 1480, when she may have been in her early forties. She already had two sons by her first marriage.

Table 6 records ten live births, the products of this union, with gaps sufficient for a couple of miscarriages or stillbirths, most of them conceived within a year of the previous birth. There were seven daughters and three sons by Edward IV, the nieces and nephews of the future Richard III. Most appear to have been healthy: only Mary (1467–82), Margaret (1472), and George (1477–78) predeceased the king.[1] Twenty associated events, ten baptisms and ten churchings, were a significant unrecorded element in court celebrations and ceremonies.

These offspring were political assets, even this train of daughters. Remember that parents normally incurred the cost of dowries for their daughters. Prince Edward became the figurehead of devolved government in Wales, Richard Duke of York was to be a territorial magnate. Marrying him to Anne Mowbray brought him a great estate at no cost to the king, principally in East Anglia and Surrey. After Anne Mowbray's death, the king contrived that the prince kept it, to the loss of his devoted servant John Lord Howard and their cousin William Lord Berkeley.[2] Even the very short-lived third son, George Duke of Bedford, though never endowed, was appointed titular lieutenant of Ireland. All moreover had potential in the diplomatic game, several featuring in international negotiations. Diplomacy involved the interaction of one royal

Table 6: Edward IV's Legitimate Children

Name	Conception	Birth date	Months until next conception	Place of birth	Date of death
Elizabeth	May 1465	(11) Feb 1466 (expected 19 Jan)	10	Westminster	
Mary	Dec 1466	(12) Aug 1467	10	Windsor	1482
Cecily	(20) Jun 1468	(20) Mar 1469	10	Westminster	
Edward	2 Jan 1470	2 Oct 1470	8	Westminster	
Margaret	June 1471	(10 Apr) 1472	7	Windsor	1472
Richard	Nov 1472	17 Aug 1473	6	Shrewsbury	
Anne	Feb 1474	2 Nov 1475	14	Westminster	
George	Jan 1477	by 15 Nov 1477	8	Windsor	1478
Katherine	mid-1478	early 1479	7	Eltham	
Bridget	Oct 1479	10 Jul 1480		Eltham	

Based on: *Annales*, ii(2), 785, 788; C. L. Scofield, *The Life and Reign of Edward IV* (1923), i 393, 428–9, 482–3, 546; ii. 163, 210–11, 253, 299.

family with another. The eldest daughter Elizabeth of York was no longer heiress apparent and was disentangled from her betrothal to George Neville, to which neither party had been old enough to give consent. In 1475 she was betrothed next to Louis XI of France's heir, Prince Charles, the dauphin and future King Charles VIII, and was known as the dauphiness at Edward's court.[3] The third daughter, Cecily, was betrothed to the future James IV of Scotland. Anne and Katherine also feature in negotiations of this kind. These matches were designed to substantiate policy, but they came to determine it, as Edward allowed his freedom of diplomatic manoeuvre to be restricted. His foreign counterparts did not. Neither Louis XI nor James III allowed these matches to pass the point of no return and both Elizabeth and Cecily were to be jilted. Crowland reports on the 'handsome and most delightful children born of the marriage', yet 'nevertheless it was not thought, at that time, that any one of these marriages would take place'.⁴ Note that it was this narrower nuclear family on which the king's attention focused rather than those of his siblings, still less his sisters-in-law. He certainly had bastards too, most probably unrecorded, but they were much lower down his list of priority if, indeed, they featured at all.

All these children took precedence over the king's two brothers and sisters and their own progeny.

George Duke of Clarence, next in age and in line, had married Isabel Neville in 1469, and had started his family at once. The first pregnancy ended prematurely on a ship off Calais early next year. Three more followed: of Margaret (d. 1541), born at Farleigh Hungerford in Wiltshire in 1473, the future Countess of Salisbury; Edward Earl of Warwick, the son and heir, born at Warwick in 1475 and King Edward's godson; and Richard, who lived only a few weeks in 1476. These too were nephews and niece of Richard III, who seems to have considered the potential of Edward as his own heir. Any family feeling that Edward experienced towards Clarence and his offspring seems to have been of the negative variety. He was quite prepared to disinherit Clarence's children.

Of his three married sisters, all duchesses, Margaret alone was childless. Richard's sister Anne bore two daughters, both called Anne. The elder, by Henry Duke of Exeter, had been married to the queen's elder son Thomas Grey, who was created Earl of Huntingdon in her own right, but she died without issue. Now childless, the duchess was divorced from the duke on 1472 – surely nullifying her first marriage bastardised her daughter, fortunately already safely married? The duchess bore another daughter, Anne, by Thomas St Leger, another brother-in-law of inferior birth, rank, and morality for Richard. This second Anne was stated to be eleven years old at her mother's death in 1476⁵ and, since the divorce cannot have permitted the duchess to remarry, the girl should have been labelled illegitimate but was not. Elizabeth

Duchess of Suffolk in contrast was highly productive: she bore another six sons after John Earl of Lincoln – Edmund (ex. 1513), Edward, Geoffrey (if he existed), Humphrey, William (d. 1539), and Richard (k. 1525) and at least four daughters. Again Richard took an interest in Lincoln once king. Lincoln was to lead his council in the north and may have been designated as heir, until he procreated his own, by Richard III. John Duke of Suffolk surely hoped for royal appointments and patronage, but Edward found no use for him outside a few months in 1478.

Note who is missing from this discussion. The older generation, the king's uncle and aunt Henry and Isabel, Countess of Essex, Cardinal Bourchier, and John Lord Berners were still at court and in government, highly influential and too easy to overlook. That Essex predeceased Edward IV by five days may have been profoundly important. But where were the Nevilles? Of Duchess Cecily's elder sisters, Eleanor Countess of Northumberland, twenty years a widow, died in 1474, Anne Duchess of Buckingham (seven years widowed again) in 1480, and Katherine Duchess of Norfolk, twelve years widowed again, about 1483. The Neville ladies may have been remarkably tough, but family direction had passed to their grandchildren. The last of Cecily's brothers, Edward Lord Abergavenny, died in 1476 without exciting remark. In the next generation, only Archbishop Neville remained of Warwick and his brothers and he was disgraced, imprisoned, and dispossessed before his death in 1476. Few of Warwick's sisters remained, and those that did, such as Alice Lady FitzHugh, fell firmly into Gloucester's sphere of influence.

The Nuclear Family of Richard Duke of Gloucester

Fans of Richard III wish to believe that his union with Anne Neville was a love match. They had been first cousins when introduced and also when they shared the same household in the mid-1460s, when Gloucester was the ward of her father Warwick the Kingmaker. They appeared in public together on several occasions. While it seems unlikely that Warwick schemed for them to marry, Richard cannot have been unaware that Anne was scheduled to become his sister-in-law when Isabel wed Clarence. If not love, liking and compatibility surely underpinned Richard and Anne's union, which they unusually contracted themselves rather than by arrangement of parents as was normal. Anne needed Richard if she was to recover her inheritance and station in life. Richard may well have fancied her, but offered the choice of her person or her inheritance he insisted on both. Materially it was a prudent match.

Richard and Anne did not marry until the 1470s. The precise date is not known because, it seems, Richard married Anne Neville ahead of a valid dispensation and indeed never secured one. She threw in her lot with him in 1471, had not yet married on 6 March 1472, but most likely did so soon after. She had been married before, to Edward of Lancaster, a match to a pretender prince of whom one did not speak in the 1470s. Certainly Edward had consummated the union, no issue resulting. Anne was no more than sixteen years of age. Richard was very likely already a father. There are no recorded pregnancies and no live births before 1475. Edward of Middleham, the only live birth known, is recorded in 1477, when he was styled Earl of Salisbury. Probably he was the king's godson. This was her only known live birth: we cannot know about any miscarriages or stillbirths, which would not have been recorded, and nothing is known of any other infants that were born alive. A reference to a son George in a version of the Tewkesbury Abbey Chronicle is probably a later error. There is more than a hint of gynaecological problems for Anne's mother, a child bride certainly sexually active in the 1440s who did not have a baby until 1451, in her mid-twenties, produced only two in all, and apparently desisted aged thirty. King Richard and Queen Anne are known to have engaged in sexual intercourse until the end of

1484, but no further pregnancies or births are recorded. The baby was styled Earl of Salisbury, a family title assigned to Clarence in 1472. Its transfer, not yet legally validated, foreshadowed Clarence's death and the transfer of his rights to the other heir. The birth of a son and heir was always to be applauded. After five years of marriage, Edward of Middleham was all the more appreciated, and he became more precious yet as the years passed without any further offspring.

Richard made a fresh start to his career from 1471. He was, after all, not yet twenty years of age. Thanks to Paul Murray Kendall, historians of the last sixty years have learnt that this was the era when Richard was Lord of the North, when he succeeded to Warwick's wardenship of the West March, to his northern estates and retinue, to his lieutenancy of the northern borders and hegemony over the whole north of England, and in 1483, in a unique distinction, secured his own palatine county of Cumberland. The Neville earls of Westmorland accepted his olive branch and all the northern nobility, including the rival House of Percy, submitted to his leadership. Edward IV, who installed him there, had not intended to give him so much, but Richard skilfully exploited exchanges to acquire such Yorkshire lordships as Richmond, Helmsley, Scarborough and Skipton too. Edward duly accepted that Richard had made himself into the greatest northern magnate of them all. He started the process and connived at Richard's self-advancement. He knew how the two countesses of Oxford and Warwick were denied their rights, but allowed Richard to do as he pleased. Richard, of course, had learnt about the north in Warwick's household and evidently liked what he saw. His late cousin and guardian had been his mentor and was now his model. Moreover, he had married Warwick's younger daughter Anne Neville. If Clarence and Isabel Neville wanted the west Midland properties, Gloucester undoubtedly wanted those in the north, not just the Neville patrimony of Middleham, Sheriff Hutton and Penrith, but Barnard Castle and Cottingham too. Moreover, he wanted them by inheritance – which was why he tolerated the trial that George Neville represented – because he could then pose as the heir rather than the conqueror of the beloved Warwick and could inherit the traditions and renown and the hereditary loyalties of the Richmondshire connection that had made the three earls of Westmorland, Salisbury, and Warwick so militarily formidable. Past glories such as the Battle of Neville's Cross (1346), the Neville chantry at Durham, St William's College at York, and the patronage of Coverham Abbey and other religious houses became his as well.

Richard married into Anne Neville's family just as much as she married into his own. A comparison of tables 1 and 4 shows how much was shared. Her grandfather Salisbury was Duchess Cecily's sister. All her ancestral lines stopped with Anne: her sister Isabel did bear a daughter with descendants alive today, but the crown of England did not pass along that route. Anne Neville herself was just as blue-blooded as Richard himself. She was the culmination of a host of noble dynasties. The four great inheritances united by her father Warwick – Beauchamp, Despenser, Montagu, and Neville – were themselves amalgamations of others, of De Clare, Monthermer, Newburgh, and Oilly, to mention but a few, each with their own noble residences and estates, each decorated with their own battle honours, religious foundations, traditions and even myths. Such 'goodwill' was a valuable asset – commercially and in this instance politically too. There was mileage in Richard posing as the continuator, perpetuator, and protector of Anne's traditions. Her family, he made very clear, was also his family. He shared her pride of lineage, and the benefits and obligations attached to it.

Anne's sister Isabel Neville was the other heiress. She had secured the old earldoms of Warwick and Salisbury, the mausoleum of her grandfather Earl Richard Beauchamp in the new Beauchamp Chapel at Warwick and of her grandmother Isabel Despenser at Tewkesbury Abbey. She and Duke George were happy with this legacy. George added their tombs to the circle of tombs that defined the east end of Tewkesbury Abbey. Anne had actually been assigned the priory of Bisham in Buckinghamshire, the mausoleum of the earls of Salisbury, where her other grandparents and her father Warwick had been laid to rest. Evidently Gloucester felt it inappropriately south for a northern magnate. Gloucester evidently was interested in new beginnings as well as continuity. In 1478 therefore he secured two other royal grants to found not one but two new colleges at Barnard Castle (Durh.) and Middleham (Yorks), thenceforth to be the spiritual home of his wife's connection and his new dynasty. We know the large size of these two establishments, the lavish scale of their endowments (mainly forfeited de Vere properties in Essex and East Anglia), the elaborate liturgy that Gloucester had planned, and that building works actually commenced at Middleham church. Barnard Castle College was the larger of the two. Probably Gloucester planned in due course to be buried there, not with his father at York or brother Edward at Windsor, nor at any existing mausoleum of Anne's ancestry.

Although not born a northerner, Gloucester's heart became set on the north. Until 1483 his interests were inward and northern-focused. His colleges were to reinforce and focus Anne's heritage and were to be the spiritual core of the new dynasty that he intended to found. He had married Anne. Together they bred an heir. A spare eluded them and of course Edward of Middleham was to be short-lived. In another sense, their family – their *familia*, household, and familiars – was very strong. Anne's hereditary connection did indeed pass from the Kingmaker to Gloucester. It provided a core of utterly devoted retainers – such as William Catesby and Sir Richard Ratcliffe – and a large number of hardened local fighters who saw the duke to the crown just as they had fortified previous generations of Nevilles. The dynasty that Richard and Anne had founded was itself very small. It was not the duke but the duchess whose fertility failed them. And Gloucester never found a solution to the conundrum of his cousin, ward and rival George Neville. He had found none when all such considerations were superseded by the succession in 1483 of King Richard III and Queen Anne. Another of Warwick's ambitions had been fulfilled.

Richard also acquired Anne's collateral relatives – apparently much more useful than his own – and the consequent inheritance disputes. Most of her close kindred – the Nevilles and Beauchamps – were already the duke's distant cousins. Thwarted rights of inheritance were never forgotten and were liable to revive at every change of generation or political regime. Anne Neville's father Warwick and grandfather Salisbury were heads of the junior house of Neville, which had been resourced from the dispossession of the senior line – the Nevilles of Raby and Brancepeth (Durh.) and earls of Westmorland. A settlement imposed in 1443 had not ended the resentments that could be ignored when the Kingmaker was all powerful, and most of the Nevilles of Raby were Lancastrian traitors. Warwick had indeed defeated and executed his cousins Humphrey and Charles Neville of Brancepeth in 1469. That era ended in 1471–72 with the permanent defeat of the Lancastrians and the reversal of an attainder of a senior Neville. Gloucester wisely resolved the dispute in 1478: Ralph Lord Neville became his retainer. Moving down the Neville pedigree, Anne's nephew George Neville, Duke of Bedford, and their cousin several times over Richard Lord Latimer (d. 1530) were rivals to her northern estates and had to be prevented from reasserting their titles.[6] Gloucester, like Warwick, was powerful enough to thwart another of Anne's cousins, a second George Neville, from 1476 Lord Abergavenny (also the duke's first cousin), from securing the half share of the marcher lordship of Glamorgan that Warwick had managed to withhold from him. Thirdly, the Countess of Warwick's last sister Elizabeth and the heirs of the two eldest, whom Warwick had overridden in 1466, were actually used by Gloucester to squeeze extra morsels from the lands held in trust for Earl Richard Beauchamp's will. No family feeling here.

The Wydeville Connection

The big extension in Gloucester's family was in the 1460s, when his eldest brother was married and the queen's extensive kin network became his own. Evidence from 1483, not least the attitude of Crowland, suggest that two decades was too short for the political establishment to reconcile itself to the rise of these parvenus. It was in the 1470s and early 1480s that the Wydeville network came to the political fore, so much so indeed that the queen's eldest son, Dorset, expected to rule on behalf of his half-brother.[7] From 1464 on it was almost as important to Gloucester to be on good terms with the queen as it was to be in the king's favour, and the evidence suggests he achieved this. They were on the same side in all the major fraternal struggles – the *Second War*, the Warwick inheritance dispute, and the destruction of Clarence. If he was actually hostile to her, as he claimed in 1483, he hid it well. Gloucester worked well enough with Anthony Earl Rivers in the Scottish war of 1482–83. Only a few weeks before King Edward's death, the queen's brother Rivers chose Gloucester to arbitrate a dispute. That Rivers placed himself in Gloucester's power on 1 May indicates that he had no inkling of hostility. The Wydevilles ranged themselves then against the older Yorkists and the household led by William Lord Hastings: not only a presiding figure at Edward's court throughout Edward's life, but also a kinsman, as husband to Katherine Neville, sister to the Kingmaker, first cousin and after their marriages to the Neville sisters uncle to all three York brothers. It is no wonder that Gloucester kept communications alive with both sides. Since the older Wydeville generation had passed away, the queen's father in 1469 and the queen's mother in 1472, the Wydeville network was somewhat diminished to the queen's four childless brothers, Anthony Earl Rivers, Lionel (from 1481 Bishop of Salisbury), Richard, and Edward, to the conjugal families of her six sisters, and to the queen's own sons.

During the late 1460s Edward had made a priority of the

advancement of his new Wydeville kin, an aim that he had generally achieved. This was far less important to him in his *Second Reign*. Initially it had been Gloucester who needed endowing, but from 1475 it had been his own sons Prince Edward and Prince Richard. His brothers-in-law Anthony Earl Rivers and Lionel Bishop of Salisbury had their own resources. Queen Elizabeth's younger brothers Sir Richard and Sir Edward Wydeville and her second son Richard Grey were really surplus to requirements. At a subordinate level they were useful militarily, at court and in the prince's household, but they received none of the peerages, high offices, substantial estates or marriages of heiresses that could be predicted if and when Prince Edward became Edward V. King Edward did not use their marriages to tie other noble houses to the crown. Earl Rivers' hand he offered somewhat casually to princesses of both Burgundy and Scotland. The earl, when he did remarry, selected in Mary Lewis a younger lady with breeding potential. Rivers, his brother Edward, his stepson Dorset and indeed his chamberlain Hastings shared in Edward's disreputable private pleasures. His brother Gloucester emphatically did not. To say with Mancini that Gloucester absented himself from court is misleading,[8] but he was not a part of the king's intimate circle of confidants.

The queen invested more heavily in her other son, Thomas Grey. He was the elder, of course, heir to a modest barony, and in 1465 she had bought for him an important heiress in Anne of Exeter, the king's niece. Since her father Duke Henry was an irreconcilable Lancastrian, Anne was expected to bring to Thomas a ducal title and an estate that was substantial if somewhat inadequate for a duke. It was in recognition of this in 1471 on the field of Barnet – was Exeter believed to have fallen? – that Thomas was created Earl of Huntingdon. But Anne died childless in 1473–74.[9] Thomas' marriage was next arranged in 1474 with the heiress Cecily Bonville, despite the opposition of her mother and stepfather Lady and Lord Hastings. In 1475 he was created marquis of Dorset, the only marquis in England with precedence next behind the six dukes. His three baronies in the south-west (Bonville), Midlands (Ferrers of Groby), and north-west (Harrington) did not enable him to dominate any region. Dorset did, however, obtain two key marriages for his offspring: Anne Duchess of Exeter's second daughter Anne St Leger for his infant son Thomas – a chunk of the estate being reserved for his own brother, the queen's second son, Richard Grey – and the royal ward Edward Earl of Warwick for his own daughter. The political upheavals of 1483 meant that none of these well-made plans came to aught. However, the queen evidently worked hard to secure for Thomas rank, wealth, and eminence second only to her sons by the king. She had to, because the king was unwilling to promote and endow his stepson at his own expense. In the king's mind Thomas was not on a par with his own princely sons, but he permitted self-help, even when it annoyed others (e.g. the Bonville marriage).

Hopeful fathers had married their daughters to the queen's sisters for immediate gains and in the expectation of substantial influence at court and hence further royal patronage. They were somewhat disappointed. Fertility-wise, when compared with their mother Duchess Jacquetta and Queen Elizabeth, the girls were somewhat defective. Five did indeed have issue, but Joan Lady Grey of Ruthin was childless and Jacquetta Lady Strange and Mary Countess of Pembroke produced only a single daughter each. William Lord Bourchier and Anthony Lord Grey of Ruthin died before succeeding their fathers. The Earl of Arundel's son Thomas Lord Maltravers featured prominently at court. Neither Henry Duke of Buckingham nor William Herbert, in turn earl of Pembroke and Huntingdon, carried much political clout: quite the reverse, in fact. Of all these, later events suggest that Richard Duke of Gloucester had already reached understandings with Buckingham and Herbert.

The Wydevilles did exercise influence both at court, where they dominated the ceremonial and the jousting, and through the substantial estates and patronage that they controlled not directly but through others. Most obvious was the queen's great estate, principally in the south, and her great household. Secondly they controlled the estates and household of the princes and in particular of Wales. This was not what Edward had intended. The management of Prince Edward's affairs that he had planned in 1473 had been for a broad-based council, to include his chief ministers and the two royal dukes, probably meeting in London. However, circumstances caused him first to intervene in Wales and then to leave his son as figurehead to rule there. Whereas Westminster was convenient to all, Ludlow was not, and those prepared to reside at Ludlow, principally Earl Rivers and Lord Richard Grey, came to dominate. Their rule appeared effective. The indentures of the marches, which subordinated such marcher lords as Buckingham, Grey of Ruthin and Herbert, were supplemented by the transfer of all other marcher lordships in the king's hands: the seventeen lordships of the earldom of March, those of the duchy of Lancaster, and those that were wrested from William Herbert the younger. Although brother-in-law to the queen and a native Welshman, Herbert was forced to exchange the lordship of Pembroke for lands of equal income – but little strategic weight – and his earldom of Pembroke for the almost random county of Huntingdon. Evidently royal kinship brought him no advantages. Rivers and Grey, under the distant eye of the queen, brought up the prince and expected in due course to extend their dominance of Wales to the rule of the whole kingdom on his accession. This was the model adopted also for the management of the affairs of the young Anne Mowbray.[10]

As intended in the 1460s, Wydeville connections did become a source of power, but not for the queen's sisters, their husbands and fathers-in-law. Buckingham, Herbert and the royal dukes originally had a say in the rule of the prince's affairs, but as things worked out they were included in the control of disruptive elements that King Edward had begun in 1473. Perhaps Clarence, who had no lands in Wales, and Gloucester, who most definitely had (Abergavenny, Glamorgan, Ogmore), were content to leave authority in the hands of the Wydevilles. The evidence of Richard III's protectorate and reign, however, demonstrates that what Buckingham petitioned for above all was the rule of Wales, and that Herbert certainly did not accept the forced transfer of his lordships, his change of title, and his exclusion from Wales. Their interests had become different from those of their royal relatives. Just as the king now focused on a narrower royal family, his nuclear family, to the exclusion of outsiders, so too did the Wydevilles. The queen had a main family of blood relatives, comprising her sons and brothers, who took priority over such collateral relatives as her sisters and their families. These rifts – hidden perhaps – offered opportunities that could be exploited and were indeed exploited by Richard Duke of Gloucester.

Conclusion

The Yorkist regime was not a stable system. Normally the principal political players were predetermined by hereditary succession, the rule of the provinces therefore predefined, and newcomers, royal dukes and favourites, were interpolated into the system gradually. Like the Lancastrian princes, their precedence was supported by honorary offices and annuities and they had to wait for the escheats or marriages to heiresses to fall in, which they might never do. Kings could not choose their magnates, their provincial rulers, or their favourites, nor could they reconsider past dispositions and switch their spheres of influence, as Gloucester had been shifted from Wales to the north. The Wars of the Roses changed that by expunging the Lancastrian nobility and placing in the king's hands a vast fund of forfeitures for him to bestow, resume, and redistribute. Montagu, Clarence, and William Herbert II are striking instances who found their regional rule terminated, transferred to others, and themselves relocated. While directed centrally, this was a decentralised system, in which the rule of whole regions was devolved on individuals. What Edward did to the Warwick, Norfolk and Exeter inheritances redrew the map in defiance of the pre-existing – and inextinguishable – rights of a string of heirs. Their claims could be overridden, the recipients hoped permanently, while the claimants awaited favourable opportunities to make their titles good. Future conflict brewed.

Richard was a pawn in these plans, the ruler of the north, a beneficiary who extended considerably what Edward IV had in mind for him, and an observer. He noted the losers in this system or those who thought themselves losers – Berkeley, Buckingham, Hastings, Howard, William Herbert II, Ralph Lord Neville – and appealed to them. He also was to confer regional hegemonies: his Council of the North, as an instrument of regional rule, reveals the limitations.

This chapter has discussed who was in, who was out, who was rising, who was falling, who was to benefit from Edward's political system and who was sidelined within Edward's royal families. For it was the royal families above all, not such long-serving and devoted servants as Dynham, Ferrers of Chartley, Hastings and Howard, who were preferred. Edward IV's *Second Reign* was when his new royal family of his own children took centre stage at the expense both of his own brothers and his Wydeville in-laws. This was an inevitable process that happened in every generation. The royal family became a collection of families, a group of dynasties each of which developed its own rationale and its own boundary awareness, all thinking themselves royal, but most of them relegated to the ranks of collaterals or king's kin. The king put his own children first. Those collaterally related directly to him, such as his de la Pole nephews and nieces, and the siblings of the queen found themselves down the order of priorities with less influence than they had expected. Always there were too many of them. But they kept hoping: only King Edward, to whom their loyalty was complete, could advance them. Edward still expected the same service. Similarly the queen and her brother Rivers preferred the two Grey brothers over her sisters' families, indeed even at the expense of them. Unfortunately the king's nuclear family had not time enough to mature and become really useful. Such fluid processes, the succession of generations, are always evolving and incomplete. Edward himself in person was needed to hold the reins. Richard Duke of Gloucester featured only in some of these families: he was no more than Uncle Richard, a collateral from a previous generation (at thirty!), to the children of his two brothers, and no more than a fairly distant collateral, a brother of a brother-in-law, to most of the Wydevilles. It seems unlikely that he was on close or intimate terms with most of them. His own family was minute, but the connection he commanded was large, formidable, and apparently devoted utterly to his Duchess Anne Neville.

It was obvious to those at court that politics took place at court: parliament was an occasional event, pre-planned and stage-managed to a great extent. For such people the court was the political system. Those who counted at court, such as the Wydevilles, the Greys, and Lord Hastings, advised and influenced the king directly, determined policy and patronage, and effectively ruled under the king, who maintained his independence with some difficulty and restrained factional infighting. The king's brothers were no part of this. However, they – and other great provincial magnates – knew well that the court was not everything – that if it ever came to brute force, it was they, rather than the courtiers, who counted. So did the king. It was his duty – and Edward failed – to prevent these multifarious tensions from becoming sides in future political strife.

7

THE SELF-DESTRUCTION OF THE HOUSE OF YORK
1483–1485

The Second Rift in the House of York

Richard was a mature adult in 1483. Aged thirty, married, and with a son, it is reasonable to suppose that his character was fully formed by the date of his accession. He was dominant in the north, Warwick's heir, and in the long term had the two college projects to fulfil. He was planning for a dynastic future. Credited with victory in the Scottish war, he had the Cumberland palatinate to implement, a permanent command on the Scottish borders, and the right to take over the debateable lands in the south-west Scottish dales. Conquests in Scotland offered him further advancement that was not at the king's expense, to whom Richard's endowment was now complete, and autonomy to which all such princes seem to have aspired. Here was the trajectory for Richard's future career. It directed him northwards and required of him the concentration of all his resources on a Scottish future. These remarkable favours conferred by Parliament can be interpreted differently of course. So exceptional are they that he could not have petitioned for them with any expectation of success. His victory was unopposed (and may have caused him to underestimate the Scots), the palatinate gave him little that he did not already hold, and his hereditary wardenship offloaded onto him an onerous burden that he might not be able to sustain. Crowland indeed thought the successful campaign a financial fiasco.[1] Yet it is difficult to believe that Richard did not accept these challenges willingly and optimistically. It is likely indeed that he suggested them. Here was the autonomous principality that so many English princes had sought but failed to realise. Edward's motives in conceding these favours demand more suspicion. Early in 1483 the future of Richard and the future of his dynasty lay on the northern borders, not in English politics or at the English court, where his status was bound constantly to recede as his nephews and nieces grew up. Although Richard was now the king's only brother, he was not his intimate, stood only tenth in line for the throne and third in precedence among the dukes. Richard had repeatedly acknowledged the superiority of his nephews. He was certainly not born to be king and had moved no closer to the throne. Yet when the opportunity came, he abandoned all that he had forged for himself in the north and on the borders, first for power in England and then the English crown itself.

Two deaths changed all this: those of Edward IV and George Neville.

The first, the least predictable, was the death of King Edward IV on 9 April 1483. The importance of Edward personally to the stability of his Yorkist regime only became really apparent on his death. It was Edward himself, too often self-indulgent and frequently unduly casual, who nevertheless maintained the uneasy equilibrium between the rival factions at his court and the conflicting ambitions of his royal families. Never were there enough promotions, preferments, and royal grants to go round: never enough to satisfy all those who thought themselves royal. Most of his Wydeville in-laws fell short of what they surely hoped. Richard and Edward Wydeville, Richard Grey, Buckingham and Huntingdon had surely hoped (legitimately) for more than this. As king, Edward's authority could not be gainsaid. It was beyond

question. He was the supreme authority. It was King Edward
who determined precedence in court, in council, in Parliament
and probably in the provinces too. He alone distributed offices
and endowments. Edward had been a nobleman himself before he
became king. He was aware also of at least some of the complex
hierarchies discussed above and of the factional rivalries at court.
He kept them under control and counted on continuing to do so
for as long as was required. He could disregard some rivalries or
override them without immediate adverse repercussions. Edward
was the linchpin. He had no plans to die. Nevertheless he had
planned ahead for when he was not around, for example in the last
will that he drew up on the eve of his invasion of France in 1475,[2]
when his son and heir Prince Edward was not yet five years old.
That his son and heir might be still underage at his accession was
why Edward IV caused his greater subjects repeatedly to swear
allegiance to the prince. He hoped and expected his son both to
reign and rule, but thought such an eventuality was remote, years
or even decades away. But Edward did die, on 9 April 1483, still
aged only forty. It was premature. It was a surprise to others,
doubtless also to the king himself. Even kings, with all the benefits
of good diet, living conditions, and medical health, could be taken,
suddenly, prematurely, as even the heroic Henry V had been.
Edward IV's victory in 1471 was sufficiently complete for Prince
Edward to succeed automatically on his father's death. Edward V
was therefore bound to reign but he was obviously too young to
rule.

On his deathbed, King Edward had a few fevered days to think
about the situation and to try to assure a stable future. He sought
at this last moment to make the dispositions that should have
been prepared earlier. He was only too aware of the fundamental
divisions between the Wydevilles (especially Dorset) and the Old
Yorkists in his household, headed by Lord Hastings. His stepson
Dorset was the son-in-law of Lord Hastings through his marriage
to the latter's stepdaughter Cecily Bonville. Kinship tied the two

together in enmity in a match that Dorset forced on Hastings through feudal law. Frictions went back a long way, to the rough deal that Hastings had forced in 1464 on the desperate lady yet to be queen, whose son (now Dorset) was contracted in marriage to a daughter of Hastings yet to be born, and perhaps back further to Elizabeth's naive hope that, as a kinsman, Hastings would take her side. Presumably the king had frequently observed frictions between these two sharers in his own sexual adventures. Edward summoned the two lords before him on his deathbed and marshalled his last authority as king to impose peace on them. Both agreed and were formally reconciled,[3] but of course no king can exercise his regal power beyond the grave. The fissures remained. Reports of a heated debate in the royal council along these old lines relate to a meeting within a couple of days of Edward's death.[4] The queen, her son Dorset and the Wydevilles thought their time had come, the golden future for which they had prepared. A Wydeville king was perhaps an opportunity for vengeance on those who had slighted them or who had done too well under Edward IV. Hastings and others like him feared their future ascendancy, even perhaps their survival. The factions were finely balanced. The Wydevilles looked for the decisive blow from the new king: was not King Edward V bound to prefer those maternal relatives who had brought him up? Hastings had been the last king's lifelong acquaintance and cousin by marriage and most trusted intimate. For more than twenty years as chamberlain of the household he had controlled access to the king and had been ever present, whispering in Edward's ear. Now that his king was dead, Hastings turned to Gloucester, whose backing he skilfully concealed. Though rivals, both factions were committed to the succession of Edward V. Gloucester himself was absent, probably still in Yorkshire.

What did Edward IV have in mind for his son's minority rule? No source suggests that he intended his queen and her family to rule. Immediate precedents, from 1422 and 1454, indicated a consensus government, headed by a representative council led by a Lord Protector, whose functions were to protect and defend king and country, not the French model of a regent (often the queen mother) who ruled there in the young king's place. The only possible protector was the late king's brother and the new king's sole uncle by blood, Richard Duke of Gloucester. One contemporary source, John Rows, explicitly states that Edward nominated Gloucester.[5] Two other contemporary sources, Crowland and Mancini, both on the spot and more authoritative, do not. At this crucial juncture Gloucester was in the country, somewhere in northern England, and unable therefore to have his say in the decision-making process. Both chroniclers make it clear that Edward V's first council, which was attended by the queen mother, brusquely disregarded Gloucester's claims and overrode the objections of the Hastings' faction. We are so important that we can do as we wish, Dorset reportedly declared.[6] The decision was made at once to proceed with the coronation, and thus with the immediate declaration that Edward V was of age, and with a meeting of Parliament to rubberstamp arrangements for the boy's government.[7] Those present took it for granted that this meant that the new regime would be dominated by the Wydevilles. Doubtless Gloucester would have a place on the new king's council, but not its chairmanship or the direction of government. Effectively this was a Wydeville *coup d'état*. Whether it was a blow at Gloucester, as Michael Jones has suggested, or whether he was merely ignored – too small and unimposing a figure? – is not established. To complete their control, the Wydevilles wanted the young king to come from Ludlow with a substantial army, but in response to Hastings' objections this was reduced to a mere 2,000 men: surely enough to impose the new king's will, even in disorderly London.

The news of these events came to Gloucester days later and at second hand. From the distant north, Gloucester penned careful conciliatory letters to the royal council and to the City corporation that were also published more widely. What the

Wydevilles apparently did not realise was that in Hastings he had inside information. Hastings was keeping him in touch, confident of his support. After struggling for a small escort, he conceded gracefully, knowing that the duke would bring no less. Evidently Gloucester also knew that he had an ally in the Duke of Buckingham, the husband of a Wydeville wife, and met up with him. Elizabeth's brother Earl Rivers, custodian of Edward V, did not view either as his foe. He did not recognise the two dukes as his enemies. Rather than keeping clear of them, which could have been so easily achieved by pursuing a more westerly route to London from Ludlow (Salop.) along the Severn and Thames, Rivers joined up with them on the Great North Road at Stony Stratford (Northants.). Admittedly this was close to Grafton Regis, his family seat, where doubtless he wished to exhibit his Wydeville king. On 1 May 1483 Gloucester seized the young king, arrested Earl Rivers, Lord Richard Grey, and Thomas Vaughan, dismissed their escort, and hence secured the only legitimate source of real power. Queen-Dowager Elizabeth in London found that she could organise no counterattack. Too many, like Crowland, thought that government by Edward V's paternal uncle was preferable to the rule of the queen and the Wydevilles, both in the interests of the young king and the public interest.[8] This was Richard's *First Coup*. Duke Richard swore allegiance to Edward V at Stony Stratford and publicised his loyalty. When Richard brought the young king to London on 4 May, he was welcomed by the Londoners and the royal council, which quickly nominated him Lord Protector. Security for the future was provided by further oaths of allegiance from the duke and everybody else of standing, by a two-month time-limit to the protectorate until the coronation, when the minority would terminate, and by the summoning of a parliament to determine how England was to be ruled until Edward V could take over himself. How Edward V, once declared of age, was to be prevented from recalling the queen, his half-brothers, Rivers and his other Wydeville uncles was not addressed at this juncture.

It was a future concern for Gloucester. Whatever his relations with the Wydevilles before the *First Coup*, the queen and other Wydevilles perceived him as their enemy now.

The plans of the queen and the Wydeville faction had taken no account of Richard Duke of Gloucester. They had underestimated him, misconstrued his desire for power, and the lengths he was prepared to take to attain it. They did not anticipate trouble with him and expected him to acquiesce. Gloucester and the Wydevilles had collaborated on multiple occasions. He did not fight battles against the queen and her family that he could not win. Yet Gloucester was in a special position in 1483 and had a special status. He was the last remaining brother of the late king. He was the sole adult male of the House of York, the only paternal uncle of King Edward V, his sole uncle of the blood royal. Only Gloucester therefore could be entitled to be Lord Protector. He was justified in resenting their exclusion of him from power, but there is no prior evidence of hostility between him and the queen's family. Hearing of his brother's death, his nephew's succession, and his own exclusion from power, Gloucester's public stance was conciliatory. He indicated by letters his willingness to accept the Wydeville takeover. His *First Coup* was therefore a surprise. The *First Coup* was an abrupt change of direction that was not anticipated by the Wydevilles or almost anybody else. It reversed a career trajectory that appeared to be fixed. It was the seizure of power by someone who had never before revealed ambitions in this direction. The *First Coup* was also much more than merely an assertion of Gloucester's guardianship over the young king or his takeover of the leadership of the minority regime. The ease with which Gloucester took control exposed the Wydevilles as a court faction dependent on royal favour and lacking local roots or power of their own. At this juncture, Richard presented the Wydevilles falsely as enemies of the new king, as having armed themselves to the teeth to enforce their will, and as embezzlers of the royal treasure.[9] He proved masterly in his manipulation of public opinion. Richard wanted Rivers and Grey executed for treasons against him – presumably for plotting his arrest or show trial, of which there is no known evidence. He appreciated how he had made them into dangerous enemies. The minority council refused, because Richard had not been Lord Protector at the time, but Richard kept them imprisoned at Pontefract Castle and had them executed anyway about 20 June. Whether or not these actions were legalised by any type of formal trial, to which Rows refers,[10] these were drastic measures. After all, Rivers was the uncle and Grey the stepbrother of the young king. They were also closely related to the two dukes of Gloucester and Buckingham – further reasons for them to exercise restraint. Rivers was brother-in-law to both dukes, Gloucester and Buckingham, and Grey as the queen's son was half-nephew to Gloucester and nephew to Buckingham. Their deaths were not necessary for the *First Coup* to succeed, but their elimination certainly made it easier for Gloucester to retain power beyond the coronation. Queen Elizabeth tried and failed to organise a counterattack. Next she took sanctuary again at Westminster Abbey with her younger children. The protectorate government sought to entice her out. Dorset's powerbase of the fleet was persuaded to desert him.

Richard's *First Coup* changed his life and his political trajectory, perhaps irrevocably. He had turned away from the fulfilment of his northern powerbase to the rule of England and he had made enemies of the other relatives of the new king, who now wanted him removed and disempowered. Perhaps they also wanted revenge. His *First Coup* alone did not presume his usurpation, but it did require him to keep hold of power to protect himself. Buckingham had taken the same risks. Buckingham's reasons for joining Gloucester when he had a Wydeville duchess who had borne him heirs may be reconstructed. He seems to have resented a marriage that disparaged him. Edward had failed to recognise him to be a royal duke and as a member of the inner royal family – by descent he was a third cousin once removed and by marriage one of eleven brothers-in-law of the king

– that he unreasonably supposed himself. And furthermore, as one of the principal marcher lords, Buckingham found himself in thrall to the Wydeville-dominated council of Wales. What Buckingham now wanted was political influence at the centre, complete power in Wales, and the other half of the de Bohun inheritance that should have devolved to him on the demise of the House of Lancaster. All these were conceded to him by Richard.[11] Buckingham needed a political regime that enabled him to keep them.

Richard found other allies in those who had lost out in Edward's *Second Reign*. William Herbert II was one such. Others were John Lord Howard and William Lord Berkeley, the rightful coheirs to the huge inheritance of the Mowbray dukes of Norfolk after the death in 1481 of young Anne Mowbray, consort of Edward IV's second son Richard, who nevertheless retained her inheritance to their loss. Howard was created Duke of Norfolk at once: his son became Earl of Surrey and Berkeley Earl of Nottingham. Ralph Lord Neville, whose military might Richard invoked, was the rightful heir to the Holland Exeter inheritance embezzled by Edward IV for his stepsons. Richard's lifelong friend Francis Viscount Lovell became knight of the Garter, chief butler of England, and, as chamberlain of the royal household, Richard's right-hand man like Edward IV's Lord Hastings. Lovell was to control access to the monarch. Francis's marriage to the Kingmaker's niece, cousin to both king and queen, made him royal kin, yet it was not such ties, but rather friendship and mutual interest, that underpinned these alliances.

It is not obvious that Gloucester wanted any such material rewards in the short term: pay as Lord Protector, grants of offices or lands. But he did have one weakness that power alone could alleviate.

This relates to the second death mentioned above, that of George Neville, formerly Duke of Bedford. Richard's apparently secure future in the north suffered from several weaknesses. Richard had produced a son and heir, but only one. It is unclear when it became apparent that there would be no more – sexual intercourse with Anne Neville continued until Christmas 1484 and was then discontinued on medical advice[12] – but only Edward of Middleham existed to continue his line and even he was to die while still a child. That was in the future. Moreover, the conundrum of George Neville was never solved. In 1478 Richard had him excluded from the House of Lords where George could have put his case. He secured his custody and marriage, but he had neither married him off and got him breeding, somehow safely, nor did he obtain the surrender of the rights of the next heir Richard Lord Latimer. Born in 1469, Latimer was a minor who could not make such releases. Latimer of course was cousin of George Neville and also of both the duke and duchess of Gloucester. Richard did try to secure Latimer's custody, but the boy had a doughty defender in his great-uncle Cardinal Bourchier, also Richard's great-uncle, who placed Latimer's interests first.[13] It was the risk that next heirs might prioritise their own interests, for example by neglecting or otherwise killing their wards, that convention forbade such men to become guardians: Richard, as we have seen, certainly did not place the interests of George Neville first and clearly intended to dispossess rather than to safeguard Latimer. Short of custody, he had to bide his time till Latimer came of age, in 1490. Richard had no insurance in place when George Neville died on 4 May 1483, whereupon the reversion to the Neville lands in the north – Middleham, Sheriff Hutton, and Penrith – passed to Latimer.[14] At this point Richard's hereditary title was reduced to a life tenancy: indeed probably less than that, as Neville retainers turned to his successor and gambled on the reversionary interest. Edward of Middleham could never succeed to the Neville patrimony in the north that had been the foundation of the power of Ralph Earl of Westmorland, Richard Earl of Salisbury, Warwick the Kingmaker, and now Gloucester himself. George's death shattered the dynastic hegemony in the north that Gloucester had been working towards. Moreover it sharply reduced Gloucester's share of the Warwick inheritance. Theoretically the partition could be adjusted, properties being transferred from Isabel Neville's share to Anne Neville's, just as Henry V in 1421 had readjusted in his own favour the division of the Bohun inheritance. Such a revision, however, demanded royal favour – difficult to obtain without an adult king – and possibly even an act of parliament. Richard's nephew Warwick would lose not less than a third of his inheritance. Such a re-partition would surely be opposed by the Wydevilles since Isabel's heir Warwick was betrothed to the daughter of the Marquis of Dorset. Ironically it was imperative for them to protect the rights of the heir of their erstwhile enemy Clarence. No resettlement of the Warwick inheritance was feasible in 1483.

George Neville's death thus undermined Gloucester's plans for the future. Was it more serious than that? Was the date of death, 4 May 1483, particularly significant? It was after Edward IV's death and after the *First Coup*, though George's demise may have been expected. Where George died and how soon Richard knew are both unknown. Bill Hampton placed his grave at Sheriff Hutton in Yorkshire.[15] No contemporary chronicler mentions this death. It gave Richard good reason to want power – to achieve re-partition of the Warwick Inheritance – and perhaps also a reason to construct his future elsewhere. Its repercussions demanded that Gloucester secured and retained political control. Of course he had another reason for this too. His *First Coup* had made enemies of the Wydevilles, who would surely seek his destruction if ever restored to power. Their restoration was actually quite likely, since the majority of Edward V was not far distant. Edward V had not agreed with the *First Coup*. The young king believed his mother, uncle, and half-brothers to be loyal and trusted friends. Retribution for his *First Coup* and in due course for his elimination of Rivers and Grey was to be expected. Gloucester thus had two defensive reasons to seek the throne. That said, these seem insufficient grounds for the huge step of usurpation. Ambition and opportunity, the desire and the means to make himself king, appear most important.

In practice, Lord Protector Gloucester did rule like another king. Apparently he made a good job of it. His *Second Coup*, on 13 June, destroyed the other court faction, drawn from Edward IV's household headed by Lord Hastings. Another cousin, Hastings, was killed, without the formality of trial. Others perceived as dangerous – or as obstacles to Richard's plans – were imprisoned. It had been Hastings who supposedly had compared Richard's bloodless coup to the shedding of blood from a cut finger.[16] Rivers, Grey, and Vaughan were executed at Pontefract. *Pace* Crowland, there was a form of trial, albeit illicit. 'This was the second shedding of innocent blood during these sudden changes,' he wrote.[17] No independent evidence has ever been found that Hastings was plotting with the queen against Richard. Without such evidence, it is difficult to regard this *Second Coup* as anything other than a preliminary step towards Richard's usurpation of the crown twelve days later. It was followed immediately afterwards by the removal of Prince Richard from sanctuary, ostensibly to the guardianship of his uncle Richard in preparation for the coronation of Edward V that was postponed that same day. Richard has a poor track record as a guardian. With both princes in the Tower of London, Richard need not fear their use as figureheads of rebellion. Those arriving for the coronation and Parliament and staying for Richard's own coronation had been disarmed, whereas Richard had camped a northern army at Finsbury Fields. A combination of overwhelming force and targeted ruthlessness regardless of family ties projected Richard to his throne. Most probably he was driven by ambition: he wanted to be king.

The most pronounced familial aspect of Richard's usurpation of the throne was that it ousted his brother's family – Edward IV's sons Edward V and Richard Duke of York, their five surviving sisters, and their mother Queen Elizabeth. These were Richard's nephews, nieces, and sister-in-law. Richard knew them well. He had repeatedly acknowledged Prince Edward's title which indeed, under primogeniture or a male entail, was undeniable.

Edward V moreover was acknowledged by the royal council and was therefore the king. Nothing could be done about that. Edward V was king by hereditary succession, by election, and by conquest. He did not need to be crowned to become king, although admittedly coronation would extend the range of his electors, would consecrate him, and would end his minority. Richard argued that all Edward's rights to reign and obligations owed by himself personally were negated because they were based on the misunderstanding that Edward V was entitled to reign. Edward V could not reign because he was a bastard. This might have been a justification before Edward acceded, but once he was indeed king it was not. Bastards did sometimes rule, both in England – William the Conqueror being an undeniable instance – or abroad, in Castile for instance. Yet it is probably true that most English people were oblivious to the legal technicalities and would have extended readily the bar on bastards inheriting in England to a bar to the succession to the crown. This fervent prejudice against bastards was one of the defining marks that distinguished the English from other Europeans.

Richard had the brute force to seize the throne, but not to retain it, unless he could carry public opinion with him. His usurpation had therefore to be justified, both to the political elite and to ordinary Londoners. Richard presented himself as the reformer of the misgovernment (probably fictional) with which he associated his brother Edward IV. Is it possible that Richard believed his own propaganda, that Edward IV's children were disqualified from rule because illegitimate? If Richard really did believe that Edward IV's children were bastards, bastards being of no account, his exposure of them and their consequent ruin was excusable. To bastardise the legitimate was an act of the utmost cruelty.

Several different arguments seem to have been rehearsed before the precontract story was settled upon. First of all the old slur that Edward V's father Edward IV was himself illegitimate was recycled, that he was the son of Cecily Duchess of York by someone other than Richard Duke of York. Edward had been born at Rouen, outside the realm of England, where, by implication, anything might happen. An act of parliament of 1351 entitled the sons of kings born abroad to succeed, but of course Edward IV and indeed George Duke of Clarence were not the sons of a king – of a rightful aspirant to kingship, perhaps. The bastardy story was current both in 1469 and 1478, and was of limited utility in 1483, since it barred not only Edward V but Edward IV from the throne, and reduced Gloucester to claiming his throne from his father York, a rightful heir who never reigned, rather than as heir to Edward IV, a reigning king. Moreover Edward IV was dead and English law did not permit the bastardising of the dead. Gloucester undoubtedly wanted to inherit the backing of Edward IV's Yorkist establishment. It seems likely that Duke Richard was behind this rumour, since his mother Cecily, whom it dishonoured, vigorously repudiated it. It does not feature in *Titulus Regius*, the statement of Richard's title written in 1483 that was enacted into law in 1484.

A better case for Edward V's inability to rule was made by discrediting the legitimacy of all Edward IV's children themselves. An earlier attempt, alleging sorcery in the match of king and queen, had been attempted in 1469, and is perhaps hinted at in 1483. What *Titulus Regius* focused on however was a precontract: that Edward IV had not been able to contract a valid marriage with Elizabeth Wydeville because he was already betrothed to another lady, Lady Eleanor Butler. This seems quite a likely story. The young Edward had several mistresses. There are marked similarities in the tales of his encounters with Elizabeth Wydeville, Eleanor Butler, and Margaret Lucy, all aristocratic widows who needed his support to recover their rights. It is conceivable that he promised marriage to each to have sex with them. The Reading great council of 1464 may have asked Margaret Lucy the question: did Edward promise marriage? The circumstances of Edward's clandestine marriage to Elizabeth Wydeville are not dissimilar. Because their parents were not married, so *Titulus Regius* explained, all Edward's children were bastards and incapable of inheriting, Edward V could not reign, and Elizabeth Wydeville, never queen, henceforth became mere Dame Elizabeth Grey.[18] Even if true, Edward could have married Elizabeth properly from 1469 after Lady Eleanor's death, so only the three eldest daughters would have been illegitimate. He did not. However Edward and his queen had lived together, he had acknowledged all his children as his own, and they had been reputed as his own at his death – the deadline before which bastardy must be established under English law. Even if the precontract was proved, the validity of his marriage and of his children most probably would have been approved. It was a matter for the Church courts, not secular courts or Parliament.

Titulus Regius stated that the evidence for the precontract would be published, but so far as is known it never was. Did it exist? 'It was put about then that the roll [*Titulus Regius*] originated in the north,' wrote Crowland, 'although there was no one who did not know the identity of the author, who was in London at the time.'[19] What a pity that Crowland did not name the perpetrator! Historians have tended to accept the identification a decade later by the French and Burgundian statesman Philippe de Commines of Robert Stillington, Bishop of Bath and Wells, who had been a government minister in the early 1460s, keeper of the privy seal at the time, and was indeed a Yorkshireman. He had been imprisoned before, in 1478, for uttering words damaging to the crown, possibly this story, though it is not recorded before 1483. The most favourable scenario for Richard was that Stillington or someone else revealed the story to him in mid-June 1483 and that he accepted that it disqualified Edward V from kingship. His brother George's children were also disqualified by their father's attainder, so Richard was obliged to take on the onerous responsibilities of kingship himself. Richard's many oaths were now excused – they were not perjury – because they were based on the misapprehension that Edward V was a legitimate king: the same argument that Richard's father York used towards the Lancastrian kings in 1460. Is that scenario credible? Richard sent a copy of *Titulus Regius* to the garrison of Calais to justify the change of monarch.[20] Richard did secure the consent of Londoners and of those at his coronation in 1483, when he wielded overwhelming military power, and also from Parliament early in 1484, when he was a king who had recently defeated Buckingham's rebellion. Fear, not belief, motivated them.

Those rebels were the Yorkist establishment. Many had been members of Edward IV's household and rulers of the southern counties. Among the leaders were the Wydevilles – the Marquis of Dorset and the queen's brother Lionel Wydeville, Bishop of Salisbury; Richard's brother-in-law Sir Thomas St Leger, widower of his eldest sister Anne Duchess of Exeter; Henry and Jasper Tudor, recalled from exile in Brittany; and Henry Duke of Buckingham, whose motives are impenetrable. Buckingham's ingratitude and betrayal especially outraged King Richard,[21] who had the pleasure of executing this cousin/brother-in-law. He also despatched St Leger, another brother-in-law. The quality of mercy was certainly not strained. Most of the rebels, however, escaped abroad and continued the fight. In place of Edward V, they backed the claims of his sister Elizabeth of York, whom they wanted to marry Henry Tudor, a nobleman (titular earl of Richmond), of royal blood of both England (through Margaret Beaufort) and France (through Henry V's queen), of marriageable age and of unimpeached character. Nobody knew him well enough to have anything against him. Henry secured a dispensation to marry Elizabeth, who had no part in securing it and indeed probably no knowledge of it.

The Fate of the Princes

Whether a bastard or not, Edward V had been king – he appears on the list of English kings and eleven weeks are allowed for his reign even by his supplanter. Official government documents of

Richard's reign designate him as both a bastard and a *de facto* king. Monarchs could not cease to be monarchs: Mary Stuart always remained Mary Queen of Scots even after losing her throne and Shakespeare's King Lear remained King Lear. That the bastardy story was not believed was nevertheless crucial for the fate of the Princes in the Tower – Edward V and Richard Duke of York, the sons of Edward IV by Elizabeth Wydeville. If they were indeed bastards and believed to be so, Ricardians may be correct that they posed little threat to Richard and could have faded into the obscurity that was the normal fate of those born outside wedlock. Public opinion was not concerned with nuances such as rightful election as opposed to illegitimacy and the consequence absence of hereditary right. But the precontract story was not believed. Alarming numbers of men plotted and rebelled on their behalf. The princes were the focus of discontent. They were bound to become more dangerous as they grew up and could then take a hand in insurrection themselves. Past kings and potential kings could never be ignored. The most effective and pragmatic solution to the disorders they fomented was to eliminate them. Had not Prince Arthur, Edward II, Richard II, and Henry VI died mysteriously, probably brutally murdered, and thus ceased to pose political threats to their successors? Here were good precedents that could indeed to be justified by the public interest, public peace rather than public disorder. As early as July 1483 Mancini and those about him, and apparently also the young ex-king, realised that their lives were at risk. Their deaths were implicit in Richard's usurpation and were almost imperative for the security of the king and his regime.

None of those who reported on the fate of the princes knew for certain what had befallen them. None of them were eyewitnesses with concrete evidence. Yet all accounts agree on two points – the violence of their deaths and the time of their deaths. When they died is the crucial question. The princes disappeared in 1483, were rumoured to be dead by November, were firmly stated to be dead in January 1484 and ever afterwards. From 2 November 1483, at least, politics proceeded on the basis that they were dead. It seems almost certain therefore that Prince Edward and Prince Richard died in 1483, during the reign of Richard III and when in the guardianship of Richard III. Who had more interest than Richard in killing them? The date eliminates almost all alternative candidates. If 1483 is accepted as the date of their deaths, the only other potential culprit is Henry Duke of Buckingham, who is named abroad principally by foreigners who cannot have known for sure. One chronicle leaves open the possibility that Buckingham acted on Richard's behalf. What interest Buckingham had in killing them is a mystery. It was King Richard that their continued survival threatened. Richard III seems to have arranged their deaths in the late summer or autumn of 1483: Thomas More's over-elaborated narrative is as likely as any.[22] Possibly – but not probably – Buckingham had a hand in it. Rumours of their death were circulated: there was no political advantage for Richard in slaying them unless their supporters knew of their deaths and were discouraged from rebelling on their behalf. Crowland seems to indicate that this news became known (was disseminated deliberately?) early in Buckingham's rebellion: a replacement monarch had to be identified and was proclaimed at Bodmin.[23]

Previous regicides had suffered no adverse consequences: why should Richard? But he miscalculated. Some anonymous brilliant propagandist seized the opportunity. The despatch of these innocent children/infants/babes – all terms were used – by their uncle/guardian was made especially shocking. It was compared to the worst of biblical stories – the murder of the Holy Innocents by wicked King Herod. Strictly speaking, such language applied only to the younger of the princes, Richard Duke of York, who was not yet ten, not his twelve-year-old brother, Edward V. The charge and the biblical comparisons feature in the propaganda of Richard's enemies, such as letters, proclamations in his own reign: Tudor propaganda existed before the Tudors. What was said at Henry VII's first parliament is beyond recovery, but the mention of the 'shedyng of infants blode' in the act of attainder is a pretty direct reference to the fate of the princes.[24] Henry VII did not know exactly what had happened to the princes, but he and his parliament had no doubt that Richard had killed them. This belief, with all the hype and horror attached to it, was accepted by chroniclers and historians both English and foreign almost without exception for five centuries. What was believed to have befallen the princes – the most ruthless and unnatural rejection of family ties – became Richard's principal crime and the main cause for him to be remembered.

Richard had miscalculated also because the disappearance of the princes did not disarm the opposition. There were also Edward's daughters: useless as fighters and rulers but capable of continuing the bloodline and of being represented by whichever men they married. Elizabeth of York passively took their place – she had no say in it – and a credible husband was found for her in Henry Tudor. The Yorkist establishment would back almost anyone against Richard. Richard could not kill Elizabeth too. The most treacherous women of the Wars of the Roses such as Lady Margaret Beaufort were exempted from the death penalty that fifty years later Henry VIII was to exact on two of his queens. Moreover, Richard needed to slay all five of Edward IV's daughters to remove that danger. The threat they posed could however be neutralised in another way if Richard himself was to marry Elizabeth of York. In the meantime Richard's victory seemed complete and Dame Elizabeth Grey negotiated the emergence from sanctuary of herself and her daughters. She did not trust Richard so the terms were defined very tightly. He promised them their lives; their freedom; no 'manner hurt ... by ravishment or defouling contrary to their wills'; residence 'in honest places of good name and fame ... as my kinswomen'; dowries of 200 marks (£133 13s 4d) each; and to marry them 'at the lawful age of marriage' to suitable gentlemen 'as their wives and my kinswomen'.[25]

This posed him a conundrum very similar to that which he had failed to resolve with George Neville. Elizabeth required him to arrange marriages for her daughters that did not disparage them and which, from Richard's point of view, needed therefore to be to men insufficiently powerful to threaten him in their own right. The option that he might marry Elizabeth himself has been mentioned. A second option was to marry her to a foreign prince, thus neatly removing her from England.[26] Cecily, the third daughter, did marry Ralph Scrope, brother of Thomas Lord Scrope of Masham,[27] a genteel match indeed but far inferior to the Scottish prince James to whom she had been betrothed in the 1470s. The much younger Anne, Katherine, and Bridget had not yet reached the lawful age of marriage. They were challenges for the future.

The Ricardian Royal Family

Richard Duke of Gloucester founded a very small dynasty: of himself, his queen, and his son. They became a very small inner royal family. They shared in his success and were indeed essential buttresses to his reign. On 6 July 1483 King Richard and Queen Anne were crowned together – the first occasion of a double coronation in England. It was not only a national event but a cause of celebration within her own family: wearing their crowns, they were celebrated both in the *Rows Roll* of the earls of Warwick and in their coronation robes in the second *Salisbury Roll*. It was the fulfilment of the dearest dream of Anne's father, Warwick the Kingmaker. Once crowned, the royal couple progressed through her territory and his territory – from Oxford to Gloucester, Warwick, and on to York – showing themselves all the way to their supporters and using their supporters to impress the unconverted in their company. There in York Minster the northern-born prince Edward of Middleham, formerly Earl of Salisbury and now Prince of Wales, heir to the Warwick inheritance and now to the crown of England, was formally invested. It was a moment of triumph for his parents, the Warwick and Neville connections, of everything they stood for. And when his parents returned south, Prince Edward remained as figurehead – as ruler of the north – to maintain and continue Richard's dominance. The prince and his council represented royal authority on the spot – a devolved system of governance – overseen by the heir to the greatest northern noble house. In January 1484 the Lords swore allegiance to the prince as King Richard's heir.[28]

Buckingham's rebellion and other conspiracies made Richard ever more reliant on his northern supporters. Notoriously he imported northerners to the south to replace those who had rebelled: a northern tyranny. His most trusted agents, Ratcliffe and Catesby, drew attention to this dependence and reminded him that he owed it to Queen Anne, to whom their primary loyalties lay.[29] All the long association and even comradeship they had enjoyed with Richard, all the rewards and influence that he had conferred on them, and all the public, secret and intimate services they had performed for him had not created a new fidelity to him that erased or superseded that due to his queen as heir to her father Warwick the Kingmaker and her mother Anne Beauchamp. The relatively passive allegiance that they, like all subjects, owed to the king did not override the active commitment that arose from their loyalties to their lord or lady, nor indeed, in this case, their own interests. They feared, so Crowland said, that Elizabeth of York if queen could wreak vengeance on the killers of her kindred.[30] That Richard had become king greatly increased their material gains and political influence without amending their primary loyalties in the short term. In the long term, had Richard reigned ten, twenty or more years, their relations could have evolved. Both Ratcliffe and Catesby were at Bosworth, where the former was killed and latter, captured, was almost alone in being executed.

Becoming king, however, changed Richard's relations with his northern affinity and with the Warwick inheritance. We have seen how he barred no holds when wresting as much as possible from his brother Clarence, from his mother-in-law Anne Countess of Warwick, and from the Neville heirs. George Neville, just like the princes, had found in Richard a guardian who definitely placed himself first. We have seen how Richard exploited the fall of his brother to enhance his share of the pickings, accruing the earldom of Salisbury, rounding off his lordships in Wales and the north, and taking attractive morsels that he had not been allocated earlier. Anne's inheritance underpinned his power and was the focus of his dynastic destiny. The death of George Neville on 4 May 1483 threatened all this. The death of his son and then his queen meant also that in strict law none of the Warwick inheritance could pass to the second family that he intended to beget.

Once king, Richard's attitude – and indeed Queen Anne's attitude – changed. Now a king, with a royal future, what had been so important to him as duke ceased to matter so much, less than the political advantages to him as king. Admittedly his mother-in-law Anne Beauchamp remains hidden. There was nothing to gain from releasing her from Middleham, apparently no advantage in her presence at court. We cannot tell whether the twin colleges of Barnard Castle and Middleham were abandoned, but certainly they were dwarfed by the much greater college of one hundred priests that Richard was to found at York. Richard was no longer determined to hang on to every scrap of property or ruthlessly fight his rivals. Four components of Anne's estate were conceded to rival heirs, perhaps to buy their support, or were given away. From the Beauchamp trust, some of her East Anglian properties were bestowed on Queens' College, Cambridge, at his queen's request: as queen she was now patroness. Richard anyway had earlier associations to the college, having financed masses there for those retainers that died fighting with him at Barnet in 1471. Also from the Beauchamp trust, he permitted the senior Beauchamp coheir Edward Grey of Astley, Viscount Lisle to recover the two manors of Chaddesley Corbet (Worcs.) and Kibworth Beauchamp

(Leics.). The injustice that the Kingmaker had inflicted on George Neville of Abergavenny and that the royal dukes had perpetuated by taking the whole Despenser inheritance for themselves, not merely Anne Beauchamp's half share, was apparently corrected. George's licence to enter his half during the Readeption had been abortive. Now he was licensed once again to enter his inheritance by the king, who was the principal loser. No formal partition is known, however, and the strategically important marcher lordship of Glamorgan remained in royal hands, but George seems at this time to have secured Mapledurwell in Hampshire.[31] Most striking of all, Richard used his kingly power not to exclude Richard Lord Latimer from his rights in the Neville patrimony, but to arrange the boy's marriage to a trusted supporter Humphrey Stafford of Grafton.[32] In the medium term it was now immaterial to Richard that the Neville patrimony would devolve to another distant branch of Neville cousins. Edward Earl of Warwick, son of Isabel Neville, was now sole heir to the rest of the Warwick inheritance of Warwick the Kingmaker and Anne Beauchamp, but was too young to sue for Richard and Anne's other half: any potential father-in-law however would include it in his calculations. Prior to this Richard contemplated sidelining Anne Neville herself, and ultimately he had to manage without her.

Richard's usurpation divided him from almost all his extensive kindred. Some accepted him and served him as king, but many did not. He had warred on them and had made them his enemies. He made little use of the wider Yorkist royal family – could make little use of them – since most of them he had offended and materially damaged. He had bastardised the daughters of his brother Edward, depreciated them on the marriage market, and had reduced their mother from royal to merely genteel status. He had deprived the extensive Wydeville clan of their royal pretensions and their expectations from the regime of Edward V. He was opposed by his brother-in-law St Leger and seems to have made no more use of his other brother-in-law the Duke of

Suffolk. However he made the most of his bastards, although both were too young to be really useful. As we have seen, Richard was contemptuous of the illegitimate, careless and ruthless in line with contemporary mores. He was a prudish king who denounced the infidelities of his brother Edward IV, of his step-nephew Dorset, and his Wydeville in-laws – deflowerers of virgins – in the belief, probably correct, that the sexual depravity of his predecessor and of his foes would shock public opinion and deter Englishmen from backing such infamous rebels and persuade them to acquiesce in the continuance of his own rule. Henry Tudor, he proclaimed, was a bastard on both sides. Yet Richard was also a practitioner of the double standard. Now he acknowledged his own two bastards and paraded them in public. He arranged a noble marriage for his daughter Katherine, as second countess to William Herbert II, Earl of Huntingdon, and dowered her appropriately. She cannot have been significantly older than fourteen. He acknowledged his son John of Pontefract too, making him grants and appointing him titular captain of Calais. Although both were put to good political use, in the absence of legitimate brothers or sons of his own, Richard also displayed here a proper fatherly concern. Crowland wrote nothing on this subject. We cannot know what observers thought of this denouncer of immorality who had practised and now shamelessly publicised it himself.

For Richard's tiny dynasty of three – the king, the queen, and the prince – was short-lived. Richard and Anne had invested their whole futures in their son. Edward of Middleham, 'this only son on whom, through so many solemn oaths, all hope of the royal succession rested, [who] died' in 1484. And then, adds Crowland, obviously an eyewitness, 'You might have seen the father and mother ... almost out of their minds for a long time when faced with the sudden grief.'[33] Husband and wife were as one. Richard's conjugal family was united by the conjugal and parental affection that we expect today. Whatever his parents' status, whether ducal or royal, Edward's death was more than a personal sorrow, it also threatened to terminate their line and indeed all their lines. Richard and Anne were the culmination and the end of the Ricardian royal dynasty. Why on earth would their supporters, in this particular context, fight for them and risk their own lives for a monarch without heirs and therefore no future beyond his own life? The solution was obvious: to beget a replacement. Richard, aged thirty-one, and Anne, aged twenty-eight, should have been young enough to conceive again. They appear to have tried. But there were no further pregnancies. This is not surprising. Anne had been first married at fourteen years of age. In the dozen years of her two marriages we learn of only one pregnancy and only one live birth: no other christened infant was named in the prayers that they commissioned. Edward of Middleham had been born not later than 1477 and probably somewhat earlier. Most probably Anne, like her mother before her, ceased to be fertile early. Richard's bastards indicate that the problem was not his. If Anne failed to conceive again, Richard could not father legitimate offspring while she lived. He could not plead non-consummation – almost the only grounds for divorce!

A short-term solution was to designate another heir – to prepare for the perpetuation of the House of York after Richard and moreover to fill the roles normally performed by the king's siblings and sons. Concrete evidence is lacking, but Richard seems to have tried two nephews in this role. Clarence's son Edward Earl of Warwick did have a serious claim to the throne. He was the male heir to the whole House of Plantagenet and heir to the house of York if Edward IV's children were illegitimate. He was also heir to the whole Warwick inheritance (bar the Neville patrimony) once Queen Anne was dead and thus the focus of loyalty of the Warwick retainers. That was why he was posted to the north. But Warwick posed two problems: born in 1475, he was a figurehead rather than a serious political operator and destined to remain one for some time. Secondly, both his titles were better than those of Richard III himself, who had used his father Clarence's attainder to sideline him. It is unlikely that the ten-year-old Warwick was particularly concerned or aggrieved, but when he grew up, what then? John de la Pole, Earl of Lincoln, the eldest son of Richard's sister Elizabeth, was a better bet. Aged about twenty, he was old enough to be of serious political use, as president of Richard's Council of the North, and his title to the crown by primogeniture was decidedly inferior to Richard's own. There were any number of next heirs after Lincoln. He had six (possibly five) brothers and four sisters. Richard III seems only to have promoted Edward, archdeacon of Richmond in 1485 and most probably destined for a bishopric. The de la Poles took their new royal title seriously: they commissioned a de luxe pedigree that culminated in John's title. It is interesting that Richard found no use for Anne St Leger, the juvenile daughter by the second marriage of his eldest sister Anne, Both earls, Warwick and Lincoln, were short-term expedients. Richard did not expect either to succeed him as he had every intention of fathering another heir himself.

This is the correct viewpoint to apply to Richard's treatment of his bastard son and nephews. They were useful as heirs apparent to his throne and as figureheads in the north and in Ireland, but he did not promote them – or any other close relatives – to higher titles, by grants of estates, or to real power. Admittedly any such grants most probably would have consisted of forfeitures, like those bestowed on Sir Richard Ratcliffe and Sir James Tyrell, and thus were bound to be revoked on his deposition, but this omission means that Richard's political heirs included no magnates of the front rank.

Richard failed conspicuously to persuade his kindred of his right to reign and to back him in the political crises of his reign. Buckingham's rebellion in 1483 was a revolt of the Yorkist establishment. Its leaders included five of the king's brothers-in-law Thomas St Leger, Buckingham, Lionel, Richard and Edward Wydeville. This same Yorkist establishment fled abroad rather than submitting to Richard – admittedly a most perilous action

– and backed Henry Tudor thereafter. They acted thus not so much because of his positive qualities as because Tudor was not Richard III. Not much familial feeling there.

It is instructive indeed that virtually none of Richard's closer relatives were with him at Bosworth. Those who were there, the Howards, Northumberland, Lovell, the old Yorkist Walter Lord Ferrers of Chartley, and John Lord Zouche, though not wholly unrelated to Richard – was anyone? – were not there primarily because of their family connection. There were none of the burgeoning Bourchier clan. There were no Nevilles – neither George Lord Abergavenny, nor the teenaged Richard Lord Latimer, nor Ralph Earl of Westmorland (formerly Lord Neville) of the senior line. Even after the king's deal with Queen Elizabeth, none of his Wydeville in-laws turned out for him: neither of her brothers Richard Lord Rivers nor Sir Edward Wydeville, nor his brothers-in-law George Lord Grey of Ruthin and Thomas Lord Maltravers. Another ex-brother-in-law, William Herbert II, admittedly, was the commander for Richard in Wales, whom Tudor skilfully sidestepped. There was an ambiguity here, to be sure. If Queen Elizabeth's son Thomas Marquis of Dorset was fearful enough to take refuge abroad, it was he whom Henry Tudor chose nevertheless to leave behind as security for repayment of his loans.[34] Another distant connection was George Lord Strange, son-in-law of the queen's late sister Jacquetta Wydeville and thus Richard's nephew-by-marriage, also as son of the Kingmaker's sister Eleanor Neville first cousin one removed of the king and first cousin of Queen Anne. George was also the son of Thomas Lord Stanley, stepson therefore of Lady Margaret Beaufort, and therefore half-brother of Henry Tudor. It was he that Richard used as a hostage to secure his family's loyalty and whose immediate execution should have followed when that failed. The king's command was not fulfilled.[35]

Meantime Anne conveniently fell ill and died on 16 March 1485. There was no need to poison her, as the rumour ran. Richard denied poisoning her. He declared that he was as sorry as he could be, which we have no reason to doubt. Yet now he could marry again to a young, fertile, lady, who could supply the children that he required. At thirty-two Richard had plenty of time, although such unions were never certain to be productive. Richard looked abroad for a suitable princess, to Portugal, who could assist in the recognition of his usurping regime.[36] Actually, Crowland reports, his preference fell on his niece Elizabeth of York, who though bastardised was his brother's next heir and offered additional advantages. To marry her, Richard would deny the rebellious Yorkist establishment their figurehead, deprive Henry Tudor of his bride and of her claim. Richard knew Elizabeth personally. Crowland tells us that she was similar in build and colouring to Queen Anne – perhaps Richard saw in her what he had liked in Anne? – and at eighteen she was in the prime of life and of excellent breeding stock on both sides. Crowland is emphatic that Richard wanted to marry Elizabeth. There is evidence also that Elizabeth fancied her uncle Richard.[37]

Richard did not wait so long. First he sought another baby with the queen, unsuccessfully, then considered carefully marriage to his niece. Crowland reports much gaiety at Christmas 1484, when Elizabeth of York, though bastardised, was prominent in the dancing and other celebrations and was attired like another queen. Richard was suspected of sloughing off his queen and marrying Elizabeth instead. This was feasible if his marriage was invalid. Crowland, who reports the king's intentions, had no idea what the problem or the loophole was. Non-consummation was one ground for divorce (nullity); sorcery another, a precontract, a third; but none of these applied. A fourth ground was if the partners were related within the prohibited degrees. Richard and Anne were very closely related, several times over, in the fourth, third, second and even first degrees. The lesser impediments had been dispensed away, but not those in the second and first degrees, which were probably too grave to be dispensable anyway. Richard and Anne nevertheless went through a marriage ceremony and lived together as man and wife, probably in 1472, certainly by 1475, when an act settling the Warwick inheritance allowed for their divorce – for the Church to force them asunder as never legitimately married. Clarence knew of the impediment of course – most probably it was he who tagged this proviso on the act – but he had died in 1478. Acts of Parliament were not printed or common currency and this proviso was, it seems, successfully concealed. Richard had every reason to keep it secret while his heir Edward of Middleham, then Prince Edward, was alive, as he would be bastardised by the nullification of his parents' marriage. Once the prince was dead, where was the problem? Anne was the only loser. However, Richard hesitated: not for long, since only a year separated the deaths of his queen and prince. While he had the means to cast off his queen, end his marriage, and to remarry, it would be revealed that his marriage was a sham and that he and Anne had knowingly lived in sin for a decade. What would the moral majority, to whose disapproval he exposed his political enemies, think of his own immorality? Fortunately little time was lost. His divorce was unnecessary because only four months after Christmas 1484 Queen Anne had died naturally.

Poor Richard accrued the discredit of plotting the removal of his queen and actually poisoning her without doing anything at all. His denials merely fed the flames. He did however conceal successfully for five hundred years the nullity of his first marriage, the invalidity of Queen Anne's coronation and of Edward's investiture, and the illegitimacy of his son and heir. Losing his queen lost him her Warwick affinity, realistically the most committed of Richard's northerners, and those on whom his dominance of the south rested. Yet this was dwarfed by his scandalous proposal to marry his niece, Elizabeth of York. Richard and Elizabeth were related in the first degree of consanguinity (by blood), far beyond what the Church taught as permissible or beyond what the Pope could dispense. The only English precedence in 1411, between

Henry IV's son Thomas Duke of Clarence (d. 1421) and his aunt Margaret Holland, had been a relationship by affinity, by marriage. Crowland reports suspicions at court, outrage at the royal council, the parading of university dons to declare the match impossible, and Richard's public denial at St John's Hall in Clerkenwell, which nobody believed. Richard's critics would surely have been even more shocked if they had known the invalidity of Richard's first marriage: that he was a serial incestor. The elevation of Elizabeth to the throne would have restored Richard his royal family: her sisters, her mother, perhaps even the rest of the Wydeville network would have been rehabilitated and might indeed have become royal again. Elizabeth as queen would be well placed to avenge her brothers. It was that which Sir Richard Ratcliffe and William Catesby feared the most. Perhaps Richard's retraction was only temporary. A decade later the Pope granted such a dispensation to Queen Joanna of Naples and subsequently such matches for monarchs became quite common. Richard was ahead of his time. Had he been able to marry Elizabeth, surely Henry Tudor's alliance with the rebel Yorkist establishment would have been severed and they could have found a way back to their allegiance. This is one of history's imponderables, counterfactual arguments or might have beens. This proposed second marriage could have been the stroke of genius that was the saving of Richard III. Had he survived Bosworth, a second family was his top priority.

RICHARD'S HEIRS

The Tudor Royal Family

Richard III's wider family included Henry VII, the victorious king who fathered a new dynasty. Through two lines Henry was Richard's second cousin once removed and his third cousin once removed. There may have been other relationships within the fourth prohibited degree. Henry's consort was Richard's niece. Three papal dispensations were needed to legitimise Henry's marriage to Elizabeth of York whom Henry, unlike Richard, managed to marry.[1] Traditionally this has been regarded as the union of the two houses of Lancaster and York and therefore the end of the Wars of Roses. Henry VII was quick to revoke *Titulus Regius* and thereby to restore Elizabeth and her sisters to their legitimacy. Following the deaths of the two princes in the Tower, Elizabeth was indeed the senior daughter and heiress of Edward IV, therefore of the House of York, and, if primogeniture is applied, to the whole Plantagenet line too. Primogeniture made Elizabeth also into the next heir to whatever right Richard had in the crown of England. Elizabeth was destined to be the ancestress of the Tudor dynasty, Stuart, Hanoverian (Brunswick/Welf), Saxon, Windsor, and Mountbatten dynasties to occupy the English, British, and imperial thrones. Elizabeth's son Henry VIII, her father Edward

IV reborn in appearance and proclivities, symbolises this success. Within eight months of her wedding, the new queen had delivered a male heir to her husband, Prince Arthur: seven live births (and at least one miscarriage) made up their clutch, although only three outlived them, two being foreign queens. However the blood royal of the House of Tudor ran very thin – from 1502 only the underage Prince Henry remained and Henry VII strangely failed to remarry. For three decades after his accession King Henry VIII found the provision of a male heir notoriously difficult to achieve. None of his known children bore issue.[2]

All monarchs need a royal family to broaden the base of the dynasty, to deputise for them, to publicise, and to extend their rule. At first sight Henry Tudor lacked this key resource. There was only one other Tudor in 1485, his uncle Jasper Earl of Pembroke, whom he promoted to Duke of Bedford. Jasper married Buckingham's widow Katherine (*née* Wydeville), probably then about forty, but they had no children together. She had children by her first husband; he had a bastard daughter. Jasper died in 1495. Henry's mother Lady Margaret Beaufort, countess of Richmond and Derby, had been the only child of her parents. Each however had offspring by others. Margaret's mother – the new king's maternal grandmother Margaret Beauchamp of Bletso, Duchess of Somerset – had married three times and bore children by her other husbands too. Henry VII had half-siblings, born St Johns and Welles, some of whom still survived and several had borne their own children before his accession.[3] Her half-brother and his uncle John Lord Welles was elevated to Viscount Welles and married to Princess Cecily of York. His modest promotion reveals how little value Henry placed on these relatives and contrasts markedly to Edward IV's treatment of his family. Henry's fourteen-year exile meant that they were not acquainted personally. Moreover his queen had a host of relatives of her own – also, of course, relatives of Richard III: a grandmother in Cecily Neville, duchess of York (d. 1495); a mother, the new king's mother-in-law, the dowager-queen

Elizabeth Wydeville (d. 1492); four sisters; at least two bastard
siblings; a half-brother in Thomas Marquis of Dorset; and a host
of de la Pole and several Wydeville uncles, aunts, and cousins.[4]
Like her mother before her, Queen Elizabeth patronised her
sisters, legitimate and illegitimate. Here potentially was a valuable
resource for Henry to exploit. But he did not. Henry of course was
raised as an only child and from twelve as an exile, so he may not
have possessed the normal family experience to replicate himself.
Notoriously stingy, he was extremely sparing in his distribution of
titles and estate and anyway could not have courted them all. He
expected committed loyalty and obedience regardless of patronage
given or withheld. More significant perhaps was that so many of
his kindred were of York or Plantagenet blood – related as much
to Richard III or those who rebelled against him – and Henry was
unwilling therefore to trust them. The stepbrother of his queen,
Thomas Marquis of Dorset, like all the other Ricardian exiles, did
secure the reversal of Richard III's attainder, but in his case the
king, although his brother-in-law, stripped him of all the grants
made to him by his stepfather Edward IV and of his share of the
Exeter inheritance too. This was quite the reverse, surely, of family
unity or even reasonable consideration to a close relative. Actually
most of these lines acknowledged Elizabeth of York and Henry
VIII as Yorkist heirs, were loyal subjects to Henry VII, and had
been alienated by Richard III. They had nowhere else to go. A few
itemised below did subscribe to Richard's cause and continued the
fight. Apart from Uncle Jasper, the only dukes created by Henry
were his three sons, Arthur Duke of Cornwall, Henry Duke of
York, and Edmund Duke of Somerset. None were old enough
in his reign to be useful. A few returning exiles such as Edward
Courtenay, Earl of Devon (d. 1509), and John de Vere, Earl of
Oxford (d. 1513), reinforced the king's power with his own, but
Henry is also famous for governing in alliance neither with his
family nor with the nobility but principally through the medium
of humbler and perhaps abler men, such as Sir Reynold Bray, Sir

Edmund Dudley, Sir Richard Empson and Sir Thomas Lovell. They did his bidding, not necessarily with political acumen, and by 1496 could be denounced as evil councillors.[5]

The Yorkist establishment was loyal to Elizabeth as her father's heir and to Henry Tudor, in turn her fiancé, husband and consort. Henry was therefore the Yorkist candidate to the throne. The Lancastrians, whose vestigial title passed to him via his mother Margaret Beaufort, were almost extinct. That Henry nevertheless insisted on ruling in his own right signals an important message: that ladies could transmit titles, but could not reign themselves. It was not until the 1550s, when all the candidates were female, that this truth had to be jettisoned. Otherwise Henry might in theory have ceased to be king in 1503 on Elizabeth's death, just as happened in Castile to Ferdinand King of Aragon following the death of his consort Isabella, who had been Queen of Castile in her own right. Mary I's consort Philip II of Spain insisted on a similar condition – their documents were dated by the regnal years of Philip and Mary – but nevertheless ceased to reign on her death. So too the Dutchman William III, who continued ruling after the death of Mary II on 1694. Margaret Beaufort, who had transmitted Henry VII's Lancastrian title, actually outlived him. She knew that she could never reign herself. Any plotting against Richard III was on her son's behalf. Crowland stressed that Henry's entitlement to rule arose principally from his consort Elizabeth of York.[6] Nobody suggested that Elizabeth could rule herself: it was her consorts who mattered. Her sisters and her nieces Margaret Pole, Anne St Leger, her four de la Pole nieces and her great-nieces were of little political account by themselves. Henry VII treated them almost humanely, allowing them to marry and to breed, so that his son Henry VIII was confronted by a host of potential heirs by primogeniture, more than he could completely pollard. Nephews were much more harshly treated. This perception that ladies were of little account except through their husbands may help explain who rebelled against the Tudor regime and why Margaret of Burgundy, obviously a woman, backed her nephews Warwick, Lincoln, and Suffolk against the husband of her niece Elizabeth of York.

The Duchess Margaret did play a key role in creating and orchestrating the opposition to Henry VII. She was the youngest sister of Edward IV and Richard III, a widowed dowager with substantial dower lands, childless but nevertheless significant in overseeing the interests of her son-in-law Archduke and Emperor Maximilian Habsburg and his son, her step-grandchild, Philip.[7] Certainly she offered shelter to the two pretenders Lambert Simnel and Perkin Warbeck, acknowledged them to be her nephews Edward Earl of Warwick and Richard Duke of York, supplied them with money and even substantial armed forces. Although both were imposters, those princes whom they pretended to be actually existed (Warwick) or could not be proved to be dead (York). Had Lambert Simnel succeeded at the Battle of Stoke in 1487, it was presumably the real Warwick who would have taken his place as king. But there was no Richard Duke of York by the 1490s. Had Perkin Warbeck succeeded, presumably he would not have been permitted by his managers to take the throne: quite who would have done so instead is uncertain. Warwick was still around. De la Pole candidates, John Earl of Lincoln in 1487 and his brother Edmund Earl of Suffolk later, were also available. Note that all these male relatives of Queen Elizabeth of York and nephews of Margaret were also nephews of Richard III.

Richard's Cause

Richard's reign was disastrous to him and his dynasty. The king was slain. His lineage was brought to an end: the House of York and the House of Plantagenet ceased. So too, not long after, did all the lineages that culminated in Queen Anne Neville. The Tudor army had been fighting principally for a negative – to get rid of Richard and to end what they regarded as tyranny – rather than for any particular positive conception of good governance. Were Richard's men fighting solely for the status quo – to keep Richard on the throne and his style of rule? It is not easy to discern quite what Richard's cause was in 1485, quite what he and his political heirs stood for. In 1483 Richard III had presented himself as the rightful heir of the House of York, heir both to his father, Richard Duke of York, and his brother Edward IV. He had declared himself to be a reformer in the tradition of York and Warwick the Kingmaker. He was committed to the correction of the defects of the regime of his brother Edward IV, to end financial oppression especially through abolishing benevolences (forced gifts), and to minister impartial justice to all of whatever rank without fear or favour. He founded the court of Requests, which offered equitable justice to ordinary people. He stopped the factional fighting at court, the corrupt Wydeville dominance of government, and the sexual immorality that had characterised his brother's regime. So Richard said. Actually, however, Edward IV's *Second Reign* had not been so bad as *Titulus Regius* portrayed it. It was not characterised by misgovernment, by excessive exactions or even by much taxation, nor by serious outbreaks of crime and disorder. Supporting evidence for Richard's strictures come principally from Richard's own utterances and appear to be of his own devising. The populace had mobilised in response to reformers when economic conditions were especially parlous and when governments particularly were strapped for cash and credit, in 1450, 1459–60, and 1469–70, not so much because of oppressive exactions as because the regime was unable to pay its debts or its suppliers or to afford proper foreign policies or defence. By the 1480s, in contrast, Edward IV had cut the debt mountain, had repaired the royal finances so that he could operate within budget and repay any short-term debt, and the economy had commenced the upward trend that marked the end of the great slump of around 1440–80 and that signalled recovery at long last from the Black Death of 1348. Modern historians have credited Richard with improved management of the crown lands and with the creation of the Council of the North, yet both built on his brother's achievements and were initiatives quite small in scale and significance. Resistance to his rule had forced Richard to distribute forfeitures as patronage rather than keeping them as sources of revenue and his expenditure on defence compelled him also to resort to the unpopular exactions that Parliament had just abolished. Richard was driven to rule the south in ways condemned by Crowland as tyrannical.[8] There was therefore no serious reform programme with which Richard was identified, no political cause for which he stood and for which his heirs could continue to fight. Moreover those self-appointed political heirs campaigned at a time of growing economic well-being, which made it much more difficult to persuade the populace of evils that demanded their irruption on to the streets to sweep away the new king's evil councillors as in 1450, 1460 or 1470. That perception did indeed re-emerge in 1496, when Perkin Warbeck denounced the evil councillors and oppressive rule that Henry VII had created, and in 1509, when his son Henry VIII culled the worst excesses of his father's rule.[9] Earlier rebels against the Tudor regime were unable to conjure up popular insurrections as Jack Cade and the Kingmaker had managed to do. The two major uprisings of the populace, in Yorkshire in 1489 and Cornwall in 1497, objected to unaccustomed taxation, but, like Cade, the insurgents sought as loyal subjects to negotiate agreements with governments rather than to overthrow the king and his dynasty.[10]

If Richard left behind no political cause, there were nevertheless those who took up his struggle against Henry Tudor. If the first two Wars of the Roses were overtly about political reform, the dynastic issue – the change of king and dynasty – being secondary and merely the means to achieve better government, the *Third War* that Richard had initiated was far more obviously a dynastic one. It was not some principled cause that had prompted Richard to usurp, but his own ambition. The cause that Henry Tudor espoused was to get rid of Richard. The primary objective of opposition leaders after Bosworth was to substitute themselves as monarchs in place of Henry Tudor. Dynasticism had become the primary motive for future conflicts within England. Two of three principal sources of support for the insurgents – popular discontent and the high nobility – had ebbed away. Civil war was too dangerous to foment. The third support, if anything, was reinforced, as foreign powers harboured, bankrolled, and even armed pretenders to invade England just as Henry Tudor had done. Moreover, repeated upheavals had made revolution almost respectable. If Richard's own claim could not withstand proper scrutiny, Henry VII was only the first to term himself king ahead of proper election and conquest. He even persuaded some French that he was the son of Henry VI![11] The letters and proclamations that he despatched to England from abroad had already adopted the royal style. Likewise Lambert Simnel was crowned King Edward VI at Dublin before conquering England, Richard IV (Perkin Warbeck) was recognised in Scotland and by the emperor, and another Richard IV (Richard de la Pole) was recognised in France. None of them, however, had defensible claims and none of them secured much support within England itself.

'With large giftes,' wrote Thomas More, Richard 'get him vnstedfaste friendshippe.'[12] Certainly Richard believed in the capacity of patronage to win him supporters and lavished the large forfeitures he had accrued from traitors to reward those who had backed him and to endow them so that they could rule the localities he placed under their control. Such rewards were recognised to be unstable. They were liable to be restored to the original possessors if they could be induced to make their peace, which Richard certainly hoped to achieve, but he was allotted too little time to bring the rebels round and to reconcile them to his rule. Many recipients of Richard's munificence were not at Bosworth, perhaps because disloyal, hostile, uncommitted or cautious, but perhaps also because posted elsewhere or lacking the time to join the lightning campaign. For all beneficiaries of

Richard's patronage, Henry Tudor's accession meant the loss of their offices and grants, generally completely, although a few were reappointed. They suffered financial loss. Those who fought on against Henry VII, like Sir Thomas Broughton, were generally those northerners of modest means who had benefited most from Richard's rule. Chief among those Ricardians who fought on was Richard's friend and cousin and chamberlain Francis Viscount Lovell: at Bosworth and attainted, he took the lead in the opening conspiracies of Richard's reign. He was apparently as loyal to Richard's heir as Edward IV's chamberlain Lord Hastings had been to Edward V and as Sir Thomas Tresham had been to Henry VI as controller of the household.[13]

The Shared Royal Family of Richard III and Henry VII

Richard III left no issue or members of his nuclear family to continue his line or to perpetuate his cause. His wife Anne Neville and his sole legitimate issue Edward of Middleham had predeceased him. The further marriage and second family that he projected proved abortive. Of his bastards, his daughter Katherine Countess of Huntingdon died childless by 1487. His bastard son John of Pontefract disappeared from the records, most probably because he died underage and childless. Richard of Eastwell, supposedly another bastard, probably never existed. If there were ever any other bastards, male or female, they are unrecorded and cannot be researched.

Failing offspring, Richard's family and Richard's heirs need to be sought up his family tree, among his siblings and their descendants. Edward IV, George Duke of Clarence, and Anne Duchess of Exeter, all deceased, had left issue. There survived two other sisters Elizabeth Duchess of Suffolk, who had eleven children, and Margaret Dowager Duchess of Burgundy. Margaret was childless: her role was as politician rather than mother. All these siblings were aunts and uncles also to King Henry VII and his queen. Their progeny were first cousins to the Tudor princes and princesses.

After Richard's death, the senior line was clearly that of Edward IV himself. There can be very little doubt that Edward's male line had terminated with the deaths of the two princes in the Tower, during Richard's reign, in Richard's custody, and almost certainly at his command. Since they lived together, they probably died together. Yet in 1491 a conspirator appeared who claimed to be the younger of the two princes, Richard Duke of York, who would then have been eighteen years of age. This was Perkin Warbeck. That both he and Lambert Simnel were reputed and are still called pretenders – that they are household names for imposture rather than the frontmen for legitimate claimants – are notable successes of Tudor propaganda. Almost certainly a fraudulent pretence, Perkin Warbeck appears to have been born to a craftsman's family from Tournai, then in Burgundy but now in France. Modern researchers in the local archives have documented the family but not yet substantiated Perkin's membership of it. Perkin was a handsome boy, of noble appearance, who was well coached in aristocratic manners, in languages, and on his past membership of the Yorkist royal family. He looked the part and played the part. Perkin was able to secure support (though not all at the same time) from Ireland; from Scotland, where he was called Richard IV and married to Lady Katherine Gordon, a connection of the Scottish king; from his supposed aunt the Duchess Margaret in Burgundy; and in the Empire, where he even attended the funeral of the Emperor Frederick III as guest of Archduke (now Emperor) Maximilian. Perkin secured enough support to launch three separate invasions of England – at Deal in Kent (1495), which received a bloody rebuff; across the Scottish border (1496), which degenerated into a mere raid; and in Cornwall (1497). This so-called Cornish Rising, which inflamed much of the West Country, was provoked by the taxation needed to oppose his

Scottish invasion and reached the outskirts of London because potential defenders had been despatched northwards. Warbeck tried to exploit widespread discontent with Henry's oppressive government. Respectable plotters in England were exposed, but not many. The danger that Warbeck posed was that if he was genuine and sufficiently successful to force men to choose, then his right to the throne was unquestionable, better than either his supposed sister Elizabeth of York, his cousin Edward Earl of Warwick, or the de la Poles. Sir William Stanley, the steward of Henry's own household, is alleged to have said that in such a case he could not oppose Warbeck.[14] After defeat in Cornwall, however, Warbeck was captured and confessed that he was an imposter. That Perkin was allowed to live and left at liberty, just like Simnel, is an indicator that Henry thought him convincingly discredited and harmless. Henry was ruthless in slaying those who posed a risk. Yet Warbeck offended again and was duly despatched in Henry's mopping-up operation in 1499.

If Edward IV's sons were dead, what of his daughters? In 1460 Richard Duke of York had claimed the crown by primogeniture, through two ancestresses, and this was the title that Edward IV had made good. Since the Wars of the Roses until 2013 primogeniture prevailed, albeit somewhat modified in 1702 in favour of Protestants. The heirs by primogeniture in 1485 were therefore Edward IV's daughters: daughters of Edward IV, whole sisters of Edward V, nieces of Richard III. Of the original seven daughters, only Mary (d. 1482) and Margaret (d. 1473) were deceased, leaving five surviving. All were Richard III's nieces whom he had bastardised and therefore hardly proud of their connection with that king. The eldest, Elizabeth of York, was Henry VII's queen. The whole right of this line to the crown focused on her: by convention however, rather than any particular law of succession. Every English monarch since 1509 has traced descent from her. Henry VII, as we have seen, made little of his Yorkist family. Elizabeth in contrast had strong emotional ties to them and accepted obligations to foster their interests. As queen, this was something she could afford, certainly for her sisters. Even Henry Tudor, it seems, could not keep them single or enclose them in nunneries, although the three who did marry were bestowed on men whose loyalty at the time appeared assured. Born in 1469 Cecily, much the oldest sister and formerly destined for James IV of Scotland, carried Prince Arthur to his christening (1486) and bore the queen's train at her coronation in 1487. Already married to Ralph Scrope of Masham (Yorks.), she was divorced. She remarried in 1487 first to John Viscount Welles, the new king's paternal uncle, who died in 1499 when she was thirty, and then, to Henry's great displeasure, to the wholly obscure Thomas Kyme.[15] There may have been two daughters Elizabeth and Anne Welles, who died in childhood, but she had no recorded issue at her death in 1507.[16] Also childless was the youngest, Bridget, who professed at Syon Abbey as a Bridgettine nun, and Anne (d. 1511), wife of Thomas Howard, from 1524 Duke of Norfolk. The Howard lines which survive today stem from his second marriage. Katherine (d. 1527) married William Courtenay, who succeeded as Earl of Devon briefly in 1511. These two marriages were arranged by their sister the queen. Katherine's eldest son Henry Marquis of Exeter in 1539 was executed for supposed treason by the paranoid Henry VIII, but the king was far too late to catch all Katherine's descendants: numerous issue survive to the present day, including the present author.

The queen also cherished at least one of Edward IV's bastards, her half-sister Grace.[17] Quite what befell her is uncertain. Another of Edward's bastards, Arthur Plantagenet, by marriage viscount Lisle, also prospered at the Tudor court. None of these close relatives of Richard III claimed the crown or rebelled, although Katherine's husband William was attainted by Henry VII and Arthur Viscount Lisle perished in the Tower, both apparently for treasons of which they were guiltless.

Neither Richard III nor the princes were the last of the Plantagenets. Arguably Plantagenets survive even today in the Somerset family headed by the Duke of Beaufort, who descend from Charles Somerset (d. 1526), bastard of Henry Beaufort, Duke of Somerset (d. 1464), grandson of John Beaufort, Earl of Somerset (d. 1410), bastard of John of Gaunt (d. 1399), son of Edward III. Lancastrian descent contributed to Charles's promotion to the peerage, but never did it bring any claim to the crown. The last legitimate Plantagenet was actually Clarence's son, Richard's nephew, Edward Earl of Warwick.[18] It could be argued – as Richard had indeed argued in 1483 – that Warwick was disabled from the succession by the attainder of his father George Duke of Clarence in 1478. That argument carries little weight, since it also applied to Richard Duke of York, whose sentence was reversed in 1460, to Henry VI when he resumed his crown in 1470, to Edward IV when he returned in triumph in 1471, and finally to Henry Tudor in 1485, when the judges ruled that, since he actually was King Henry VII, the sentence carried no weight. Recognising the danger that Warwick represented, King Henry seized his person at once and kept him confined until his execution unmarried at the age of twenty-four in 1499. The young earl's title to the crown was formidable and was promoted by rebels both in 1486 and 1487. It was Warwick who Lambert Simnel pretended to be. Warwick was potentially a great magnate – the last of the overmighty subjects. He was the heir of the Beauchamp earls of Warwick, of Warwick the Kingmaker, and of George Duke of Clarence, all of whom had held sway over the west Midlands. Adherents of Warwick led by his former retainers the Staffords of Graftons sought in 1486 to mobilise the traditional Warwick connection in Warwickshire and Worcestershire. Once again their supporters donned the badge of the bear and ragged staff.[19] Simnel was in Ireland in 1487, where Warwick's grandfather Richard Duke of York and his father Clarence had both been lieutenants. From there he embarked to Lancashire, passing through and recruiting from the Richmondshire heartlands of the Kingmaker and Richard III, en route for decisive defeat at Stoke by Newark on 16 June. Henry VII rode young Warwick through the streets of London to demonstrate that the real earl was in his hands and that Simnel in Ireland was an imposter. Perhaps this deterred the undecided.[20] At least some of the rebels must have known of the imposture and were not put off, such as John Earl of Lincoln, for whom Simnel was a means to raise the army to defeat King Henry. The Irish probably knew nothing of the parade in London.

Henry curtailed the military threat that Warwick posed, at least in theory, by seizing his lands. Firstly in 1485 Henry confiscated the lands of Richard III including the half-share of the Warwick inheritance that Richard had held only for life and that should have accrued to Warwick as son of the other heiress. Secondly, in 1487, by restoring the boy's grandmother Anne Countess of Warwick, the widow of the Kingmaker, who was 'persuaded' to surrender all her rights to the king.[21] In theory, for traditional loyalties were surprisingly enduring, even a generation or so. As late as the 1536 Pilgrimage of Grace some rebels demanded the restoration of their ancient lords. Had young Warwick been allowed to come of age, he would have found himself entitled only to his father's Salisbury inheritance in southern England, and would surely have been aggrieved by this chicanery and by his unjust treatment. Warwick was a conundrum for Henry VII very like that which George Neville had presented to Richard Duke of Gloucester: could he ever be safely released or married? Execution, however unjust, resolved that issue.

Warwick was not Clarence's only child. Two brothers died at birth or infancy. The earl also possessed an elder sister Margaret, born at Farleigh Hungerford in Somerset in 1473, who seemed less dangerous to Henry VII. Early in the 1490s she was permitted to marry the relatively obscure Sir Richard Pole – however Margaret Beaufort's step-nephew and the king's second cousin – and on her brother's death in 1499 she was allowed to succeed as Countess of Salisbury. She bore five children who reached maturity. Four bred. Margaret did not forget her royal antecedents, nor the injustice of her father's death: witness her chantry chapel at Christchurch Priory (now in Dorset), the most splendid of cage chantries emblazoned with her royal arms that Henry VIII's agents defaced, and the surviving portrait that shows her wearing a bracelet with a barrel pendant in memory of the supposed death of her father Clarence in a butt of malmsey wine. Being short of issue of his own, Henry VIII came to fear her bloodline too, executing the aged countess aged sixty-eight in 1541 and her eldest son Henry Lord Montagu in 1539. By then, however, her children and grandchildren had proliferated and in 1907 her 11,723 descendants filled a whole volume of pedigrees.

Further down the order of succession surely were the offspring of Richard's two elder sisters, Anne Duchess of Exeter and Elizabeth Duchess of Suffolk, whether the inheritance system was by primogeniture or a male entail.

Richard's eldest sister Anne Duchess of Exeter bore two daughters called Anne, the eldest being Anne Holland, who predeceased her, and the second being Anne St Leger (Selenger, d. 1526), her sole legitimate heir. Originally betrothed to a future Marquis of Dorset, this girl made a good marriage to George Manners, Lord Roos, and was ancestress of the Manners earls and dukes of Rutland. Her royal blood was not forgotten either. When created first earl in 1525, her son Thomas Manners was allowed elements of the royal arms of England and France in recognition of his descent from Anne Plantagenet, Duchess of Exeter and sister of King Edward IV.[22] This line also never dabbled in the crown. In 1907 25,552 descendants of Anne's descendants were traced in the Anne of Exeter volume.[23] It is to this line that Michael Ibsen, Wendy Duldig, and the present author belong.

The case that Richard made for his accession was based on the discrediting of the claims of others and the arguments that were put forward are not very convincing and indeed failed to persuade many of his contemporaries. Yet Richard undoubtedly was King of England and did reign. Henry VII's regime, like Richard's own, and Edward IV's regime, was obliged to recognise its predecessors, kings in fact (*de facto*) if not of right (*de jure*), to accept much that they had done, and to build on the foundations that they left. It was not so much Richard's hereditary right to which his de la Pole successors laid claim, but rather that Richard had designated them – specifically John Earl of Lincoln – as his heirs. Most politically important and certainly most numerous of Richard's collateral relatives were the de la Poles, the offspring of his second sister, who at Edward IV's death rated from fifteenth to twenty-second in line for the throne: far behind the issue of the brothers Edward IV and Clarence. Neither Richard's sister Elizabeth nor her spouse John Duke of Suffolk seem to have counted for much politically in the reigns of her brother Edward IV, her nephew Edward V, her brother Richard III, or her nephew by marriage Henry VII. She was unfortunate that her husband was the poorest of dukes and that his mother survived until 1475. He was never advanced or enriched by his kingly brothers-in-law. This was particularly regrettable since the couple were remarkably fecund, bearing six (or possibly seven) sons and four daughters who attained maturity: John Earl of Lincoln (k. 1487), Edward (d. 1485), Edmund Earl of Suffolk (ex. 1513), Dr Humphrey (d. 1513), William (d. 1539), Geoffrey (if he was more than a misprint), Richard (k. 1525), Katherine Lady Stourton, Anne, Dorothy, and Elizabeth Lady Morley (d. after 1489). The duke died in 1491–92 and the duchess in 1503. But who they were came to matter for more than their personal qualities. That is the nature of a hereditary system. Nonentities can become rulers. Royal blood – and belief in its transforming qualities – brings both opportunities and risks. The belief of some de la Poles in their title to the crown, as demonstrated by the pedigree roll that they commissioned and maintained[24] – and the decision of the first two Tudors to tar them all with the same brush – was fatal for the whole family and explains why there is no Suffolk or de la Pole volume to trace living descendants of Edward III. Through this line there were none; none recorded in the standard genealogies, anyway.

So large a brood was difficult to provide for, the duchess's brothers Edward IV and Richard III being little help, and from 1504 the family estate was forfeited. John Earl of Lincoln, the eldest, did marry at his own level, to Margaret, the daughter of Thomas Earl of Arundel (when still Lord Maltravers) and his Wydeville wife. This may have been during the reign of Richard III, when John – the king's nephew and perhaps heir – was especially eligible. The duke and duchess of Suffolk did educate their offspring, two or possibly three sons attending university. They settled jointure on John and Margaret, and presumably found marriage portions for two daughters – though marrying into the peerage, they were marrying below the high nobility. The family's straitened circumstances may explain why two sons Edward and Humphrey became clergymen (and perhaps a third, Geoffrey, was so intended), the Church being a profession that offered livings at no cost to the parents. None of them rose to the episcopacy surely anticipated for clerics of royal blood. Relative poverty may also explain why Anne became a nun of Syon, why Dorothy and Richard never married, and why Elizabeth – the only de la Pole born in the next generation – was also professed as a nun at Syon in 1510, after the forfeiture and during the exile of her father Earl Edmund. Five did marry: John, slain at the Battle of Stoke in 1487; Edmund, father of the nun Elizabeth, executed in 1513; William, imprisoned in the Tower from 1503 to 1539, who married a twice-widowed lady in Catherine Lady Grey of Codnor (formerly Berkeley of Beverstone, *née* Stourton); and Katherine Lady Stourton and Elizabeth Lady Morley, who were both childless. Elizabeth Morley apparently vowed herself to chastity after her husband's premature death in 1489. Her example warns us not to presume that nunneries were only the last resort of ladies of slender means. Professing as a nun in a fashionable house moreover was not without cost. Failure to marry might have happened because the boys lacked the estate to support a wife and the girls a marriage portion suitable to attract a husband of appropriate means. Relative poverty rendered them ineligible to wed their social equals and they declined to seek out partners of lower rank. It was prudent of William to choose a wife with two dowers, but his wife Catherine was already childless by two previous husbands, perhaps past the age of childbearing, and was probably denied conjugal rights when visiting her husband in the Tower.[25] Sating lust need not, of course, require marriage: whether Edmund in exile or Richard in exile or on campaign fathered children by foreign women is not recorded and cannot be accounted for. Not just violent deaths in the Wars of the Roses explain the expiry of the de la Poles: just as important were multiple failures to reproduce, and such failures were attributable to their inability to marry, to cohabit, and to bear children which was also a consequence of the Wars of the Roses. The Beauforts and Hungerfords are other instances of this kind of consequence of civil war.

In retrospect it was poor judgement by Edward IV and Richard III not to advance and employ their de la Pole nephews.

John Earl of Lincoln set the family on this disastrous course in 1486. He had been Richard III's favourite nephew, a royal prince who bore the orb at his coronation and was appointed lieutenant of Ireland, presided over Richard's Council of the North and was designated his successor failing direct issue. It was the latter that the de la Poles recorded in the splendid genealogy that they commissioned. Whether at Bosworth or not, he submitted to the new king and resumed his former position, less the roles in Ireland, as heir apparent, and as a royal prince. John had not forgotten his royal expectations – that he was Richard III's designated heir was fatal to him and all his family. No doubt Henry VII remained suspicious of him. Either way John defected, fleeing abroad and joining the Simnel conspiracy that sought ostensibly to put his cousin Edward Earl of Warwick on the throne. Was this defensive, about self-preservation from a hostile king? Was it an entirely straightforward backing of an alternative candidate? Or was it Lincoln himself, the highest-ranking adult in the plot, who intended to take the throne? Regardless, the plot failed. Simnel's Irish and Germanic army failed to recruit sufficiently in England. Although proceeding rapidly to the heart of the kingdom and skilfully

outmanoeuvring the king's forces, it was decisively defeated at the
Battle of Stoke on 16 June 1487. This was a battle, Paul Murray
Kendall pointed out, that could have gone either way. Lincoln was
among those killed. The death, attainder and forfeiture of the heir
apparent to the family title and estates was disastrous for the de
la Poles. When Duke John died, his inadequate estate was further
reduced, so that the next heir, Edmund, was obliged to negotiate
away the dukedom for sufficient endowment. Edmund Earl of
Suffolk was a chivalric ornament at court. He does not appear to
have wanted to make his succession to Richard III a reality, and
he was not a committed plotter, but Henry's oppression drove him
into opposition, into flight, and into conspiracy that he probably
never intended. When Suffolk fled abroad for a second time, this
time with the crown of England in his sights, he and his next
brother William were attainted. Extradited from France with a
promise of his life in 1506, he was nevertheless executed in 1513.
Richard, the youngest brother, wisely remained abroad, called
himself Richard IV, and was periodically recognised by the French
as a pawn in the diplomatic game. His death in 1525 was at the
Battle of Pavia, in the Italian Wars. The last surviving brother,
William, mouldered in obscurity until his eventual death in 1539,
aged about sixty, after thirty-six years in prison. For the de la
Poles, the crown was a mirage that lured them only to catastrophe.

Of course Richard III had many other relatives after 1485.
Another of Ruvigny's genealogical volumes itemised solely the
many thousand descendants then living or recently living of
his aunt Isabel Plantagenet, Countess of Essex.[26] There were
numerous cousins, first, second, third or fourth – notably numerous
Bourchiers and Nevilles who did not dabble in dynastic politics –
and in-laws. From these descended many more connections today
than the descendants of the 54,040 itemised by the marquis of
Ruvigny and Raineval in 1907.[27] Those with rights emanating
from Richard, like the earls of Westmorland, the lords Latimer,
and Anne Beauchamp's rivals, wisely kept quiet about them.

9

THE POSTHUMOUS LIFE OF
RICHARD III

Richard's End[1]

Richard was definitely killed at the Battle of Bosworth on 22 August 1485. Given precedents such as William Trumpington, who pretended for many years to be Richard II, Henry VII was determined to leave no doubt that his rival was dead. The battered body of King Richard III was retrieved, carried to Leicester naked across a horse's back with his genitals visible – possibly it was at this stage that a minor wound was inflicted on his buttocks – and was publicly exhibited, still nude, at Newark College for two days. Thereafter, no doubt already decomposing in the August warmth, the corpse was interred in the choir of Leicester's Franciscan friary. The large complex was by this time served by a mere handful of friars. The burial was Christian: Catholic, but apparently without solemnity. An epitaph inviting prayers 'for my offences/That my punishment may be lessened by your prayers' must be pre-Dissolution and was most obviously composed by friars seeking offerings from visitors who read Latin, therefore ecclesiastics rather than the laity. It was more probably on a placard rather than the marble stone(s) mentioned: an effigy as suggested by Raphael Holinshed (1577) and Sir George Buck

(1619), who cannot have seen it in situ, seems unlikely. One may have been intended in the alabaster monument commissioned ten years later from the Nottingham sculptor William Hilton, possibly in alabaster: Richard had been a king, like Henry himself, who 'thus honours my bones/And you cause a former king to be revered with the honour of a king'. Although rubbed, the chancery record of a lawsuit seems to be about non-fulfilment of the contract and the sums cited to be the penalties in a recognisance rather than the cost of the monument.² The friary was dissolved in 1536, unroofed, and soon demolished. If any masses were dedicated to the good of the late king's soul, they stopped, and he ceased to benefit from others in the friary church as well. For the past five hundred years, it would be nice to say that Richard rested in peace. Indeed, until the Victorians removed his feet when constructing an outhouse and Jo Appleby (Leicester's human bioarchaeologist) smote his head with a mattock, he was. Yet all around him was transformed. The buildings were demolished, the site was divided, developed and redeveloped several times, latterly as a school, public buildings, and as the now famous Social Services Department car park. Here the bones were allegedly found by Philippa Langley, the Leicester University archaeology unit, Leicester Cathedral Chapter, and other interested parties that wish their identity as Richard to be believed. Their message has been beamed across the world. Near the site there is to be a splendid new visitor centre, and in the cathedral across the road the bones and tomb of Richard III himself.

Richard III's Posthumous Reputation

The Wars of the Roses petered out early in the sixteenth century and the last significant claimant to be Richard III's heir was surely Richard de la Pole, the White Rose of York, who perished at the Battle of Pavia in 1525. By failing to father a male heir and by initiating the English Reformation as a by-product, Richard's great-nephew Henry VIII set off other divisions. He embarked too late on pollarding Yorkist descendants to exterminate them entirely. Established orthodoxy, Tudor orthodoxy but also Lancastrian and Yorkist orthodoxy, was that Richard III had been wrongfully a king, a bad king, a tyrant, the murderer of innocent children, and that he had suffered God's rightful verdict at the Battle of Bosworth. So-called Tudor propaganda began in Richard's own reign as Yorkist propaganda: some was a matter of fact. Richard's usurpation of the crown was damaging to the king's reputation alone. Other slurs were developed during his reign and afterwards and were not stilled by denials. A wicked and wrongful king like Richard, who had been exposed by God, could be expected to display outward evidence in his twisted body. His unnatural life should have been anticipated by his unnatural birth. Testimony to this effect appears both in the *Life of Richard III* of around 1513, written by Sir Thomas More, and before him in the *History* of John Rows (d. 1491).[3] Today, of course, such mirroring of later character in the face and birth are discounted as credulous.[4] Some of these superstitions, such as the hunchback story and accounts of his birth, at least contain some truth. Stories about Richard's last day on earth – his troubled rest, the absence of breakfast or any chaplain to shrive him – were reported by Crowland, who, remember, was thereabouts. His chronicle dates as early as November 1485.[5] Thomas More was writing too late to invent the stories and both Crowland and Rows may have imbibed stories already current. No men – and certainly no priests – attended childbirth. There was scarcely time for Richard's enemies to invent these tales. Once ousted, discredited and apparently damned, Richard attracted no sympathetic biographers. Crowland and Rows, both Yorkists rather than Tudor propagandists, inaugurated the long-dominant tradition that presented Richard as the bad king from whom England was saved by the Tudors. Until about 1950 the best account of the reign was that of Sir Thomas More – St Thomas More – and Richard was best known through the gripping drama of Shakespeare's *Richard III*. As late as 1966, A. L. Rowse could confirm Shakespeare's portrait using only Shakespeare's sources.

Dissenting voices were few. Only an inferior abridgement of Sir George Buck's distinguished Renaissance *History* of 1619 was published in 1646, and Horace Walpole's *Historic Doubts* (1759) was more ingenious than reliable.[6] Even the creation of the Richard III Society (then the Fellowship of the White Boar) made little impact. After the Second World War, critical scholarship addressed the traditional story and its sources, academic historians like Alec Myers and Paul Murray Kendall took Richard's line,[7] and in the 1970s Peter Hammond, Anne Sutton, and others provided the Richard III Society with reputable historical leadership. The Richard III exhibition of 1973 and the Richard III Quincentenary of 1983–85 were triumphs for the society. The message that Richard III was maligned by Tudor propagandists became universally known and believed. The society has made a reality of its mission to enhance understanding of Richard III through its journal *The Ricardian* and the publication of sources. Such investment has made Richard III and his era particularly well studied. Richard has benefited also from popular literature, notably Philippa Gregory's *The White Queen* and *The Cousins' Wars*. All this activity has not, however, brought Richard III academic acclaim.

The King under the Car Lot

A major fillip in Richard III's posthumous life has come with the 2012 discovery of bones that are alleged to be his at Leicester. It is the latest attempt to bring science to bear on fifteenth-century mysteries. This perhaps began with the accidental discovery in the seventeenth century of two sets of children's bones in the Tower, one set being identified as the bones of the Princes in the Tower and honourably reinterred at Westminster Abbey, where they remain to this day. These bones were forensically examined in the 1920s by Professor William Wright and Lawrence Tanner, who took the identification for granted and did not, therefore, question their gender. No cause of death was established.[8] Subsequently Theya Mollason's reconsideration noted genetic features similar to their relative Anne Mowbray (d. 1481), whose bones in the ruins of the London Greyfriars had been forensically examined. Anne was married to the younger prince: more importantly, her great-great-grandmother was the boy's great-grandmother, but the physical peculiarities may have been widely shared. Mollason could not re-examine the bones or apply carbon dating to them, which might at least have fixed them to the right era if not to a specific year.[9] Researchers into Richard III have tried to re-examine the bones in Westminster Abbey and others at Tiverton and Mechlen in Belgium, so far without successful research outcomes.[10]

Meanwhile, science has developed new tests applicable to ancient remains, notably DNA fingerprinting, which could, for instance, demonstrate whether Edward IV had the same parents as his siblings.[11] Unfortunately, the remains of medieval aristocrats were often located in monasteries in England or abroad that have been dissolved or were moved or otherwise disturbed. Such matching remains therefore need identifying themselves before being used for comparison. The bones of George Duke of Clarence probably remained intact at Tewkesbury Abbey until the eighteenth century, when the Hawlings family took over his vault and moved his remains, which are now lost.[12] Instead of comparing historic skeletons with other historic remains, why not compare them with present-day descendants? After all, everybody inherits DNA from each parent and everybody's DNA is different. After seventeen generations, however, the legacy from Richard III's siblings to present-day relatives is too diluted – not all ancestors can be represented – and anyway it is impossible to establish which element comes through which line. For this purpose, frankly, such simple DNA data is no use. However, two types of DNA supposedly do not change over the generations[13] and thus permit comparison with relatives living today. There are scientific tests regarding mitochondrial DNA and the Y chromosome. Mitochondrial DNA reveals the direct maternal line – whether a modern descendant and the fifteenth-century individual share a common ancestress: a mother, maternal grandmother, maternal great-grandmother, etc. The female line cannot be broken. The Y chromosome reveals a common male ancestor – whether today's donor and the medieval man are both Plantagenets, for instance. Here is the potential to add significantly and perhaps conclusively to such debates as the fate of the princes.

Dr John Ashdown-Hill, to his enormous credit, was the first to appreciate this potential. He confirmed that Richard III was buried in the choir of Greyfriars friary in Leicester, located the precincts within the town, and argued that the king's remains most probably were still there. Moreover, he greatly increased the chances of identifying any surviving remains of Richard III by DNA fingerprinting. Firstly he traced Joy Ibsen and Wendy Duldig, two modern descendants of Richard III's sister Anne Duchess of Exeter, who should share the mitochondrial DNA of Cecily Duchess of York and therefore her children. Testing the remains of Margaret Duchess of Burgundy or Richard III against the results of the two modern relatives should have established descent from a common maternal ancestor. Secondly, he recognised that a male line of the Plantagenets did still exist in the Somerset family of the Duke of Beaufort. Charles Somerset, Earl of Worcester (d. 1526), illegitimate son of Edmund Duke of Somerset, executed by Richard in 1471, was descended from the first Beaufort, John Earl of Somerset (d. 1410), son of John of Gaunt, son of Edward III. Testing the Y chromosome from Richard's remains against results from the Somersets should prove Plantagenetness. No mitochondrial match was found for Margaret. For the bones, some matches were established.

Ashdown-Hill also assisted Philippa Langley, who overrode all obstacles to archaeological investigation. A preliminary desktop exercise established convincingly the original place of Richard's burial under the Leicestershire Social Services car park within what had been the choir of Leicester Franciscan friary, which was then precisely located by excavation. A small-scale, short-term dig achieved all its objectives including the discovery of an articulated skeleton identifiable as Richard III. If not the best archaeology – levels were dug through to reach the friary – this was a brilliantly conceived research project. It was also remarkably well supported, notably by the University of Leicester, which committed a galaxy of archaeological and scientific expertise – on biology, biochemistry, genetics, medicine, statistics, and art history. The utmost care was taken by the archaeologists to avoid contamination of the bones with other DNA and by the scientists to undertake multiple tests of the data at different institutions. It seems impossible to fault their research. In an age of immediate communication and instant gratification, of public impatience with delayed results, of research impact and media interviews, of news flashes and public excitement, academic publications and proof have lagged well behind rather than coming first as ought to be the case. Research, life, and debate has proceeded as though it was proven that the bones belonged to Richard. It will probably be several years before the full archaeological report is available for detailed study, but the results have already been announced by the Leicester team: firstly, that they have found the skeleton of Richard III and most recently, on 3 December 2014, that all scientific tests had identified the bones as his, with 99.999 per cent certainty.[14] Public impact justified breaking all the normal academic rules. Philippa Langley and other Ricardians embarked at once on plans for a monument and the funeral. A whole range of spin offs relate to his appearance, physique, health, cause of death and much else. On 26 March 2015 the body of Richard III was interred in Leicester Cathedral, both the archbishops of Canterbury and Westminster having contributed to the exequies. The Richard effect has been calculated to be worth £45 million to the district and was especially beneficial to the cathedral and to Leicester's museums. The discovery of the king in the car lot – in American parlance – captured the imagination of the world. Newsreels and newspapers, primetime television programmes, to date four highly readable and indeed gripping books – others are forthcoming – have resulted. The membership of the Richard III Society has burgeoned. The University of Leicester has enormously magnified its research impact.

However, all is not what it seems. How can one prove the authorship of an anonymous chronicle or the identity of an assemblage of bones five hundred years old? There are a range of obvious criteria for the bones to be Richard's. They have to belong to an adult male aged about thirty, to have been buried in the Leicester friary choir, and to have perished violently. All these criteria fit this skeleton Moreover the bones are of a man, small, with uneven shoulders, suffering from scoliosis, all features which tally with fifteenth-century testimony that Ricardians up to now have been anxious to discount as Tudor propaganda. Ironically Ricardians are now committed to the scoliosis while rebutting as pejorative terms like 'hunchback' and 'deformity'. As Philippa Langley rightly recognised, proving that some Tudor propaganda is true will rehabilitate other Tudor evidence that Ricardians since Josephine Tey have sought to discredit. At first carbon dating precluded 1485, but re-testing, suitably adjusted for a marine diet, dated the bones within the bracket 1455–1530. None of these criteria are conclusive, of course – any number of small men aged about thirty with scoliosis might have perished violently at any of the battlefields of the Wars of the Roses or foreign wars within this timeframe. Thus far there was nothing to prove death at the Battle of Bosworth or the precise identity with the remains. Nobody knows who else was buried in the priory choir: most of the priors, for a start, should be there. Fulfilment of a whole series of criteria, none of them exclusive, constructs a formidable case, but not a watertight one. Doubts were registered along these lines by the present author and the quality of the excavation was criticised by the renowned archaeologist Professor Martin Biddle,[15] but such caveats were overridden by the team. There remain other discrepancies to explain: the wounds to the head of a man undoubtedly helmeted, for instance, deductions to be drawn from them that contrast with the historical narratives, and the mismatch of the rough, ill-fitting grave and the fine alabaster monument.

Historians have to make the most of the evidence that is available to them, which is often imperfect – the fate of the Princes in the Tower being a case in point. They are not content with its imperfections and try through further research and argument to make their deductions more secure. These bones are an example where such further opportunities existed and further research was called for, which is why the Leicester team subjected their data to further tests.

Why does it matter? Why does not a high probability suffice, given that the date and circumstances of death and place of burial are well known? It matters because deductions are already being made from the bones about Richard III's appearance, physique, pathology, pathogens, diet, character and psychology. In future, apparently, historians will have to engage with scientists on the deductions to be drawn from such evidence. In the meantime, if such conclusions are to be fed into mainstream history, it is crucial that the identification is reliable. Mere probabilities, even Bayesian probabilities, do not suffice. Statistical probabilities depend on the quality of the underlying evidence, and here our ignorance of the incidence of battlefield mortality, burials at Leicester friary, and scoliosis among the aristocracy, to name just three, drastically reduce the likelihood. Until identification is certain, any scientific tests should be regarded as capable of supporting or refuting this identification.

A forensic reconstruction of the corpse's face in life was also commissioned. Richard III is well-known from Tudor descriptions and portraits to have possessed a white, drawn face, dark-brown hair and hazel or green eyes. The head created by the reconstruction bore so striking a resemblance to Richard III as depicted in his portraits that it was greeted enthusiastically by Philippa Langley among others as the face of Richard III. When the image was superimposed on the portraits there was an exact match. Deductions from his facial appearance were made: Richard was not unhandsome; this was not the face of a psychopath or murderer. Such reconstructions, of course, are modern interpretations of the evidence. Developed originally to identify modern-day murder victims, techniques have moved on from the familiar sticking of pegs into a cast of the skull, which depended heavily on estimates of soft issue and the experience of the technician, to computerised 3D simulations. This work was undertaken by Professor Caroline Wilkinson, professor of Craniofacial Identification at the University of Dundee. She had seen a portrait as a child, but claimed not to be influenced by it.

But the bones by themselves lead only so far: whether the subject was clean-shaven, bearded, or bald, ruddy in complexion or pale, a blonde or brunette, red- or black-haired, blue-eyed or hazel, cannot be deduced from the skull alone. These details, dress and styling were therefore added from the portraits by Janice Aitken, digital artist at Dundee University. No wonder the likeness was so good! Such dependence on the portraits corrupted Wilkinson's and Aitken's reconstruction and renders it derivative, not independent. Indeed this type of contamination might be argued to be necessary. Given that Richard's appearance in his portraits is universally known, not to produce a match might have discredited in the public eye not only the identification of Richard III but the whole of this experimental technique, with possible perilous effects among jurors for forensic identifications in modern cases.

This gap in evidence could be bridged however, declared Sir Alec Jeffreys, the world-renowned professor of Genetics at Leicester University. By tracing Richard III's genome from the bones, the colour of the king's hair and eyes could be established.[16] When this was first reported, the present author realised that such a result could not *prove* the bones belonged to Richard III (though it would be yet another piece of supporting evidence) but could *disprove* it, if it showed the dark-eyed and black-haired king to be blonde or red-haired. Whether he shaved, grew a beard, or was bald would not emerge. The results of the DNA investigation did indeed produce this result: Richard III was blonde and blue-eyed in contradiction to the portraits. Not to identify the bones as Richard's, however, was not an acceptable conclusion for the team. They pre-empted criticism ahead of their announcement by arguing firstly that the portraits were deficient, selecting out of many surviving copies that portrait belonging to the Society of Antiquaries as most compatible with the DNA colouring, and by stating that many children start fair and darken with age. This is perfectly true – witness the present author, his siblings, uncle, cousins, and nieces – but in no case have they darkened to the extent of the portrait. Moreover, eye colour does not change. Nevertheless, the team asserts a 77 per cent probability that the corpse was blond.[17] The result ought to be evidence that the bones are probably *not* those of Richard III, but predestination by DNA, in the eyes of the team, takes precedence over contemporary evidence. A 77 per cent probability allows for 23 per cent exceptions: the show remains on the road.

Fortunately for the Leicester team, the DNA did survive intact, uncorrupted and uncontaminated, making possible modern comparisons with modern descendants of the Yorkists. Here was the chance to prove beyond reasonable doubt that the bones are those of Richard III. If demonstrated to belong to a Plantagenet violently slain between these dates who was descended in the female line from Cecily Duchess of York or her direct ancestresses, then Richard was almost the only possible candidate.

Unfortunately, the tests failed.

No match was produced between the bones and the Somersets on the Y chromosome test.[18] If a match had been achieved, the Leicester team would unquestionably have claimed this evidence that the bones were those of a male Plantagenet as further proof that they belonged to Richard III. That they did not tally, on the same basis, is evidence that the bones are not Richard's. The bones cannot belong to a male Plantagenet, not the last Plantagenet king, as has always been claimed.

Only the mitochondrial DNA test worked. This proves the kinship of the modern individuals to the bones, not (repeat, not) to Richard III, whose identity with the bones is not proven by this test. Extremely thorough tests recently carried out on the mitochondrial DNA have established a relationship between two living relatives (Michael Ibsen and Wendy Duldig) eighteen generations down the family tree and the bones. The assertion of the Leicester team that the bones are 99.999 per cent certain to be those of Richard III was just that, assertion.[19] Any male sharing a maternal ancestress in the direct female line could qualify. If so, these bones are not proven to belong to Richard III. That the Leicester team also produced considerable evidence that none of Richard's known relatives in the maternal line were killed at Bosworth is not relevant because it is not established that the bones belonged to anyone killed in 1485 at Bosworth. Apart from the hypothesis that they belonged to Richard III, the only dating evidence is the radiocarbon dating, which produces a bracket of 1450–1540 at its widest, within which 1485 falls. Richard III is eligible on dating grounds, but so are many others. The whole of the Wars of the Roses falls between these dates. Anybody slain at any battle between the First Battle of St Albans in 1455 and the battles of Flodden and Spurs (Guinegate) in 1513 could qualify. There are plenty of qualified descendants of Richard's maternal ancestresse whose graves are unknown, from Thomas Lord Egremont (1460) and Richard Perry (1461), to John Earl of Lincoln (1487), who could count. Improbably even Richard de la Pole, White Rose of York, slain at Pavia in 1525, could have been shipped home. Indeed, anybody who suffered the reported injuries outside battle, in a skirmish, brawl, or ambush, could count. We cannot know if any of these suffered from scoliosis.

The high-blown assertions of proof should therefore be shelved, for now. Unfortunately the Leicester team presumed the bones were Richard's and set out only to prove that without considering other possibilities. Excellent though their research appears to be, their conclusions cannot be regarded as impartial, independent, or open-ended. When the results of the Y chromosome test were negative, the Leicester team rejected them. Astonishingly, Professor Kevin Schűrer ignored the significance of the negative finding: 'The fact that we have a break means just that we have a break – it doesn't mean that the skeleton isn't Richard.'[20] As Pro-Vice-Chancellor for Research and Enterprise at the University of Leicester, Schűrer here allows his commitment (and consequently the university's commitment) to the identification of the bones as Richard III to take precedence over the findings of the scientific investigation and his objectivity as a historian. Schűrer's historical expertise anyway lies in areas irrelevant to this study, in modern history and especially the census. The team desperately needed an expert in the medieval aristocracy.[21]

Faced by this negative finding, the team resorted as explanation, apparently instantly, casually and without forethought, for a break in paternity because of illegitimacy in one of the lines. Dr Turi King (the project manager) stated the statistical probability of such undetected illegitimacy is quite high. The data underpinning her assertion cannot be drawn from medieval evidence. One such hiatus must explain the different Y chromosome results for two branches of the Somerset family.[22] However, unsubstantiated slurs of this kind were commonplace in the late Middle Ages. It is highly unlikely that in 1342 John of Gaunt, the Lancastrian patriarch, was the son of Queen Philippa of Hainault (d. 1369) by a Flemish butcher, fairly unlikely that Richard of Conisborough (d. 1415) – grandfather of Richard III – was the son of Duchess Isabella de Padilla by the serial seducer John Holland (k. 1400),[23] almost inconceivable that Prince Edward of Lancaster (k. 1471) was not the son of Henry VI or that Edward IV was the son of a French archer. A mix up is possible in the Beaufort family in the

1370s, when Katherine Swynford was bearing both her Swinford and Beaufort sons,[24] or much later, when virtually nothing is known of the relationship between Edmund Duke of Somerset (ex. 1471) and Joan Hill. The illegitimacy hypothesis at present is undocumented speculation. King's statistics about the incidence of paternity breaks within marriages are not based on evidence from the aristocracy in the late medieval English cultural environment at this time and such statistics anyway are never definitive – there is always the exception to prove the rule. Similarly, the team insist from the DNA evidence that Richard was blond with blue eyes in his youth is in direct contradiction of the well-known portraits.[25] The DNA evidence at five hundred years' remove is not superior to hard evidence from the time.

The current position is therefore that the identification of the bones with Richard III is not established. Indeed, the identification with Richard III is more unlikely than likely. This is a considerable nuisance to researchers like the present author, since it impedes deductions from the findings and more effective use of the Tudor evidence which up to now Ricardians have successfully barred. That is for now. It is a real shame that the conclusions drawn by the Leicester team fall so far short of their excellent research. Their commitment to a particular result and their search for public acclaim was allowed to override appropriate scholarly caution. What should have been a model of multidisciplinary academic collaboration faltered in the final stretch. Decisions about the reburial of the king and the participation of the archbishops are somewhat premature. All is not lost. As long as researchers do not accept the Leicester team's claim that all the work is done, there remain other lines of inquiry to pursue, most obviously matching the DNA of Richard's siblings to the bones. That, however, may be even more difficult than hitherto, since the Leicester team could not resist the temptation of extrapolating from their illegitimacy hypothesis an impugnment of the legitimacy of the Lancastrian kings, Yorkist kings, Tudor and all subsequent monarchs down to today. How right was Queen Elizabeth

II to refuse permission to test the Yorkist royals at St George's Chapel Windsor and how right was the current Duke of Beaufort to decline the test himself! The greatest danger for future understanding is that the Leicester case is accepted, so that funding and research stops before conclusive proof either way can be assembled.

This story, therefore, is not yet over and will continue for some time. This discussion will certainly be overtaken by new contributions before the publication of this book. The debate can be settled, more or less conclusively, quite simply. Comparison of the corpse's DNA with that of a much closer relative than seventeen generations and many centuries away could achieve this. It is known where in Fotheringhay church his father and elder brother Edmund were reinterred by Queen Elizabeth. The burial places are known of Richard's siblings Edward IV and Anne Duchess of Exeter at St George's Chapel, Princess Mary, Prince George, and Anne St Leger at Windsor, and Elizabeth Duchess of Suffolk at North Wingfield. Several bodies have been moved, which may create problems. Even if Edward IV was a bastard, he shared his mother with Richard. The difficulty is in gaining permission to exhume and forensically examine remains. If Queen Elizabeth II and St George's Chapel are understandably opposed to the disinterring of royal ancestors to test out current theories,[26] how much more opposed will they be now that the Leicester team have flung around wild assertions of bastardy at all and sundry? Even Richard III realised that he could not bastardise the dead. The best bet, therefore, is comparison with Elizabeth at North Wingfield. If a match is found with the bones, the identification is almost proved. But if not, will the result be accepted?

The Family of Richard III Today

Richard III, of course, has no descendants – all his known children died childless – but he has nephews and nieces distanced from him by many generations, many times his great-nephews and nieces. Michael Ibsen and Wendy Duldig are separated from him by eighteen generations. Each had two parents, four grandparents, eight great-grandparents and so on, 131,068 great-great-great-great-great-great-great-great-great-great-great-great-great-great-great-great-great-grandparents (sixteen greats) to the generation of Richard III's sister Anne Duchess of Exeter, only three generations in common. Writing early in 1907, the Marquis of Ruvigny and Raineval calculated that there were 53,000 living or recently living descendants of Richard III's siblings Edward IV, George Duke of Clarence, and Anne Duchess of Exeter. 'The Exeter volume contains the names of some 25,052 living (or very lately living) descendants of the Duchess of Exeter,' wrote Ruvigny. The index for his Anne of Exeter volume alone contained 3,200 surnames. He had found 11,723 descendants of Edward IV and 17,265 of Clarence. Many, of course, were the same, due to intermarriage: one individual occurred fifteen times. Clarence's line was markedly less interbred, because more plebeian, than the others. Ruvigny presumed there were no descendants of Edward IV's daughter Cecily and the de la Poles, both doubtful propositions.[27] More than a century later, four generations on from the present author's grandfather, who featured in the Exeter volume, each should have sixteen times as many ancestors – a total of 848,000 each and cumulatively much more than the population of England at the time. That, of course, is because, as Ruvigny pointed out, there was a lot of interbreeding, as most people at all times marry people they know from within their class. Aristocrats married aristocrats. This is how it is possible not to be descended in this way at all while others, like the present author, are descended several times. Several hundred thousand people can claim to be as closely related to Richard III as it is possible to be without being descendants, of which there are none. Indeed, so many are descended in this way that such trickles of diluted royal blood are commonplace and scarcely worthy of remark.

This point was made to the thirty members of the Plantagenet Alliance who styled themselves Richard's descendants – his closest relatives. All, of course, are related by blood, by consanguinity: affinity is not regarded as relevant. While admitting they were a tiny minority of similarly related people, they asserted that York rather than Leicester was his spiritual home and pursued a judicial review of the decision to inter him at Leicester Cathedral rather than York Minster. '"Who do we think we are?", says Vanessa Roe, the group's spokesperson. "We don't think we are anyone – we know who we are. We are the collateral [non-direct] descendants of Richard III. We speak on behalf of him. The only people who can speak on behalf of him."'[28] They were right that Richard did not wish to be buried at Leicester, the heartland of his Lancastrian enemies and home, in Newark College, a Lancastrian mausoleum, or in a friary church that he had probably never visited. Medieval people did think about the end of their extremely transitory lives and planned their funerals at much earlier ages than we do today. Most children were buried where they dropped. As Richard grew up, the obvious place for his final resting place was the Yorkist mausoleum at Fotheringhay in Northamptonshire where his father and brother Edmund were interred in 1476, and thereafter perhaps Barnard Castle chapel in County Durham or even Middleham parish church in Yorkshire, at both of which he was licensed to found a college in 1478. That implies that Richard rejected options provided by his wife at her family mausolea: with her father, Warwick the Kingmaker, and paternal grandfather, Richard Earl of Salisbury (d. 1460), at Bisham Priory (Berks.); with her maternal grandfather, Richard Beauchamp, Earl of Warwick (d. 1439), at the Beauchamp Chapel at Warwick; or her maternal grandmother, Isabel Despenser, Countess of Warwick and Worcester (d. 1439), at Tewkesbury Abbey; or with her great-grandfather (and his grandfather) Ralph Neville, Earl of Westmorland (d. 1425), at the Neville college at Staindrop (Durh.). Edward IV may have offered Richard a space at his new chapel of St George at Windsor when Richard also endowed it. Once king, of course, everything changed. Windsor remained an option – he moved the sainted King Henry VI there – or Westminster Abbey, where he buried his queen in what may have been intended as a temporary tomb. The problem with Westminster was that it lacked the space for a grand royal monument or chantry chapel, a problem that Henry VII was to resolve by demolishing the existing Lady Chapel and constructing the vast existing Henry VII chapel. At York Minster Richard founded a college to dwarf all previous chantries, for a hundred priests, initially scattered around the existing buildings. Richard never finished – and indeed scarcely begun – his colleges at Barnard Castle, Middleham and York and so his plans for them remain obscure. No will of Richard III was proved or survives.[29] Neither the Plantagenet Alliance, nor anybody else, knows for sure where Richard wished to lie. Death at Bosworth passed the choice to Henry VII: determining Richard's resting place was a fruit of victory.

Ruvigny's research was inevitably incomplete. Naturally, he relied on the work of previous genealogists who had relied on existing genealogies and heraldic visitations of the sixteenth to eighteenth centuries relating principally to top families. *The Complete Peerage* and *Burke's Peerage, Baronetage and Knightage*, now in its 107th edition, are in this tradition. Early non-inheriting children, younger sons and especially daughters and their daughters, and of course bastards may have been overlooked. Moreover, tracing all descendants when they were born outside the aristocracy in the era before parish registers and the IGI (International Genealogical Index) was difficult, if not impossible. Regarding Clarence's line, for instance, which plunged below the aristocracy sooner than the others, Ruvigny gave up on two of the five children of Margaret Pole: 'It is probable that numerous descendants of his still exist, but the author has been unable to trace them further than the beginning of the eighteenth century.'[30] Presumably this was because too many of them were too humble to be easily traced, which suggests that the total descendants today should be inflated by two-thirds.

Mitochondrial DNA is different from general DNA. It differs because it is transmitted only in the direct female line, from mother to daughter to granddaughter. Whereas Michael Ibsen and Wendy Duldig have double the number of ancestors in each generation, only one line out of 2, 4, 8, 16, 32, 64, 128 and so on represent the mitochondrial line. Mitochondrial DNA drastically diminishes the numbers of those sharing it. The incidence of any particular type depends of course on how many maternal lines there are. Richard had two sisters who bore daughters, only one of whom is known to have bred (Anne). However, he had six aunts sharing the same mother (Joan Beaufort), who as daughter of Katherine Swinford is believed to be the only breeding daughter of the three daughters of Payn Roet: Isabella was a nun, and the daughter of Philippa Chaucer also became a nun. Any female issue of Mrs Roet, her mother, grandmother, and so on should also have shared the same mitochondrial DNA, but it cannot be tracked back further because Mrs Roet is unidentified. If of English descent, such unidentified issue (and issue of her direct female ancestresses) presumably lived and bred in England and descendants are most probably located in Britain. If a Hainaulter like her husband, which is quite likely, such descendants are probably Belgian and can be discounted. That Mrs Roet has not been identified does not mean that she never will be: Laura Tompkins' magnificent work on Alice Perrers has shown how obscure bourgeois can be identified.[31]

Schűrer identified 144 such people around this date. Not all lived at the same time and few were males slain in battle. This total is likely to be incomplete due to poor recording of various types of non-inheriting daughters, who scarcely mattered at the time. At least there should be no bastards. Tracking the transmission of mitochondrial DNA to the present is much more difficult. Most genealogists in all periods focus on the direct male line and drop collaterals: mitochondrial DNA almost always passes through collaterals. The surname changes in every generation: in Michael Ibsen's case from St Leger to Manners to Constable to Babthorpe to Belsasyse to Slingsby to Talbot to Yelverton to Calthorpe to Gough Calthorpe to Spooner to Vansittart Neale to Frere, Stokes, and Brown; for Duldig from St Leger to Manners to Constable to Craythorne to Maltby to Wentworth to Grantham to Holt to Winstanley to Truman to Read to Villebois to Plunket to Gardiner to Lysaght to Morre and to Whitehorne. When checking – and Schürer, heroically, did check – the more aristocratic early generations are much more recorded in the herald's visitations than rustics through parish registers. The lower orders are less well recorded than the aristocracy, rustics than townsfolk, and daughters than sons. The descent of manors and other landed property which is documented in records, county histories, etc., only passes via daughters in default of sons. The early genealogies focus on the inheriting line: the direct male line or line by primogeniture. Often they included all offspring at the date of writing, but when continued pursued one line only and ignored the descendants of those who did not inherit.[32] Mitochondrial genealogy is therefore exceptionally difficult: congratulations once again to John Ashdown-Hill. Many mitochondrial chains were broken when marriages were childless or ended in males – Michael Ibsen is an example – but it is likely that other ladies than Catherine Constable (*née* Manners) bore several daughters who themselves mothered daughters. The Leicester team declares the haplogroup of mitochondrial DNA of the bones to be rare: it is not among the 26,000 European haplogroups or 2,000 British haplogroups recorded to date.[33] Their sample is too small and probably skewed. Rarity in this case means that it does not occur in their highly selective sample, perhaps because such people are seldom forensically tested and are socially disinclined to commit testable crimes. How many unbroken female lines derive from Richard's siblings and maternal ancestresses is quite unknown at present, but more probably is in the dozens or scores than the tens of thousands.

If Richard's family has never been more extensive, it is unlikely that Richard would have appreciated it. He was a king with little time or consideration for quite close collateral relatives, several of whom he killed. The collateral relatives, however, are pleased to discover their royal connections. Joy and Michael Ibsen were obviously thrilled. So were the Plantagenet Alliance, who thought their royal ancestry gave them public standing and a public role. The whole debate about the bones has made millions of people more aware about Richard III and his history, about the potential of archaeology, and about such sciences as genetics. What a pity therefore that, like *Time Team*, what is popular and televisual is not the best archaeology and that the scientists have overplayed their case. Let us hope that it does not all end in tears. An unfortunate by-product has been the doubt cast on the legitimacy of the royal family, indeed all the royal families dating back to 1352. Instead of responding to the negative Y chromosome test by admitting that they had got it wrong, the Leicester team asserted that there must be a paternity break: in the line of the Somerset family; the line of the Beauforts, impugning the title of Henry VII and all subsequent monarchs; perhaps in the parentage of John of Gaunt, which impugns the title of the Lancastrian kings and all monarchs from Henry VII on; or in the parentage of Richard Earl of Cambridge, which impugns the legitimacy of all monarchs since the Yorkists. All these suppositions are speculative and mostly unprovable, even if more bones are located, exhumed, and tested. Yet it is that which made the headlines. Exonerating the most vilified of kings has strangely enveloped all his successors in scandal and cast doubt over their rights to reign. All those kinsfolk who rejected Richard and his right to reign and all their descendants find themselves involuntarily tied to their disgraced relative. His disgrace and scandal is shared by his huge posthumous family.

NOTES

List of Abbreviations

Annales	'Annales Rerum Anglicarum', *Letters and Papers Illustrative of the Wars of the English in France*, ed. J. Stevenson, Rolls Series (1864), ii (2).
Arrivall	*The Arrivall of Edward IV*, ed. J. O. Halliwell, Camden Society i (1836)
BL	The British Library, London
Crowland	*The Crowland Chronicle Continuations 1459–86*, ed. J. C. Cox and N. Pronay (1986)
E.H.R.	*English Historical Review*
GEC	*The Complete Peerage*, ed. H. V. Gibbs et al. (13 vols. London 1910–59)
Hammond & Sutton	*Richard III: The Road to Bosworth Field*, ed. P. Hammond and A. Sutton (London, 1985)
Hicks, *Anne Neville*	M. Hicks, *Anne Neville, Queen to Richard III* (Stroud, 2005)
Hicks, *Clarence*	M. Hicks, *False, Fleeting, Perjur'd Clarence: George Duke of Clarence 1449–78*, rev. edn (Bangor, 1992)
Hicks, *Edward V*	M. Hicks, *Edward V: The Prince in the Tower* (Stroud, 2003)
Hicks, *Richard III*	M. Hicks, *Richard III* (Stroud, 2000)
Hicks, *Wars*	M. Hicks, *The Wars of the Roses* (2010)
Lander	J. R. Lander, *Crown and Nobility 1450–1509* (1976)
Mancini	D. Mancini, *The Usurpation of Richard III*, ed. C. A. J. Armstrong, 2nd edn (Oxford, 1969)

More   T. More, *History of King Richard III*, ed. R.
                    Sylvester (New Haven, Conn., 1963)
Paston L & P   *Paston Letters and Papers of the Fifteenth*
                    Century, ed. N. Davis, 2 vols (Oxford, 1971–76)
Ruvigny   M. A. H. D. H. de la Caillemotte de Ruvigny,
                    Marquis of Ruvigny and Raineval, *The*
                    Plantagenet Roll of the Blood Royal, 3 volumes
                    (Edinburgh, 1905–08)
TNA   The National Archives, Kew
THRS   *Transactions of the Royal Historical Society*
Vergil   *Three Books of Polydore Vergil's English*
                    History, ed. H. Ellis, Camden Society xxxix
                    (1844)
Waurin   J. Waurin, *Recueil des Chroniques et Anchienne*
                    Istoires de la Grant Bretaigne, ed. W. & E. L. C.
                    P. Hardy, Rolls Series (London, 1891), v

1 *Richard III in Context*

1. T. More, *History of Richard III* (New Haven, Conn., 1963); W. Shakespeare, 'History of King Richard III', *The Complete Works*, ed. P. Ackroyd (2006); J. Gairdner, *History of Richard III* (1878); A. L. Rowse, *Bosworth Field and the Wars of the Roses* (1966).
2. E.g. by Pietro Carmeliano, Thomas Langton, and John Rows, M. Hicks, *Richard III* (2000), 207–08.
3. J. Potter, *Good King Richard?* (1985).
4. R. E. Horrox, *Richard III: A Study of Service* (Cambridge, 1989).

2 *Types of Families*

1. C. D. Ross, 'Some "Servants and Lovers" of Richard III in His Youth', *Richard III: Crown and People*, ed. J. Petre (1985), 146–48.
2. *Crowland*, 174–75.
3. There is a mass of literature on the family; see bibliographical essay below for works used here.
4. P. D. Clarke, 'English Royal Marriages and the Papal Penitentiary in the Fifteenth Century', *E.H.R.* cxx (2005), 1025.
5. *GEC* iii.259.
6. See below, chs 5, 7; M. Hicks, Anne Neville, 206.

7. I am indebted to Mrs Victoria Sood for this information.

8. M. Hicks, 'Heirs and Non-Heirs: Perceptions of the English Nobility *c.* 1300–1500, *Meeting and Breaking the Rules: Succession in Medieval Europe, c. 1000–c. 1600,* ed. Frédérique Lachaud and Michael Penman (Brepols, Turnhout) esp. 196; 'English Monasteries as Repositories of Ancestral Memory', *Monuments and Monumentality Across Medieval and Early Modern Europe,* ed. M. Penman (Stamford, 2013).

9. T. B. Pugh and C. D. Ross, 'The English Baronage and the Income Tax of 1436', *Bulletin of the Institute of Historical Research* xxvi (1953), 7–8; M. Hicks, 'Cement or Solvent? Kinship and Politics in Late Medieval England: The Case of the Nevilles', *History* lxxxiii (1998).

10. More, 8.

11. *Somerset County Gazette,* 28 August 2014, 9.

12. Ruvigny, *passim.*

13. E.g. *Handbook to the Maude Roll,* ed. A. Wall (Auckland, 1919).

14. M. Hicks, 'Edward IV's *Brief Treatise* and the Treaty of Picquigny 1475', *Historical Research* 83 (2010), 256–57, A. Crawford, *The Yorkists: The History of a Dynasty* (London, 2007), 44.

15. See below, ch. 9.

16. K. B. McFarlane, 'Had Edward I a Policy Towards the Earls?', *England in the Fifteenth Century* (1981), 257–58.

17. Notably the resettlement of the Neville of Raby lordships on the offspring of Joan Beaufort, Pugh and Ross, 'Income Tax', 7–8, 17–18.

18. Hicks, *Edward V,* 43–44.

19. D. A. L. Morgan, 'The King's Affinity in the Polity of Yorkist England', *TRHS* 5th ser. xxiii (1973), 18n–19n.

20. R. E. Archer, 'Parliamentary Restoration: John Mowbray and the Dukedom of Norfolk in 1425', *Rulers and Ruled in Late Medieval England,* ed. R. E. Archer and S. Walker (London, 1995), 99–116.

21. M. Bennett, 'Edward III's Entail and the Succession to the Crown', *E.H.R.* cxiii (1998).

22. M. Hicks, 'The Royal Bastards of Medieval England', *Bâtards et la Bâtardise au moyen âge,* ed. A. Marchandisse (Turnhout, 2015). Intriguingly DNA tests on the supposed bones of Richard III suggest that John Beaufort was a Swinford all along: see below, ch. 9.

23. As suggested in M. Hicks, *Wars,* 45.

24. C. Rawcliffe, 'Richard, Duke of York, the King's "Obeisant Liegeman": A New Source of the Protectorates of 1454 and 1455', *Historical Research* lx (1987), 237–38.

25. *PROME* xii, 516–17.
26. C. Given-Wilson, 'Chronicles of the Mortimer Family, c. 1250–1450', *Family and Dynasty in Late Medieval England*, ed. R. Eales and S. Tyas (Donington, 2003), 67–77.
27. See below, ch. 9.

3 Cadet in the House of York

1. W. Dugdale, *Monasticon Anglicanum*, 8 vols (1846), vii.1600–02.
2. P. A Johnson, *Duke Richard of York 1411–60* (Oxford, 1986), 2.
3. A. Hanham, *Richard III and his Earlier Historians 1483–1535* (Oxford, 1975), 120.
4. C. Rawcliffe, 'Richard, Duke of York, the King's "Obeisant Liegeman": A New Source of the Protectorates of 1454 and 1455', *Historical Research* lx (1987), 237.
5. Four offspring were born at Fotheringhay.
6. *Richard III*, ed. P. Tudor-Craig (National Portrait Gallery, 1973), 26.
7. Rawcliffe 'Obeisant Liegeman', 237.
8. Hanham, *Earlier Historians*, 120; More, 7.
9. Johnson, *Duke Richard*, 119–20.
10. Why had Duke Richard not used his own name for one of his seven previous sons?
11. C. T. Allmand, *Lancastrian Normandy 1415–50* (1983), 62. York had no known bastard called Edmund.
12. T. B. Pugh, 'The Magnates, Knights and Gentry', *Fifteenth-Century England 1399–1509: Studies in Politics and Society*, ed. S. B. Chrimes, C. D. Ross and R. A. Griffiths (Manchester, 1972), 118n.
13. *Crowland*, 170–71.
14. T. B. Pugh, *Henry V and the Southampton Plot of 1415* (Gloucester, 1988), 88–89; J. J. N. Palmer, 'England, France, the Papacy and the Flemish Succession', *Journal of Medieval History* ii (1976), 339–64.
15. A. Goodman and D. A. L. Morgan, 'The Yorkist Claim to the Throne of Castile', *Journal of Medieval History* xii (1985), 61–9; M. Hicks, 'Edward IV's *Brief Treatise* and the Treaty of Picquigny of 1475, *Historical Research* lxxxiii (2010), 256–57. Duke Edmund was not included in the Treaty of Bayonne.
16. Pugh, *Southampton Plot*, 90; *The Times*, 4 December 2014. Presumably Richard inherited a third of the children's third share

of the chattels of his father Edmund Duke of York anyway, so his absence from his father's will need not be significant.

17. A Sutton and L. Visser-Fuchs, *The Reburial of Richard Duke of York, 21–30 July 1476* (1996), 2.

18. Dugdale, *Monasticon*, vii.1600–02; Given-Wilson, 'Mortimer Chronicles', 67–77.

19. Lander, 96–97.

20. M. Hicks, 'Three Unusual Features of Richard Neville's Succession to the Earldoms of Warwick in 1449–50', www. *MappingtheMedievalCountryside.ac.uk*.

21. M. Hicks, 'Cement or Solvent? Kinship and Politics in Late Medieval England: The Case of the Nevilles', *History* lxxxiii (1998).

22. Lander, 97.

23. M. Hicks (Oxford, 1998), 16 & ch. 3.

24. Rawcliffe, 'Obeisant Liegeman', 238–39. The recipient is corrected by T. B. Pugh, 'Richard, Duke of York and the Rebellion of Henry Holand, Duke of Exeter, May 1454', *Historical Research* lxiii (1990), 256.

4 Edward IV's New Family in the 1460s

1. TNA PSO 1/64/41. Richard's majority is deduced from his actual officiation on a commission of oyer and terminer in autumn 1468, *CPR 1467–77*.

2. Philippa Langley & Michael Jones, *The Search for Richard III: The King's Grave* (London, 2013), 74.

3. He created him Earl of Lincoln in 1467, *GEC* vii.688, which dates his birth to around 1462.

4. Hicks, *Clarence*, 6–7.

5. See e.g. M. Hicks, 'Lancastrian Dynasty and Lancastrian Dynasties: The Misplaced Priorities of Henry IV', *The Lancastrian Legacy: Re-Evaluating the Kingship of Henry VI*, ed. D. Grummitt (forthcoming); 'A Failure in Foresight: The Lancastrian Kings and the Lancastrian Dukes', ed. P. Fleming and D. Newton (forthcoming).

6. *Plumpton Letters and Papers of the Fifteenth Century*, ed. J. Kirby, Camden 5th ser viii (1997), 38; M. K. Jones, 'Richard III and the Stanleys', *Richard III and the North*, ed. R. E. Horrox (Hull, 1986), 39–40; M. Hicks, 'The 1468 Statute of Livery', *Historical Research* xliv (1991), 20.

7. Hammond & Sutton, 36; 145.

8. *Issues of the Exchequer*, ed. F. Devon (1837), 490.

9. Hicks, *Warwick*, 230–31.

10. *Waurin*, v.458–59.

11. *Annales*, ii(2).786.

12. For the latest discussion, see Hicks, *Edward V*, 25–37.

13. *Ibid.*, 38–48.

14. When bestowed on Katherine, Buckingham was a royal ward.

15. *The House of Commons 1386–1421*, ed. J. S. Roskell, L. Clark and C. Rawcliffe, 4 vols. (Stroud, 1993), iii.324–27.

16. Hicks, *Edward V*, 134.

17. J. Lander, *Crown and Nobility*, 110; *Annales*, 783–6.

18. *Annales*, ii (2), 785. Although the couple had several children, Buckingham allegedly resented his Wydeville relatives: *Mancini*, 76–77.

19. *Annales*, ii (2).783–6.

20. Hicks, *Clarence*, 23; M. Hicks, 'The Changing Role of the Wydevilles in Yorkist Politics to 1483', *Patronage, Pedigree and Power in Later Medieval England*, ed. C. D. Ross (Gloucester, 1979), 67–69.

21. Hicks, *Clarence*, 26.

22. Hicks, *Edward V*, 29–30.

23. Hicks, *Anne Neville*, 155–59.

5 Brothers at Odds: Gloucester, Clarence and Edward IV, 1469–1478

1. *Paston L & P* i.162.

2. Lander, 110–11.

3. *Mancini*, 60–63.

4. Hicks, *Clarence*, 135–36.

5. M. Hicks, '1468 Statute of Livery', *Historical Research* lix (1991), 18–20.

6. Hicks, *Clarence*, 33.

7. Jones, 'The Stanleys', 39–41.

8. Eleanor Cobham's sorcery conviction in 1441 involved her divorce *de mensa et thoro* from Humphrey Duke of Gloucester. On that precedent, once divorced Edward could not have remarried or fathered legitimate children.

9. Hicks, Clarence, 45–50; *Edward V*, 51–4

10. *Arrivall*, 12.

11. *Ibid.*, 10.

12. L. Visser-Fuchs, 'Edward IV's *Memoir on Paper* to Charles, Duke of

Burgundy: The so-called "Short Version of the *Arrivall*"', *Nottingham Medieval Studies* xxxvi (1992), 172–73.

13. *Arrivall*, 12; *Crowland*, 124–25.

14. More, 8.

15. *Crowland* 132–33.

16. *Ibid.*, 132–33.

17. M. Hicks, *Richard III as Duke of Gloucester: A Study in Character*, Borthwick Paper 70 (1986).

18. For the story that follows, see M. Hicks, 'Descent, Partition and Extinction: The "Warwick Inheritance"', *Bulletin of the Institute of Historical Research* li (1979); Hicks, *Clarence*, ch. 3; Hicks, *Anne Neville*, ch. 4.

19. *Paston L & P* i.447.

20. Crowland, 132–33.

21. Hanham, *Earlier Historians*, 121.

22. M. Hicks, 'What Might Have Been: George Neville, Duke of Bedford, 1465–83: His Identity and Significance', *The Ricardian* 95 (1986); 'Richard Lord Latimer, Richard III, and the "Warwick Inheritance"', *The Ricardian* 154 (2001).

23. *Crowland*, 144–45. The fullest discussion is in Hicks, *Clarence*, ch. 4.

24. *Crowland*, 142–43.

25. *Ibid.*, 139–40. For friary, read priory, A. Sutton and L. Visser-Fuchs, *The Reburial of Richard Duke of York, 21–30 July 1476* (1996).

26. Sutton & Visser-Fuchs, *Reburial, passim.*

27. Hicks, *Clarence*, 129–31.

28. *Crowland*, 142–43.

29. *Ibid.*

30. Hicks, *Anne Neville*, 152.

31. The promotions of Buckingham and Suffolk were very brief.

32. *GEC* xii (2).395.

33. Hicks, *Clarence*, 127–29.

34. Hicks, *Clarence*; 'The Beauchamp Trust 1439–87', *Bulletin of the Institute of Historical Research* liii (1981), 141–42.

35. Crowland, 146–47.

6 Brothers in Law: The Evolution of the Royal Family During Edward IV's Second Reign

1. L. Visser-Fuchs and A. Sutton, *Royal Funerals of the House of York at Windsor* (2005).
2. Hicks, *Edward V*, 129–30. The justifiable dissatisfaction of these loyal subjects was exploited by Richard III in 1483.
3. *Ibid.*, 67.
4. *Crowland*, 148–49.
5. *GEC* v.216n.
6. Both were minors. George was Anne's first cousin/Gloucester's first cousin once removed. Richard was Anne's second cousin and first cousin once removed and Gloucester's first cousin once removed.
7. *Mancini*, 74–75.
8. *Mancini*, 62–63.
9. They had married in 1466, so her mother's divorce, while bastardising her, did not destroy her prospects.
10. Hicks, *Edward V*, 114; *Clarence*, 135.

7 The Self-Destruction of the House of York, 1483–1485

1. *Crowland*, 148–9.
2. *Excerpta Historica*, ed. S. Bentley (1831) 366sqq.
3. *Mancini*, 69.
4. M. Hicks, 'The Minority of Edward V', *The Royal Minorities of Later Medieval and Early Modern England*, ed. Charles E. Beem (Basingstoke, 2008), 199–200.
5. Hanham, *Earlier Historians*, 118.
6. *Mancini*, 62–63.
7. Hicks, 'Minority', 200–01.
8. *Crowland*, 153.
9. Hicks, *Richard III*, 167–68, 171–73.
10. Hanham, *Earlier Historians*, 119.
11. Hicks, *Richard III*, 190–91.
12. *Crowland*, 174. The English translation (p. 175) is incorrect.
13. Possibly Richard expected the aged cardinal to die (as he did in 1486) before Latimer came of age in 1490 and hoped to secure the latter's wardship and marriage in that window of opportunity.
14. M. Hicks, 'What might have been? George Neville, Duke of Bedford,

1465–83: His Identity and Significance', *The Ricardian* 95 (1986); 'Richard Lord Latimer, Richard III, and the "Warwick Inheritance"', *The Ricardian* 154 (2001), 316, 318.

15. W. E. Hampton, *Memorials of the Wars of the Roses* (Upminster, 1979), 230–31.

16. *Crowland*, 158–59.

17. *Ibid.*, 161–62.

18. Sutton & Hammond, 155–59.

19. *Crowland*, 161–66.

20. Hicks, *Richard III*, 138.

21. Hammond & Sutton, 145.

22. For a fuller discussion, see Hicks, *Edward V*, 176–89.

23. *Crowland*, 162–63; I. Arthurson and N. Kingwell, 'The Proclamation of Henry Tudor as King of England, 3 November 1483', *Historical Research* lxiii (1990), 100–06.

24. *The Parliament Rolls of Medieval England*, ed. C. Given-Wilson, 16 vols (2005), 24.

25. Sutton & Hammond, 166–7.

26. A. Crawford, *The Yorkists. The History of a Dynasty* (2007), 146.

27. R. E. Horrox, *Richard III: A Study of Service* (Cambridge, 1989), 295.

28. *Crowland*, 170–71.

29. *Ibid.*, 174–77.

30. *Ibid.*, 176–77.

31. Hicks, 'Beauchamp Trust', 145; Corpus Christi, Twyne Transcripts, 203–04; Hicks, 'Latimer', 319.

32. Hicks, 'Latimer', 317–18.

33. *Crowland*, 170–71.

34. R. A. Griffiths and R. S. Thomas, *The Making of the Tudor Dynasty* (Gloucester, 1985), 131.

35. *Crowland*, 179, 181; *Vergil*, 212, 218.

36. Crawford, *Yorkists*, 146.

37. Discussion of this topic is based on Hicks, *Anne Neville*, 194–210.

8 Richard's Heirs

1. P. Clark, 'English Royal Marriages and the Papal Penitentiary in the Fifteenth Century', *E.H.R.* cxx (2005), 1025–26.

2. It is difficult to believe that Henry VIII's sexual shenanigans resulted

only in Henry FitzRoy, Duke of Richmond, but no other bastards were acknowledged.

3. M. K. Jones and M. Underwood, *The King's Mother: Lady Margaret Beaufort, Countess of Richmond and Derby* (Cambridge, 1992), pedigrees 2 and 4.

4. Most of these are discussed further below.

5. Hicks, *Wars*, 250.

6. *Crowland*, 194–95.

7. See C. Weightman, *Margaret of York, Duchess of Burgundy, 1446–1503* (Gloucester, 1989).

8. *Crowland*, 170–71.

9. Hicks, *Wars*, 259.

10. M. Hicks, 'The Yorkshire Rebellion of 1489 Reconsidered', *Northern History* xxiv (1986); I. Arthurson, 'The Rising of 1497: A Revolt of the Peasantry?', *People, Politics and the Community*, ed. C. Richmond and J. Rosenthal (Gloucester, 1987).

11. Hicks, *Wars*, 228, 230.

12. More, 8.

13. D. A. L. Morgan, 'The King's Affinity in the Polity of Yorkist England', *TRHS* 5th ser. xxiii (1973), 7.

14. S. B. Chrimes, *Henry VII* (1970), 85.

15. Jones & Underwood, *King's Mother*, 134–35.

16. *GEC* xii.ii.448–49.

17. Hicks, *Edward V*, 30.

18. *GEC* xii.ii.846. The credit for recognising the significance belongs to John Ashdown-Hill.

19. C. H. Williams, 'The Rebellion of Humphrey Stafford in 1486', *E.H.R.* xliii (1928), 181–89.

20. The best account is still M. Bennett, *Lambert Simnel* (Gloucester, 1987).

21. M. Hicks, *Richard III and his Rivals* (1991), 333.

22. GEC xi.253–54n.

23. Ruvigny, *The Anne of Exeter Volume*, 8nn.

24. P. Morgan, '"Those were the days": A Yorkist Pedigree Roll', *Estrangement, Enterprise and Education in Fifteenth-Century England*, ed. Michalove, S. and Compton Reeves, A. (Stroud, 1998), 111–16 & plates.

25. *GEC* xii(1) appx I 22–25; ix.220n. Katherine predeceased her husband.

26. Ruvigny, *The Isabel Plantagenet Volume*.

27. Ruvigny, *The Anne of Exeter Volume*.

9 *The Posthumous Life of Richard III*

1. For this summary, see J. Ashdown-Hill, *The Last Days of Richard III* (History Press, Stroud, 2010); P. Langley and M. Jones, *The Search for Richard III. The King's Grave* (John Murray, London, 2013); M. Pitts, *Digging for Richard III: How Archaeology found the King* (Thames and Hudson, London, 2014); M. Morris and R. Buckley, *Richard III: The King under the Car Park* (University of Leicester, rev. edn. Leicester, 2014); A. J. Carson, J. Ashdown-Hill, D. Johnson, W. Johnson, & P. J. Langley, eds., *Finding Richard III: The Official Account of Research by the Retrieval and Reburial Project*, Imprimis Imprimatur, Horstead (2014). Unless otherwise stated, this chapter is based upon these books.

2. TNA C1/206/69.

3. More, 7; Hanham, *Richard III and His Earlier Historians* (Oxford, 1975), 120.

4. Strangely some deductions about Richard's character have been made from the reconstruction of his face.

5. *Crowland*, 180–81; M. Hicks, 'The Second Anonymous Continuation of the Crowland Abbey Chronicles 1459–1486 Revisited', *English Historical Review* xxx (2007).

6. G. Buck, *History of King Richard III*, ed. A. N. Kincaid (Gloucester, 1979); H. Walpole, *Historic Doubts on the Life and Reign of Richard III*, ed. P. Hammond (Gloucester, 1987).

7. A. R. Myers, 'Richard III and Historical Tradition' *History* liii (1968); P. M. Kendall, *Richard III* (London, 1955).

8. L. E. Tanner and W. Wright, 'Recent Investigations regarding the Fate of the Princes in the Tower', *Archaeologia* xxxiv (1934); see also P. W. Hammond and W. J. White, 'The Sons of Edward IV: A Re-Examination on their Deaths and on the Bones in Westminster Abbey', *Richard III, Loyalty, Lordship and Law*, ed. P. Hammond (1986), 104–47.

9. T. Mollason, 'Anne Mowbray and the Princes in the Tower: A Study in Identity', *London Archaeologist* 5 (1987), 258–62.

10. Mitochondrial DNA examination of Margaret of Burgundy's bones at Mechlen failed to produce a match.

11. This discussion derives its scientific explanations in T. E. King *et al.*, 'Identification of the Remains of King Richard III', *New Communications* 5 (2014), 1–8; Ashdown-Hill, Langley and Jones, and Pitts, see note 1.

12. M. Domnall and R. K. Morris, 'The Bones in the Clarence Vault', *Tewkesbury Abbey: History, Art and Architecture*, ed. R. K. Morris and R. Shoesmith (Logaston, 2004), ch. 4.

13. Of course nobody has ever proved this by testing multiple generations. Do mutations never occur? 26,000 European haplogroups suggests they do. The tests on Richard III's bones do support the efficacy of the Leicester mitochondrial test.

14. www.bbc.co.uk/news/science-environment–3028133.

15. www.historyextra.com/news/was-skeleton-found-leicester-car-park-really-richard iii?

16. www.bbc.co.uk/news/uk-england-leicestershire–26142693.

17. www.BBC.co.uk/news/zcience-environment–3028133.

18. *Ibid.*

19. www.bbc.co.uk/news/science-environment–3028133. See my letter in *The Times*, 5 December 2014. The probability ratio is assessed at 6.7 million:1, but of course no geneticist has ever tested 6.7 million people.

20. www.historyextra.com/news/richard-iii-latest-dna-study-%E29680%99.

21. Schűrer's research from published sources on 144 known bearers of the same mitochondrial DNA is competent, but is incomplete and presumes death must occur in 1485.

22. www.bbc.co.uk/news/science-environment-3028133.

23. T. B. Pugh, *Henry V and the Southampton Plot of 1415* (Gloucester, 1988), 90; *The Times*, 3 December 2014.

24. Sir Thomas Swinford had some difficulty in asserting his right to inherit.

25. www.bbc.co.uk/news/science-environment-3028133.

26. www.lovescience.com/4569-richard-iii-fna-controversy.html.

27. Ruvigny, *The Exeter Volume*, vii–viiin; *The Clarence Volume*, v–vii.

28. www.bbc.co.uk/news/uk-england-leicestershire–23929989.

29. www.historyextra.com/feature/five-places-richard-iii-may-have-wanted-to-be-buried-and-none-and-none them-are-leicester.

30. Ruvigny, *The Clarence Volume*, vi.

31. L. Tompkins, 'Alice Perrers and the Goldsmiths' Mistress: New

Evidence concerning the Identity of the Mistress of Edward III', *E.H.R.* (forthcoming).

32. M. Hicks, 'Heirs and Non-Heirs. Perceptions of the English Nobility *c.* 1300–1500', *Meeting and Breaking the Rules: Succession in Medieval Europe,* c. *1000–c. 1600,* ed. Frédérique Lachaud and Michael Penman (Brepols, Turnhout), 191–200.

33. As stated by Turi King on BBC Four's *Inside Science*, 4 December 2014.

BIBLIOGRAPHICAL ESSAY

Unless otherwise stated, all books are published in London. Biographical and genealogical information taken from *GEC, The Complete Peerage of England, etc.*, ed. H. B. Gibbs and others, 12 vols (1910–59) is not separately identified. Many individuals discussed feature in *Oxford Dictionary of National Biography*, 64 vols (2004), www.oxforddnb.com.

The best overview of medieval England down to 1461 is G. L. Harriss, *Shaping the Nation: England 1360–1461* (Oxford, 2005). For the Wars of the Roses I have relied on M. Hicks, *The Wars of the Roses* (2010). Of books on Richard III, there is no end. Most exhilerating is P. M. Kendall, *Richard III* (1955); most accessible D. Hipshon, *Richard III* (Abingdon, 2011); still the best overview C. D. Ross, *Richard III* (1981); most detailed on service R. E. Horrox, *Richard III: A Study of Service* (Cambridge, 1989); fullest on propaganda M. Hicks, *Richard III* (Stroud, 2000). A. J. Pollard, *Richard III and the Princes in the Tower* (Stroud, 1991) is readable and authoritative. Apart from the standard editions, key sources are usefully extracted by K. Dockray, *Richard III: A Reader* (Gloucester, 1988) and collected by P. Hammond and A. Sutton, *Richard III: The Road to Bosworth Field* (London, 1985) and illustrated from the public records by S. Cunningham, *Richard III: A Royal Enigma* (Kew, 2003). Jonathan Hughes assembles a mass of Yorkist propaganda in his *Arthurian Myths and Alchemy: The Kingship of Edward IV* (Stroud, 2002).

1 Richard III in Context & 2 Types of Families

There is a mass of literature on the family. This discussion has been influenced particularly by: R. A. Houlbrooke, *The English Family 1450–1750* (London, 1984); L. Stone, *The Family, Sex and Marriage in England 1500–1800* (London, 1977); P. W. Fleming, *Family and Household in Medieval England* (London, 2001); D. Youngs, *Family and Life-Cycle The Life Cycle in Western Europe*, c. *1300–c. 1500* (Manchester, 2006); and M. Hicks, 'Cement or Solvent? Kinship and Politics in Late Medieval England: The Case of the Nevilles', *History* lxxxiii (1998). On contemporary genealogies, I have drawn on A. Allan, 'Yorkist Propaganda: Pedigree, Prophecy and the "British History" in the Reign of Edward IV', in *Patronage, Pedigree and Power in Later Medieval England*, ed. C. D. Ross (Gloucester, 1979); C. Given-Wilson, 'Chronicles of the Mortimer Family, *c.* 1250–1450', *Family and Dynasty in Late Medieval England*, ed. R. Eales and S. Tyas (Donington, 2003); M. Hicks, 'Heirs and Non-Heirs: Perceptions of the English Nobility *c.* 1300–1500', *Meeting and Breaking the Rules: Succession in Medieval Europe,* c. *1000–c. 1600*, ed. Frédérique Lachaud and Michael Penman (Brepols, Turnhout); M. Hicks, 'English Monasteries as Repositories of Ancestral Memory', *Monuments and Monumentality Across Medieval and Early Modern Europe*, ed. M. Penman (Stamford, 2013). On bastardy, see K. Thomas, 'The Double Standard', *Journal of the History of Ideas* 20 (1959); P. Laslett, *Family Life and Illicit Love in Earlier Generations* (Cambridge, 1976); *Bastardy and its Comparative History*, ed. P. Laslett, R. M. Smith and K. Osterveen (1980); R. E. Helmholz, *Marriage Litigation in Medieval England* (1974); C. Given-Wilson and A. Curteis, *The Royal Bastards of Medieval England* (1984); and M. Hicks, 'The Royal Bastards of Medieval England', *Bâtards et la Bâtardise au moyen âge*, ed. A. Marchandisse (Turnhout, 2015).

3 *Cadet of the House of York*

T. B. Pugh and Paul Johnson are the principal historians of the three dukes of York: T. B. Pugh, *Henry V and the Southampton Plot of 1415* (Southampton, 1988); 'Richard Plantagenet (1411–60), Duke of York, as the King's Lieutenant in France and Ireland', in *Aspects of Late Medieval Government and Society*, ed. J. G. Rowe (Buffalo, Can., 1986); 'The Estates, Finances and Regal Aspirations of Richard Plantagenet (1411–60), Duke of York', *Revolution and Consumption in Late Medieval England*, ed. M. Hicks (Woodbridge, 2001); P. A. Johnson, *Duke Richard of York 1411–60* (Oxford, 1986); see also A. Crawford, *The Yorkists: The History of a Dynasty* (2007). The overall narrative is taken from my *Wars of the Roses* (2010).

4 *Edward IV's New Family in the 1460s*

Modern discussion commenced in 1963 with J. R. Lander, 'Marriage and Politics in the Fifteenth Century: The Nevilles and the Wydevilles', *Crown and Nobility 1450–1509* (1976) and was developed by M. Hicks, 'The Changing Role of the Wydevilles in Yorkist Politics to 1483', *Patronage, Pedigree and Power in Later Medieval England*, ed. C. D. Ross (Gloucester, 1979), in his *False, Fleeting, Perjur'd Clarence: George Duke of Clarence 1449–78*, rev. edn. (Bangor, 1992), and retold and refined in his *Edward V: The Prince in the Tower* (Stroud. 2003). For the discussion of Edward IV's mistresses, bastards and marriage, see Hicks, *Edward V*.

5 *Brothers at Odds: Gloucester, Clarence and Edward IV, 1469–1478*

An overview is provided by M. Hicks, *The Wars of the Roses* (2010). For the second phase of the Wars of the Roses, see also M. Hicks, *False, Fleeting, Perjur'd Clarence: George Duke of Clarence 1449–78*, rev. edn (Bangor, 1992); *Warwick the Kingmaker* (Oxford, 1998), and A. J. Pollard, *Warwick the Kingmaker: Politics, Power and Fame* (2007). For the Warwick inheritance, see M. Hicks, *Richard III and his Rivals* (1991); *Clarence*, ch. 3; *Anne Neville*, ch. 4; and 'Richard Lord Latimer, Richard III, and the "Warwick Inheritance"', *The Ricardian* 154 (2001). For Clarence's fall, see Hicks, *Clarence*, ch. 4.

6 *Brothers in Law: The Evolution of the Royal Family in Edward IV's Second Reign*

This is an understudied area. The development of Richard III's family has been treated by M. Hicks, *Richard III as Duke of Gloucester: A Study in Character*, Borthwick Paper 7 (1986). The evolution of the Wydeville affinity is solely treated by Hicks, *Edward V*, which now seems to miss a good deal. Evidently more work is needed.

7 *The Self-Destruction of the House of York, 1483–1485*

The fullest discussion of the usurpation story is in M. Hicks, *Richard III* (2000), ch. 3, as refined in 'The Minority of Edward V' in *The Royal Minorities of Later Medieval and Early Modern England*, ed. C. E. Beem (Basingstoke, 2008). For the fate of the princes, see Hicks, *Edward V*, and the proposal to marry Elizabeth of York, see Hicks, *Anne Neville*. For Richard's reign, see especially R. E. Horrox, *Richard III: A Study of Service* (Cambridge, 1989). For the Tudor opposition, see R. A. Griffiths and R. S. Thomas, *The Making of the Tudor Dynasty* (Gloucester, 1985); M. K. Jones and M. G. Underwood, *The King's Mother: Lady Margaret Beaufort, Countess of Richmond and Derby* (Cambridge, 1992); J. A. Ross, *The Foremost Man in the Kingdom: John de Vere, Earl of Oxford* (Woodbridge, 2013).

8 Richard's Heirs

Currently the best overview of Henry VII's politics is S. Cunningham, *The Reign of Henry VII* (2007); see also *Who was Henry VII?* ed. M. R. Horowitz (2009). For Henry VII's family, see M. K. Jones and M. G. Underwood, *The King's Mother: Lady Margaret Beaufort, Countess of Richmond and Derby* (Cambridge, 1992), and for the Duchess Margaret, see C. Weightman, *Margaret of York, Duchess of Burgundy, 1446–1503* (Gloucester, 1989). For the two pretenders, see M. Bennett, *Lambert Simnel* (Gloucester, 1987); I. Arthurson, *The Perkin Warbeck Conspiracy 1491–99* (Stroud, 1994); A. Wroe, *Perkin: A Story of Deception* (2003). There is no modern study of the de la Poles, but for individual lives, see *The Oxford Dictionary of National Biography*, 64 vols (Oxford, 2004).

9 The Posthumous Life of Richard III

This chapter is based on J. Ashdown-Hill, *The Last Days of Richard III* (Stroud, 2010); P. Langley and M. Jones, *The Search for Richard III. The King's Grave* (London, 2013); M. Pitts, *Digging for Richard III: How Archaeology Found the King* (London, 2014); M. Morris and R. Buckley, *Richard III: The King under the Car Park* (rev. edn.; Leicester, 2014); A. J. Carson, J. Ashdown-Hill, D. Johnson, W. Johnson, & P. J. Langley, eds, *Finding Richard III: The Official Account of Research by the Retrieval and Reburial Project*, Imprimis Imprimatur, Horstead (2014); T. E. King *et al.*, 'Identification of the Remains of King Richard III', *New Communications* 5 (2014), 1–8. It has been supplemented by other publications, principally on the internet, as indicated in references. The author also drew on earlier consultations with news media as the story unfolded. Most of these are readily pursued via google searches.

LIST OF ILLUSTRATIONS

INDEX

Key: C = Countess, D = Duke/Duchess, E = Earl, K = King, Ld = Lord, Ldy = Lady, M = Marquis, Q = Queen, Vct = Viscount/Viscountess, w = wife, da = daughter, fam = family, Abp = Archbishop, s = son, stepda = stepdaughter

Richard III from Amberley Publishing

RICHARD III
David Baldwin

'A believably complex Richard, neither wholly villain nor hero'
PHILIPPA GREGORY

£9.99   978-1-4456-1591-2   272 pages PB 81 illus, 57 col

ANNE NEVILLE
Amy Licence

'Timely ... the real life of the daughter of Warwick the Kingmaker'
WI LIFE

£10.99   978-1-4456-3312-1   304 pages PB 30 col illus

THE FAMILY OF RICHARD III
Michael Hicks

'The greatest living expert on Richard III' **BBC HISTORY MAGAZINE**

£20.00   978-1-4456-4228-4   240 pages HB 40 illus, 30 col

THE PRINCES IN THE TOWER
Josephine Wilkinson

'What really happened to them' **ALL ABOUT HISTORY**

£9.99   978-1-4456-1974-3   192 pages PB

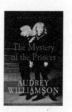

ELIZABETH OF YORK
Amy Licence

'Very accessible' **THE HISTORIAN**

£10.99   978-1-4456-3314-5   272 pages PB 51 illus, 47 col

MARGARET OF YORK
Christine Weightman

'Brings Margaret alive once more' **THE YORKSHIRE POST**

£10.99   978-1-4456-0819-8   256 pages PB 51 illus

THE MYSTERY OF THE PRINCES
Audrey Williamson

'Brilliant and readable' **THE TRIBUNE**

£9.99   978-1-84868-321-1   192 pages PB 40 col illus

CECILY NEVILLE
Amy Licence

'Vivid, very readable, and wonderfully detailed' **SARAH GRISTWOOD**

£9.99   978-1-4456-4480-6   336 pages PB

RICHARD III
Terry Breverton
£9.99 978-1-4456-4479-0 PB

ELIZABETH WOODVILLE
David MacGibbon
£9.99 978-1-4456-3313-8 PB
19 illus, 14 col

THE MAN WHO KILLED RICHARD III
Susan Fern
£18.99 978-1-4456-1980-4 HB
21 illus, 18 col

RICHARD III: THE ROAD TO LEICESTER
David MacGibbon
£9.99 978-1-4456-3313-8 PB
75 col illus

RICHARD III: THE YOUNG KING TO BE
Josephine Wilkinson
£9.99 978-1-84868-513-0 PB
40 illus, 25 col